Shakespeare's Fathers and Daughters

Oliver Ford Davies

THE ARDEN SHAKESPEARE

LONDON · NEW YORK · OXFORD · NEW DELHI · SYDNEY

THE ARDEN SHAKESPEARE
Bloomsbury Publishing Plc
50 Bedford Square, London, WC1B 3DP, UK

BLOOMSBURY, THE ARDEN SHAKESPEARE and the Arden Shakespeare
logo are trademarks of Bloomsbury Publishing Plc

First published in Great Britain 2017
Reprinted 2017, 2018

Cover design: Irene Martinez Costa
Cover image: Photo by Ellie Kurttz © RSC

A catalogue record for this book is available from the British Library.

ISBNs: HB: 978-1-350-63846-2
         PB: 978-1-474-29013-5
         ePDF: 978-1-474-29015-9
         eBook: 978-1-474-29014-2

Library of Congress Cataloging-in-Publication Data
Names: Davies, Oliver Ford, author.
Title: Shakespeare's fathers and daughters / Oliver Ford Davies.
Description: New York : Bloomsbury Arden Shakespeare, an imprint of Bloomsbury Publishing
Plc, 2017. | Includes bibliographical references and index.
Identifiers: LCCN 2016056089 | ISBN 9781350038462 (pbk.) | ISBN 9781474290135 (hardback)
Subjects: LCSH: Shakespeare, William, 1564-1616–Characters–Fathers. | Shakespeare,
William, 1564-1616–Characters–Daughters. | Shakespeare, William, 1564-1616.–Family. |
Fathers and daughters in literature. | Domestic drama, English–History and criticism.
Classification: LCC PR2992.F3 D38 2017 | DDC822.3/3–dc23 LC record available at https://lccn.
loc.gov/2016056089

Typeset by Fakenham Prepress Solutions, Fakenham, Norfolk NR21 8NN
Printed and bound in Great Britain

To find out more about our authors and books visit www.bloomsbury.com
and sign up for our newsletters.

CONTENTS

List of illustrations vi
Preface vii
Acknowledgements viii

Introduction 1

1 Early plays 11

2 Comedies 45

3 Tragedies and tragicomedies 73

4 Late plays 125

5 Shakespeare and his daughters 157

6 Fathers and daughters in contemporary society 163

7 Fathers and daughters in drama 1585–1620 173

Conclusion 181

Notes 191
Select Bibliography 201
Index 207

LIST OF ILLUSTRATIONS

Figure 1 Leonato (Oliver Ford Davies), Beatrice (Zoë Wanamaker), Hero (Susannah Fielding) and Friar Francis (Gary Pillai) in *Much Ado About Nothing* at the Olivier, National Theatre, London, 2007 (© Catherine Ashmore/National Theatre) 58

Figure 2 Polonius (Oliver Ford Daves) and Ophelia (Mariah Gales) in *Hamlet* at the Royal Shakespeare Theatre, Stratford-upon-Avon, 2008. Photo by Ellie Kurttz (© Royal Shakespeare Company) 77

Figure 3 King of France (Oliver Ford Davies), Helena (Michelle Terry) and Bertram (George Rainsford) in *All's Well That Ends Well* at the Olivier, National Theatre, London, 2009 (© Simon Annand/National Theatre) 101

Figure 4 Lear (Oliver Ford Davies) and Goneril (Suzanne Burden) in *King Lear* at the Almeida Theatre, 2002 (© Ivan Kyncl) 111

Figure 5 Lear (Oliver Ford Davies) and Cordelia (Nancy Carroll) in *King Lear* at the Almeida Theatre, 2002 (© Ivan Kyncl) 124

PREFACE

I first had the idea for this book at a seminar at Warwick University in 2007. I mentioned that I was going to the National Theatre to play Leonato in Nick Hytner's production of *Much Ado about Nothing* with Zoë Wanamaker and Simon Russell Beale, and to my surprise Paul Edmondson said, 'You do know it's the second longest part in the play'. It turned out to be only fifteen lines shorter than Benedick and over fifty lines longer than Beatrice. I was immediately fascinated – why had Shakespeare chosen to write Leonato at such length (it's often severely cut, as in the 1993 Branagh film)? I'd always been interested in why Shakespeare chose to foreground certain characters: why Polonius is longer than Gertrude, Portia than Shylock, even Goneril than Cordelia. It seemed a conundrum worth examining.

I have played a number of Shakespeare's fathers of daughters. For my first Duke Senior, at the Birmingham Rep in 1967 (aged twenty-seven), my Rosalind, Andrée Melly, was actually older than I was. Over the years I have played Capulet, Leonato, Duke Frederick, Polonius and Lear. I have also played a number of surrogate fathers: Boyet in *Love's Labours Lost*, Friar Laurence, Pandarus, Duke Vincentio and the King of France in *All's Well That Ends Well*. I felt intrigued, and qualified, to write about these father figures, but it was unthinkable not to link them to their daughters. I should also declare an interest, as Jenifer Armitage and I are the parents of a single daughter, the presciently named Miranda.

There have been a number of studies of these father–daughter relationships, which seemed so to absorb Shakespeare, mostly by American academics who have tended to concentrate on the daughters. Apart from the obvious heavyweights, Shylock, Polonius, Lear, Leontes and Prospero, fathers have been often taken for granted, so I have tried to give equal weight to both sexes. Sometimes Shakespeare is more interested in one than the other – Leonato more than Hero, Rosalind more than Duke Senior – but no two families are the same. Shakespeare worried away at this relationship from Titus and Lavinia through to Prospero and Miranda. Is there any discernible pattern or development in his treatment of fathers and daughters, and do I, as an actor, have anything particular to contribute?

ACKNOWLEDGEMENTS

The staff of the British Library, the Shakespeare Centre and the Shakespeare Institute (University of Birmingham) in Stratford-upon-Avon have been unfailingly helpful, and I have spent many happy hours there when not rehearsing and playing.

I have learnt so much about Shakespeare in the rehearsal room from so many actors and directors in my fifty years in the theatre, and I would like to thank in particular John Barton, Cicely Berry, Adrian Brine, Michael Bryant, Tony Church, Nevill Coghill, Howard Davies, Judi Dench, Peter Dews, Gregory Doran, Richard Eyre, Ralph Fiennes, Terry Hands, Ronald Harris, Alan Howard, Nick Hytner, Emrys James, Jonathan Kent, Daniel Massey, Adrian Noble, Trevor Nunn, Michael Pennington, Simon Russell-Beale, Paul Scofield, Anthony Sher and Juliet Stevenson. I am indebted to my stage 'daughters' who have contributed to the four play sections entitled from 'An Actor's Perspective': Anna Calder-Marshall (recollecting her Juliet nearly fifty years ago), Suzanne Burden (Goneril), Nancy Carroll (Cordelia), Susannah Fielding (Hero), Mariah Gale (Ophelia) and Lizzy McInnerny (Regan).

I wish to thank Ian Buck, Hannah Turner, Susan Furber and all at Bloomsbury Arden Shakespeare, my excellent copy-editor Sue Cope, and Kim Storry and all at Fakenham Press. My especial thanks go to my editor Margaret Bartley, who believed in my project at first reading, and has given me so much good advice.

I am also grateful to those who have read this book in preparation: Jenifer Armitage, Michael Cordner, Gregory Doran, Miranda Emmerson, Carol Rutter and Elizabeth Schafer. They have made many suggestions and saved me from numerous blunders, and bear no responsibility for the misjudgements that remain.

Introduction

Shakespeare is a great dramatist of the family. Almost all his major characters are in thrall to family ties, and Shakespeare lavished attention on these bonds throughout his career, from Baptista and his daughters, the children of York and Lancaster and the Capulet household, right through to the late romances where Pericles, Cymbeline and Leontes struggle with the varying turns of fortune that overtake their wives and children. As Jonathan Miller writes: 'I think what is common to both Shakespeare and our time is simply the fact ... that we have parents and siblings, and share a grammar of relationships ... He seems to me to be the great chronicler of the family that survives, of a species that reproduces as we do.'[1] At the same time Coppelia Kahn cautions: 'An intense ambivalence towards the family runs through Shakespeare's works, taking the familiar shape of a conflict between inheritance and individuality, and between autonomy and relatedness'.[2] *Hamlet* is the story of two families, linked through a love and a rejection which leads to their total destruction. In *King Lear* Shakespeare grafted on to his main plot the story of Gloucester and his sons, as he had with Polonius and his children. He was intrigued by both individuals and families contrasting and mirroring one another, and this is particularly noticeable when compared with his most successful rivals, Marlowe, Jonson, Beaumont and Fletcher. Two aspects of the family dominate Shakespeare's attention: he had, Stephen Greenblatt noted, 'a special, deep interest in the murderous rivalry of brothers and in the complexity of father-daughter relations'.[3] Claudius' rivalry with his brother leads to assassination; Polonius dominates Ophelia, but his death leads to her madness. Edmund plots to dispossess Edgar; Lear demands a love test from his daughters. Seventeen of the plays have significant father–daughter relationships, and surrogate fathers feature in many others.

In his early career Shakespeare was much concerned with fathers and sons, mainly through his concentration on the history chronicle plays. In military conflicts Talbot, Clifford, York, Henry VI and many others are naturally linked to their sons. *Richard II* examines three family connections: Gaunt and Bolingbroke, Northumberland and Harry Percy, York and Aumerle. They are contrasted with one another, and in turn with the absence of Richard's son and heir. The culmination comes with the relationship Hal has with Henry IV and with his surrogate father, Falstaff. The early comedies contain various fathers and sons – Vincentio and Lucentio, Egeon and the Antipholi, Gobbo and Lancelot, Page and William – but none of these is central to the action. After 1598 fathers and sons occur less frequently: Polonius and Laertes, Priam and his sons, Polixenes and Florizel, Cymbeline and his two sons, Alonso and Ferdinand are not relationships examined in depth. The two significant exceptions are *King Lear* and *Macbeth*. Gloucester, Edgar and Edmund form the parallel plot to Lear and his daughters; Duncan and his sons, Banquo and Fleance, Macduff and his children, Siward and his son are set, as in *Richard II*, against the Macbeths and their lack of heir.

The canon does of course contain several mothers of sons – Tamora, Margaret, Emilia, Constance, Gertrude, the Countess of Rossillion, Lady Macduff, Volumnia and Cymbeline's Queen – but there are at least a dozen plays that do not feature mothers at all. This may reflect the way women were often sidelined in the public sphere: both sons and daughters were firmly identified with their fathers, as Rosalind, Celia and Orlando demonstrate in *As You Like It* (see p. 65). For a dramatist the comparative powerlessness of mothers meant that they were frequently left absent, or dead – though Shakespeare seldom enlightens us about their end. Married couples also feature little in Shakespeare, and even the requisite unions at the end of the comedies seem questionable (Angelo and Mariana, Bertram and Helena?). As has been often remarked, Hotspur and Kate, Master and Mistress Page, Brutus and Portia, York and his wife may have a basically loving relationship, but they are only seen quarrelling. The two most examined marriages are both dysfunctional in their different ways; the Macbeths, and Leontes and Hermione. Mothers and daughters are even rarer. Lady Capulet's concern for Juliet promises much but soon turns to rejection – 'I would the fool were married to her grave'. From this play onwards wives are banished from most of the comedies. Shakespeare clearly changed his mind about giving Hero a mother, Innogen, in *Much Ado about Nothing* (see p. 55), and Anne Page's mother's main concern is for her to marry the eccentric and unwelcome Dr Caius in *The Merry Wives of Windsor*. Thaisa and Marina meet only at the denouement of *Pericles*, as do Hermione and Perdita in *The Winter's Tale*. In fact the most detailed and interesting scenes are in *All's Well That Ends Well* between Helena and her surrogate mother, later mother-in-law, the Countess of Rossillion, and between the Widow and her daughter Diana.

Shakespeare's interest in fathers and daughters must stem partly from his education, and in particular the Roman dramatists Plautus, Seneca, Menander and Terence, whose plays had been studied and performed in schools and universities since the thirteenth century. The typical Plautine plot concerns the bringing together of a young couple, after overcoming the hazards of unsympathetic parents and unsuitable suitors, aided by cunning and resourceful servants out to further their own interests. The plays figure prominently a father, the *senex iratus* (angry old man), bent on marrying his *filia astuta* (wily daughter) to a rich, unwelcome and sometimes stupid man, while ignoring his daughter's own chosen lover. Wives are usually absent, or play little part in the plot. This was the template that most dramatists adopted, and Shakespeare followed suit in his early plays *The Two Gentlemen of Verona* and *Romeo and Juliet*, though rarely thereafter. Jonson was later to write in his commendatory verse to the First Folio (F1) that Shakespeare surpassed 'all that insolent Greece or haughty Rome / Sent forth', ensuring that 'Neat Terence, witty Plautus ... antiquated and deserted lie.'

Plays were not however the only influence that education provided fledgling dramatists. The grammar school education that Shakespeare presumably received at Stratford would have been very similar to Jonson's three or four years at Westminster School, or Marlowe's time at The King's School Canterbury (where I myself learnt to read Virgil and Homer with some fluency by the age of fifteen). The core Latin curriculum would have included Cicero, Horace, Virgil and, of course, Ovid, and in particular his *Metamorphoses*, 'which in some schools boys in the upper forms memorized, word for word, at the rate of a book a year'.[4] 'In the traditional liberal arts course, Ovid's *Metamorphoses* stood squarely between lower-level work in grammar, rhetoric and logic, and upper-level work in natural philosophy. His fables served as exercise books in grammar schools, but their subject matter was Nature.'[5] References to Ovid bespatter Shakespeare's plays, whether Holofernes' 'Dictynna' (*Love's Labours Lost*, 4.3.36); Lucentio's quotation to Bianca (*The Taming of the Shrew*, 3.1.28–9); Juliet recalling Narcissus and Echo (*Romeo and Juliet*, 2.2.158–63); or the Mechanicals' Pyramus and Thisbe play. What is remarkable is how frequently Shakespeare would have encountered women's feelings and their sufferings at the hands of men in *Metamorphoses*, whether in *Hamlet* 'Niobe all tears' sitting among the corpses of her husband and her seven sons and daughters; in *The Two Gentlemen of Verona* Julia playing 'the woman's part', ''Twas Ariadne, passioning / For Theseus' perjury and unjust flight' (5.1.157, 164–5); or in *Titus Andronicus* Lavinia/Philomel's rape and disfigurement. When Hamlet calls for a speech from the Player King he chooses the slaughter of Priam and Hecuba's grief, running 'barefoot up and down, threatening the flames / With bisson rheum' (2.2.508–9), taken from Virgil's *Aeneid* 2.[6] A knowledge of Greek drama's Antigone, Electra, Medea and Iphigenia seems to have been sadly denied Shakespeare, certainly in the original.

Shakespeare has proved not alone in finding motherless young women a rich source of drama. Jane Austen, for example, started her career by creating the rather ineffectual Mrs Dashwood in *Sense and Sensibility*, and the heavily satirized Mrs Bennett in *Pride and Prejudice*. In *Northanger Abbey* and *Mansfield Park* she kept Catherine Morland and Fanny Price's mothers at a distance, while in her two final novels she dispensed with mothers altogether: both Emma Woodhouse and Anne Elliot have difficult, overbearing fathers, who partly rule their lives. Among playwrights Chekhov has Ranyevskaia and her daughter Anya in *The Cherry Orchard*, but Nina in *The Seagull*, Sonya and Yeliena in *Uncle Vanya* and the Three

Sisters are all motherless. Fathers dominating their daughters and directing their choice of husband remained a stock device for the three centuries after the Elizabethans – *Clarissa, Tom Jones, Persuasion, Dombey and Son, Rigoletto, Père Goriot, Eugénie Grandet, Silas Marner* are witness to that. The twentieth century saw fewer examples. Female writers were more interested in mother-daughter relationships, and even male writers felt the tyrannical patriarch and the rebel/victim daughter was too well-mined a genre. Nevertheless, O'Neill in *Strange Interlude*, Harold Brighouse in *Hobson's Choice*, Githa Sowerby in *Rutherford and Son*, Bernard Shaw in various plays from *Widower's Houses* onwards and John Osborne in *Inadmissible Evidence* continued to examine the hold fathers, alive or dead, exercised over their daughters.

The reasons for this device are not hard to find. A dead, or absent, mother leaves a young daughter without the support of the adult who has largely brought her up and understands the trials and tribulations of a woman in a male-dominated society (though Shakespeare does not dwell on the daughter's sense of loss), and at the mercy of a father who has been distant in her development. Father and daughter are naturally and socially the two most opposed members of a family, through gender, age, status and expectation. The dramatic possibilities for conflict and/or growing dependence are endless, and Shakespeare particularly relished writing such clashes, perhaps because of his delight in creating a whole range of elderly men, fathers to a single daughter. 'Elderly' is a relative term. Lear and the Old Shepherd tell us they are over eighty, and we can deduce Capulet is around sixty and Prospero around forty-five, but we can't tell how old Shylock, Leonato, Duke Senior, Polonius, Cymbeline and others are, though they *feel* 'elderly' – in a time of short life expectancy fifty was considered by many to be on the brink of old age. The fact that the daughters are so young (Juliet thirteen, Marina and Miranda fourteen and Perdita sixteen) is related of course to their marriageability, but also perhaps the fact that they were to be played by teenage boys. Although Shakespeare may have thought of them as female, and in my experience most modern actresses would endorse this, there are those who argue that the plays work best, and bring out the text's ambiguities most fully, with male actors. It is worth noting that Shakespeare created his great comic heroines between 1595 and 1600, when his own daughters were in their teens. I have, however, approached the influence that his own experience of family had on his writing with great caution. Shakespeare, unlike Ben Jonson, seems adept at removing himself from his creation of drama, however much he was influenced by contemporary social and political events. There is, for example, no suggestion that he felt any 'murderous rivalry' with his own younger brothers.

General studies of the father's role in the family, and his relationship with his daughters, have been sparse. Eileen Fairweather commented: 'Our culture is top-heavy with images ... about what constitutes good *mothering*: our concept of good fathering is almost non-existent.'[7] Freud has proved

an unreliable guide to father-daughter relations, with his theories
envy and the daughter's submission to patriarchy as a form of mas
Jung has had more influence with his theory of the 'psychic revolution'
a daughter feels at the awakening sexuality of puberty, which results in
either a throwing off of paternal authority and a greater assertiveness, or
a retreat into childhood to gain approval and a deference to the father or
lover. I shall examine how Shakespeare's stage daughters demonstrate all
these traits, while his fathers, particularly in the later plays, learn in Jungian
terms to recognize their 'anima' (their 'unconscious feminine potential')
and embrace patience, humility and compassion. 'Birth Order' is a recently
developed topic among psychologists, in which only daughters (much
favoured by Shakespeare) emerge as mature, conscientious, controlling
achievers (Juliet, Rosalind, Helena, Marina?), and second daughters as a
mixture of people-pleasing and rebellious (Bianca, Regan?).[8]

It is impossible to read studies on father-daughter relationships without
encountering references to incest. David Wilbern writes, 'a degree of sublimated
incestuous desire is nearly always present in the mixture of concern, posses-
siveness and love that Shakespeare's fathers feel for their daughters ... In *The
Winter's Tale* the incest syndrome is a highly complex entity to which the
feelings of Leontes, Antigonus and Polixenes all contribute.'[9] Thus Leontes is
briefly attracted to Perdita, though arguably only because he sees the mother
in the daughter. The only clear example of incest is in *Pericles,* where Gower
says that Antiochus took a liking to his (unnamed) daughter, 'and her to
incest did provoke' (1.Ch.27), and several commentators uphold the idea that
Pericles is plagued throughout his life by shame at being attracted to a woman
in an incestuous relationship (see pp. 124–5). Despite these rare examples
many psychologists have discerned sublimated, emotional or 'pseudo' incest
in certain of the plays – witness how Shylock seems castrated by Jessica's
escape and her stealing of 'two stones, two rich and precious stones', or
Lear's dependence on Cordelia, hoping 'to set my rest / On her kind nursery'.
It does seem, however, that Shakespeare went out of his way to play down
overt representations of incest: witness how Pandosto's desire for Fawnia in
Greene's prose story *Pandosto,* the source for *The Winter's Tale*, is reduced
to Leontes' momentary attraction to Perdita (see p. 135). Many productions
of the plays have tried to compensate for the lack of textual justification for
sublimated incest by extra-textual business. *King Lear* is a case in point. Lear
has entered the first scene with his arm round Cordelia, as Olivier did in his
1983 television film. Both John Wood at the Royal Shakespeare Company
(RSC) in 1990 and Jonathan Pryce at the Almeida in 2012 impulsively kissed
their elder daughters on the mouth in a way that might hint at incestuous
desire.[10] When I myself played Lear in 2002, also at the Almeida, I was
accused of the same in my treatment of Regan (see p. 116).

Most writers on Shakespeare's father-daughter relationships have
marshalled them into categories. Diane Elizabeth Dreher divides fathers into
Reactionary (Polonius, Brabantio, Cymbeline); Mercenary (Silvia's father,

Baptista, Capulet, Egeus, Portia's father, Polonius); Egocentric (Shylock, Leonato, Lear, Prospero); Jealous (Egeus, Brabantio, Lear, Pericles).[11] Such treatment is not without problems. In what sense is Capulet mercenary (he never discusses money with Paris), Pericles jealous (of whom?) or Prospero more egocentric than most of the others? Egeus and Lear would fall into every category apart from mercenary; Polonius might fit into every single category. Dreher has a somewhat easier time categorizing daughters. They are Dominated (Hero, Ophelia, Desdemona); Defiant (Silvia, Kate, Hermia, Juliet, Jessica, Anne Page, Innogen and all three Lear daughters); Androgynous (Julia, Beatrice, Portia, Rosalind, Viola, Helena); Redeemers (Marina, Innogen, Perdita, Miranda). But in what sense are Beatrice and Helena androgynous while Cordelia (army leader) is not, Miranda and Perdita redeemers (Paulina and Hermione are surely Leontes' major redeemers) or Desdemona dominated rather than initially defiant?

Lagretta Tallent Lenker has a more conceptual categorization: the Sacrificial Lamb (Juliet, Ophelia, Cordelia); the Temptation of Incest (in *Pericles*, *Cymbeline*, *The Winter's Tale*); Fantastic Interaction (the four romances); Theatrical Intervention – Playwriting Fathers (Portia's father, Lear, Simonides, Leontes, Prospero), and Role-playing Daughters (Rosalind, Innogen, Perdita); and Gender Blenders (Portia, Rosalind, Viola, Cordelia, Innogen).[12] There are problems here too, in addition to the supposed 'temptation of incest'. Shakespeare was obsessed by playwriting and role-playing characters. Surely Leonato and Polonius are also playwrights; and Kate, Juliet, Hero, Marina, Innogen and many others are role-players? It is always tempting to put any woman who puts on male attire, whether willingly or not, as 'androgynous' or a 'gender blender', but their characters and motives are always more complex. Barbara Goulter and Joan Minninger in *The Father-Daughter Dance* and Mark Taylor in *Shakespeare's Darker Purpose* attempt similar categorizations.[13]

This labelling of characters is not only a limiting concept but a dangerous one, particularly for the director and actor in production. Is Leonato 'gullible', Ophelia 'weak', Prospero 'wise', Cordelia 'pure'? Directly we label Juliet as a sacrificial lamb, Portia as androgynous, Marina as a redeemer, Baptista as mercenary, we have in some way predetermined our approach to them, seeing in them only the aspects of their character that fit the label. Actors and directors must be free to interpret from scratch – all performances are an act of re-creation. Much of the ambiguity, opacity and omissions in the texts, I believe, is there to allow, even encourage, individual interpretations, and these may differ widely and be equally justifiable. Although Shakespeare regularly recycles ideas and situations, his characters almost always have their own individuality. Marina, Innogen and Perdita are quite different young women – they are not just 'the redemptive daughters in the romances'. Harriet Walter recalls how, faced with playing Viola, Portia and Innogen in the same 1987 RSC season, she tried to find a distinctive voice for each, but soon came to realize that they were so different that there was no need to impose artificial distinctions upon them; their individuality would play itself.[14] From my own experience I know that Capulet, Leonato and Polonius may all come into the *senex* category, but in performance they are not remotely similar. Shakespeare constantly shifts their circumstances, alters their options, changes the way they react. No two tragic or comic developments are the same.

I have quoted widely from the texts.[15] Shakespeare's characters are lines in a play, performing actions which the text indicates: there is a great danger in divorcing them from the text and treating them as real people. Shylock and Romeo, for instance, have broken free from their moorings and become archetypes far beyond the careful limits their author envisaged. Of course to the actor all characters are 'real' at one level, human flesh and blood that the actor has endowed with aspects of him/herself. Simon Callow writes that the actor feels 'another person is coursing through your veins, is breathing through your lungs. But of course it's not. It's only you – another arrangement of you'.[16] In many cases actors and directors feel the need to invent motives and intentions that Shakespeare has ignored: why is Lear abdicating and what is the nature of his madness; how long have Gertrude and Claudius been attracted to one another, and does Gertrude suspect, or even know, that Claudius murdered her husband; why is Don John intent on destroying the Claudio–Hero marriage? Once a decision has been taken about these questions, should this be communicated to the audience, and, if so, how? However much Gertrude and Claudius fondle one another, how can the audience tell whether their relationship is a two-month or a five-year affair? However clinically 'accurate' the actor's playing of Lear's apparent insanity on Dover Beach, he has to be largely recovered days later at his meeting with Cordelia. The text always brings speculation down to earth: this is the sum total of what Shakespeare tells us about his creations.

I have also paid particular attention to Shakespeare's use of source material as a guide to where his taste and interests lay. We know so little of his working methods. Did he write shut up in a room and present a finished article, with scarcely a line blotted, to the company, or did they have considerable input? Did he rewrite and cut after the first few performances; was *Hamlet* ever presented in its 3,800-line, 4½-hour version? Who edited the texts/foul papers for quarto and folio publication? Since we know that Middleton slipped Hecate and two of his songs into the *Macbeth* witches scenes, is this the tip of an iceberg? Our one sure guide to both his concepts and methods is the way he handled his sources. Comparing the sources with the finished plays is, as Geoffrey Bullough writes:

> The best, and often the only, way open to us of watching Shakespeare the craftsman in his workshop – not indeed of 'explaining' the mystery of his artistic genius, but at least of perceiving his constructive powers in operation, of seeing the ingenious collocations and associative energies

which underlie the dynamic balance of the plays and which fuse plot, character, dialogue, and imagery into a poetic unity.[17]

In this way we can appreciate how he shaped and altered his source material, so that his Viola is not already in love and in pursuit of Orsino, Don John is not a rejected suitor of Hero's and Cordelia does not put her father back on the throne. In an early play like *The Taming of the Shrew* he follows the accepted version fairly closely. By *King Lear* he felt confident enough to re-imagine almost totally the last three acts. But in all the plays we can see small, but significant, changes. Petruccio and Kate's treatment of their servants is toned down, Duke Frederick is not killed in battle but achieves an improbable conversion and Goneril's criticism of her father's knights seems justified. Nowhere is both his craft and his personal taste more clearly identifiable.

Character analysis has not been in vogue, but as a performer it naturally concerns me. I have paid particular attention to four fathers and, because I have played them, I have personalized my account of Capulet, Leonato, Polonius and Lear (marked as 'an actor's perspective'), describing how I went about preparing and performing them: they represent, I think, four significant stages in his development of the *senex*. I have also quoted freely from personal correspondence with my six stage daughters. Perhaps because I was trained as a historian (I was briefly a history lecturer at Edinburgh University) I have attempted to place Shakespeare's treatment of fathers and daughters in some sort of context, to contrast his individual experience and dramatic output with the society in which he lived and wrote and to maintain a hazardous balance between our knowledge of Elizabethan *mores* and our twenty-first-century mindset. Would the Globe audience have condemned Leonato for wishing his daughter dead or Jessica for swapping her father's ring for a monkey, or applauded them for behaving as betrayed fathers and Christian Jewish daughters should? It sets the modern actor a perplexing choice. To present some background to this problem I have outlined what little we know of Shakespeare's own daughters; summarized the position of fathers and daughters in contemporary society; and attempted a brief overview of how other dramatists of the period treated this relationship. I have placed this material, familiar to most academics but I hope of interest to students, at the end of the book (Chapters 5–7). In the first four chapters I discuss twenty-four of the plays chronologically, rather than in categories, while remaining aware that the dating of some of the plays is uncertain. Several of the plays where the father-daughter relationship is peripheral to the main action (as in *A Midsummer's Night Dream* and the histories) are necessarily dealt with more briefly. As an actor in twenty-five of Shakespeare's plays (some three times) I am very aware of the nuts and bolts of his development as a playwright, of how the language changes, theme and structure become more complex, the treatment of the central character waxes and wanes, the approach grows more tortured and questioning – and the development of the father–daughter relationship is reflected in all this. Some pattern may, or may not, emerge.

1

Early plays

The plays that Shakespeare wrote, or collaborated on, through to 1594/5 show him experimenting in a wide variety of genres: the history chronicle plays of *Henry VI* and *Richard III*, the tragedies of *Titus Andronicus* and *Romeo and Juliet* and the comedies of *The Two Gentlemen of Verona*, *The Taming of the Shrew*, *The Comedy of Errors*, *Love's Labours Lost*, culminating in the wild originality of *A Midsummer's Night Dream*. If he had then died, aged thirty, he would have been feted, as one of the great writers of the period who had finally found his voice. Already, in both tragedy and comedy, his particular interest in the father-daughter relationship had come to the fore and been examined in growing diversity.

The Two Gentlemen of Verona: Duke of Milan and Silvia

This may be Shakespeare's first surviving play and, though an ambitious mess, it is clearly a prototype for his later comedies. It highlights certain themes that fascinated him for the rest of his writing career: the friendship and rivalry of young men, the relationship between father and daughter and the young woman at the centre of the comedy who adopts male disguise. Both the ambition and the mess derive from his use of sources. The two male friends, Valentine and Proteus, come from Boccaccio via Sir Thomas Elyot's *The Governor* (1531). The young woman disguised as a page, Julia, comes from Bartholomew Yonge's English version of the Portuguese *Diana Enamorada* (1582), where Celia falls in love with Felisma, disguised as the page Valerius, and dies of chagrin when she/he fails to respond. Shakespeare was to use this plot in *Twelfth Night*, though without the fatal consequences. The young woman with two lovers, Silvia, comes from Lyly's *Euphues*, where Lucilla doesn't want to marry Philautus, loves Euphues, but finally abandons them both and marries 'one Curio, a gentleman of Naples of little wealth and less wit'.[1] These sources provided Shakespeare with a heady, complex mixture, and he decided all these plot strands could be combined in a comedy that ends in happy unions. It was beyond his technical capacity, which was at this stage limited largely to soliloquies, duologues and asides, with a clumsy handling of scenes with many characters. His love of linking various plot lines, each of which would suffice for an orthodox play, never left him – *King Lear* and *Cymbeline* are witness to that. Implausible as parts of the play are, it can play better than it reads, as RSC productions in 1991, 1998 and 2014 have demonstrated.In most versions of the story the parents of the two young women are absent. Lyly, however, in *Euphues* gives Lucilla/Silvia a father, Don Ferardo, 'one of the chief governors of the city'. Lucilla is an only child, 'heir to his whole revenues', who declares her father 'shall sooner martyr me in the fire than marry me to Philautus'. Don Ferardo attempts to persuade her in the most decorous language:

> Dear daughter, as thou has long time lived a maiden, so now thou must learn to be a mother, as I have been careful to bring thee up a virgin, so I am desirous to make thee a wife. Neither ought I in this matter to use any persuasions, for that maidens commonly nowadays are no sooner born, but they begin to bride it ...[2]

This gentle template Shakespeare abandons in favour of a tyrannical *senex* in the Plautine mode.

The duke, or emperor (Shakespeare can't quite make up his mind about his title, but as in so many of his plays he ups the father's status to aristocratic ruler), wants Silvia to marry Thurio, 'for his possessions are so huge' (2.4.175), as Valentine reports. Valentine plans to elope with Silvia, and when Proteus, in love with Silvia himself, decides to betray his friend the Duke bathetically reveals 'This love of theirs myself have often seen, / Haply when they have judg'd me fast asleep' (3.1.24–5). To prevent this, the Duke, in true fairy-tale style, locks Silvia every night 'in an upper tower', which Valentine intends to climb with the aid of his rope ladder. At this point the scene descends into farce. The Duke, begged by Proteus not to reveal his informant, decides to unmask Valentine by devious cunning. Valentine, not the brightest of romantic leads, tries to disarm suspicion by talking up Thurio, and asks 'Cannot your grace win her to fancy him?' The Duke's eloquent reply is Lear-like in his anger at his daughter's 'pride':

No, trust me, she is peevish, sullen, froward,
Proud, disobedient, stubborn, lacking duty,
Neither regarding that she is my child,
Nor fearing me as if I were her father.
And may I say to thee, this pride of hers
(Upon advice) hath drawn my love from her,
And where I thought the remnant of mine age
Should have been cherish'd by her child-like duty,

I now am full resolv'd to take a wife,
And turn her out to who will take her in.
Then let her beauty be her wedding-dower;
For me and my possessions she esteems not.

(3.1.68–79)

This verse is typical of early Shakespeare: regular iambics, many lines end-stopped. But the speech, so redolent of themes in later plays, has a certain ambiguity about it. The Duke seems genuinely angry at his daughter's rebellion, but he is also trying to lull Valentine into revealing his planned elopement. He does this by seeking Valentine's advice about the wooing of a lady, and by a rather unconvincing stratagem 'discovers' the rope ladder. He then proceeds to banish Valentine in language that shows Shakespeare's debt to Marlowe, demonstrating that he can write euphuistic, bombastic verse with a classical bent as well as any university wit:

Why, Phaeton, for thou art Merops' son
Wilt thou aspire to guide the heavenly car?
And with thy daring folly burn the world?
Wilt thou reach stars, because they shine on thee?
Go, base intruder, overweening slave,
Bestow thy fawning smiles on equal mates,
And think my patience (more than thy desert)
Is privilege for thy departure hence.

(3.1.153–60)

When Silvia begs for Valentine's reinstatement, the Duke, according to Proteus, puts her in a 'close prison'. He then assures Thurio that Silvia will love him now Valentine is gone.

The Duke is revealed as foolish and mercenary in his championing of Thurio, devious in his manipulation of Valentine and tyrannical in his imprisoning of his daughter. He can appear the fairytale wicked father, obsessed by ancestry and gentlemanly behaviour, his actions only tempered by the atmosphere of farcical comedy; or, alternatively, a worldly and ironic observer of youthful folly, determined to test the sincerity of both Valentine and Silvia, as Paul Daneman showed in the 1983 BBC television version directed by Don Taylor. From this point on Shakespeare has to make the Duke display nobility and forgiveness in order for the happy ending to work. In the forest, captured by outlaws, he suddenly discovers that Thurio is 'degenerate and base', applauds Valentine's spirit 'and think thee worthy of an empress' love', gives him Silvia, pardons the outlaws, so that they 'will include all jars / With triumphs, mirth, and rare solemnity' (5.4.134, 139, 158–9). It is as near to a pantomime ending as Shakespeare ever came. Nevertheless the Duke is almost entirely Shakespeare's invention, and the space and variety he is accorded shows that right from the start of Shakespeare's career he was fascinated by the potential, both comic and serious, for patriarchal complexity.

Silvia, however, is not a complex creation, and reveals little of her inner life. She has to represent steadfastness in her love for Valentine, just as Julia does for Proteus, but her journey is not nearly as interesting. She also represents courtly love, one of Shakespeare's few experiments in this genre. She is the 'mistress', Valentine her 'servant', and there is a lot of fun to be had in her offering back his love letter, written at her behest as for another, and Valentine's complete misunderstanding of this courtly gesture, a lack of response that continues even when Speed explains it to him. Silvia evidently spelt out her feelings to the dim but nice Valentine because by the next scene he tells Proteus they are 'betrothed' (though not apparently before witnesses) and their 'marriage hour ... determin'd of'. She is obviously a woman of spirit, because she has agreed to climb down from her 'upper tower' by rope ladder, and elope with him, 'all the means / Plotted, and 'greed on' (2.4.179–83). Her father sees her as 'proud, disobedient, stubborn, lacking duty'.

Shakespeare tells all this in reported speech, and this continues with Valentine's banishment. Proteus is again made to report that she wept 'a sea of melting pearl ... but neither bended knees, pure hands held up, / Sad sighs, deep groans, nor silver-shedding tears / Could penetrate her uncompassionate sire' (3.1.224, 229–31). Silvia behaves in true heroic style, but Shakespeare is not interested enough in her to give her scenes to play: the contrast with the space later given to Julia is evident. Proteus next reports that when he pressed his suit, Silvia 'twits me with my falsehood to my friend', and 'how I have been forsworn / In breaking faith with Julia, whom I lov'd' (4.2.8, 10–11). But after 'Who is Silvia?', the only heroine in Shakespeare to have a song sung to her, she is at last allowed to appear and berate Proteus in grande-dame style:

> Thou subtle, perjur'd, false, disloyal man,
> Think'st thou I am so shallow, so conceitless,
> To be seduced by thy flattery ...
>
> (92–4)

She decides to pursue Valentine but, unlike Julia, needs a man, Sir Eglamour, to escort her after she has confessed at Friar Patrick's cell. She is at last allowed a speech of some length, though it is largely to explain the plot. She has a heightened sense of the dramatic: the Thurio alliance is 'a most unholy match, / Which heaven and fortune still rewards with plagues' (4.3.30–1). Her exemplary behaviour continues with the disguised Julia, even handing over her own purse 'for thy sweet mistress' sake, because thou lov'st her' (4.4.173–4). When the outlaws capture her it is

Proteus who rescues her, and Silvia extravagantly declares she would have preferred to be breakfast for a hungry lion. Proteus says he will 'force thee yield to my desire' (5.4.59), Silvia exclaims 'O heaven!', Valentine rescues her, Proteus apologizes and Valentine declares: 'All that was mine in Silvia I give thee.' This is a much debated line. Is it heroic generosity? Several recent productions have, by various gestures, hugs and kisses, made the line appear to mean 'the love that I have given to Silvia I also extend to you', though this doesn't square with the Boccaccio/Elyot source, where 'Silvia' is handed over, and indeed marries the Proteus figure. Shakespeare's happy ending, with the two men and the two couples reconciled, is implausibly achieved and, significantly, Silvia is given no lines at all. Shakespeare's main interest in the play has always lain with the two men and Julia, so Silvia's silence can be interpreted either as due to her low priority, or that Shakespeare can't imagine what she would have to say on being handed over to her rapist. Various productions have tried to explain her silence by having her faint or be gagged by Proteus, and in 1762 Benjamin Victor's version provided her with a speech. But her silence is not uncommon among Shakespeare heroines at the denouement, witness Hero, Celia and Marina, as if acknowledging that it was not appropriate for a daughter to speak out while her father and her lover decide her future. Such a patriarchal notion has already been endorsed by Lance: 'To be slow in words is a woman's only virtue' (3.1.328).[3]

Shakespeare never again wrote such a stylized idealization of a young woman. Valentine calls her 'a heavenly saint', 'sovereign to all the creatures on the earth' (2.4.144, 152); Proteus declares her 'too fair, too true, too holy'; the song calls her 'holy, fair, and wise' (4.2.5, 40); Julia finds her 'a virtuous gentlewoman, mild, and beautiful' (4.4.177). Despite these paeans of praise Shakespeare does manage to give her some wit and spirit in her teasing of Valentine and her determination to run away with him, but her verse is pedestrian and uninspired:

> Had I been seized by a hungry lion,
> I would have been a breakfast to the beast
> Rather than have false Proteus rescue me.
> O heaven be judge how I love Valentine,
> Whose life's as tender to me as my soul.

> (5.4.33–7)

Shakespeare's later handling of Juliet, Jessica and Olivia, who share some of her characteristics, shows how far he had developed in humanizing his rebellious young women. Despite the Duke's eloquence on Silvia's betrayal, the relationship between the two is hardly explored. In their first scene together (2.4) the Duke scarcely acknowledges her; when Proteus reports to Valentine Silvia's entreaties on his behalf the Duke simply puts her in 'close prison' (3.1); and in the final scene he doesn't speak to his daughter, but brusquely concedes, 'Take thou thy Silvia, for thou hast deserv'd her' (5.4.145), as if she were barely related to him. But then fathers in Shakespeare are often shown to be more interested in who their son-in-law and successor is to be than in pleasing their daughter. Silvia remains a two-dimensional creation, sidelined partly because Julia is the best drawn character in the play, prefiguring in her spirit and disguise both Rosalind and Viola. Julia has a father, who 'stays' for her at dinner (1.2.131), but he is not taken into account when she decides to pursue Proteus in male clothes (2.7). Shakespeare's delight in writing an intimate scene for two young women is evident – and contains the only discussion of the cod-piece problem in adopting male attire. Her desire to read Proteus' letter, which she has disdainfully torn up, is a scene worthy of Restoration comedy (1.2), and her musings over Silvia's portrait is verse reminiscent of Helena in *A Midsummer's Night Dream*:

> O thou senseless form,
> Thou shalt be worshipp'd, kiss'd, lov'd, and ador'd;
> And were there sense in his idolatry,
> My substance should be statue in thy stead.
> I'll use thee kindly, for thy mistress' sake
> That us'd me so; or else, by Jove I vow,
> I should have scratch'd out your unseeing eyes,
> To make my master out of love with thee.

> (4.4.195–202)

From the start of his career Shakespeare was prepared to put a young woman at the centre of a comedy, to show both women as more intelligent, moral and assertive than their lovers, and *The Two Gentlemen of Verona* announces many of the themes that he will continue to develop: the cross-dressed heroine, the constancy of young women, the jealous bond between young men, their transformation through love and a father's failed attempt to control his daughter.

Titus Andronicus: Titus and Lavinia

Shakespeare was first drawn to the story by Ovid's tale of Philomel, and it demonstrates his obsession from early in his career with the father-daughter relationship. Central to the play's plot and language is the mutilated body of Lavinia, which appears to be both a symbol of female suffering and a mirror image of her father's destructive violence. Lavinia is first protected by the males in her family, abused, then avenged and finally killed – a progress that recurs in various forms in tragedies that follow. In Ovid's

Metamorphoses Philomel is raped by her brother-in-law, the Thracian king Tereus; her tongue is then cut out so that she cannot reveal his identity; but she finds a way of communicating this through sewing a picture into a sampler. The two sisters then kill Tereus' son and serve him up in a pie. Shakespeare's play seems to have been his first great success, a challenge to Kyd and Marlowe that he could write a Senecan revenge tragedy that would emulate, even outdo, any predecessor in cruelty, suffering, black farce and high rhetoric. The consensus seems to remain that, on stylistic grounds, the first act may be by George Peele with possible revisions by Shakespeare, and that the version we have in the first quarto of 1594 was written in late 1593, though an earlier version may have been in existence in 1591/2. Indeed the play was probably much revised, as a scene (3.2) is added to F1, which does not exist in earlier quartos.[4]

No source has survived for the play as a whole, though it owes much to Kyd, Marlowe and Peele's *The Battle of Alcazar* (1590?), where a dish of heads is served at a banquet. The character and actions of Titus may therefore be Shakespeare's invention. It is his most ferocious and absolute picture of patriarchal authority, in which Titus appears both as a righteous avenger and enemy to injustice, and a monstrous egoist, prepared to sacrifice his children. He has been a soldier for forty years, his latest campaign has lasted ten years, in which time twenty-one of his twenty-five sons have been killed. The Roman people by 'common voice' have chosen him to be emperor, but Titus declares his body 'shakes for age and feebleness', and bids them crown Saturninus: he seeks a staff of honour, not 'a sceptre to control the world' (1.1.191, 202). This honourable withdrawal is contrasted with his insistence on killing his hostage, Tamora's son, in an action of religious sacrifice which precipitates the entire tragedy. From the outset Titus speaks with passion and high wrought imagery, tempered with controlled rhetoric in the approved Senecan form (thought this first-act speech may be by Peele):

> Lo, as the bark that hath discharged his freight
> Returns with precious lading to the bay
> From whence at first she weighed her anchorage,
> Cometh Andronicus, bound with laurel boughs,
> To resalute his country with his tears,
> Tears of true joy for his return to Rome.

> (74–9)

Lavinia is given a considerable build-up. Bassianus names her 'Gracious Lavinia, Rome's rich ornament', and Saturninus offers to make her his empress, 'Rome's royal mistress, mistress of my heart' (55, 245). Lavinia enters to greet her father's return more in the role of wife or mother than daughter: 'And at thy feet I kneel with tears of joy / Shed on this earth for thy return to Rome' (164–5). When Coriolanus enters Rome the first thing the general Cominius says is, 'Look, sir, your mother', though, significantly, it is Coriolanus who kneels. Titus calls Lavinia 'the cordial of mine age to glad my heart', a pre-echo of Lear and Cordelia.

Twenty lines after proposing to Lavinia, Saturninus makes a play for Tamora, promising to make her 'greater than the queen of Goths'. This would seem to amount to a declaration of marriage, and when he checks that Lavinia is not 'displeased with this', her reply is graciously ambiguous: 'Not I, my lord, sith true nobility / Warrants these words in princely courtesy' (273–6). Bassianus then claims that he and Lavinia are betrothed and tries to take her away. Titus' sons hustle her out, Titus kills his son Mutius for barring his way, orders Lucius to 'restore Lavinia to the emperor', though Lucius points out that Tamora is now his 'lawful promised love' (301, 303). Lavinia is silent throughout, and the effect of this is to make her a passive victim, a property to be fought over and owned. When we next meet her, at the hunt, she is married to Bassianus, apparently contented, though the actions of the first scene had suggested a form of rape.

Before this, however, Aaron has plotted her downfall (Shakespeare may by now have taken over the authorship). Chiron and Demetrius, Tamora's sons, both lust after her, and Aaron suggests they take advantage of the 'deaf and dull' woods to 'revel in Lavinia's treasury'. He compares Lavinia's chastity to that of Lucrece (raped by Tarquin and the subject of Shakespeare's later poem), so that Lavinia's rape and subsequent death are anticipated in an almost ritualistic way. When Bassianus and Lavinia come upon Tamora and Aaron in a clearly compromising situation, Lavinia takes up Tamora's reference to Actaeon's horns in a taunt, which shows a rash sense of moral superiority worthy of her father:

> Under your patience, gentle empress,
> 'Tis thought you have a goodly gift in horning,
> And to be doubted that your Moor and you
> Are singled forth to try experiments.

> (2.2.66–9)

Lavinia's fate is sealed. Bassianus is killed and Tamora incites her sons not only to rape Lavinia, but to kill her – 'Let not this wasp outlive, us both to sting'. Lavinia begs her, 'O, keep me from their worse-than-killing lust … and be a charitable murderer' (175, 178). Shakespeare is here close to endorsing the stereotype that women are either victims or monsters. He then piles on the torment. Unlike Philomel, Lavinia is raped by two men and has both her hands cut off in addition to her tongue. Kermode writes that this horrific act is in a sense 'Senecan', but as in *The Rape of Lucrece* 'there is a distancing of horror, which is treated with a kind of formality', but is intended to make Lavinia's suffering 'an object of contemplation'.[5]

I well remember Vivien Leigh's entrance, in the Peter Brook production of 1955/7, with scarlet ribbons hanging from her wrists and mouth, a stylization that both distanced and magnified the cruelty. Titus' reaction is in stoical vein:

MARCUS This was thy daughter.
TITUS   Why, Marcus, so she is.

(3.1.63–4)

On the one hand he tells the kneeling Lucius, 'Faint-hearted boy, arise and look upon her'; on the other he asks, 'Give me a sword, I'll chop off my hands too' (66, 73). Slowly his grief and loneliness begin to flood out, once more sea imagery to the fore:

For now I stand as one upon a rock,
Environed with a wilderness of sea ...
Dear Lavinia, dearer than my soul.
Had I but seen thy picture in this plight,
It would have madded me; what shall I do
Now I behold thy lively body so?

(94–5, 103–6)

Lavinia sobs and weeps, her father offers to kiss her lips, and begins to cry himself. Titus, who has buried twenty-one sons in action and seen innumerable deaths in five campaigns, is overcome by his only daughter's suffering. Shakespeare is using his invented story to test out for the first time the particular bond between father and daughter.

In an inspired piece of plotting Shakespeare now shifts to Aaron's report of Saturninus' offer to spare the falsely accused Martius and Quintus if Titus will chop off his hand. Titus does so, and is rewarded with his two sons' heads plus his own severed hand. Here Shakespeare's growing psychological astuteness comes to the fore: Titus can only laugh at this, 'I have not another tear to shed'. In fact a kind of madness overtakes him, symbolized by the 'employment' he finds for Lavinia: 'Bear thou my hand, sweet wench, between thy teeth' (267, 283). This madness is compounded by the next scene, which may have been added in the late 1590s.[6] Titus laments with Lavinia, she handless, he one-handed, that she cannot strike her beating heart, but encourages her instead to 'Wound it with sighing, girl, kill it with groans' (3.2.15). He feels so close to her, presumably for the first time in his life, that 'I can interpret all her martyred signs ... In thy dumb action will I be as perfect / As begging hermits in their holy prayers' (36, 40–1). When Marcus kills a fly, Titus demands 'how if that fly had a father and a mother', and only relents when Marcus claims it is a black, ill-favoured fly, like to Aaron. He then retires to his closet to read with Lavinia 'sad stories chanced in the times of old' (61, 84). Shakespeare never again approached this degree of intimate empathy between father and daughter until Lear tells Cordelia, 'We two alone will sing like birds i'the cage'. And yet, unlike the Lear scene, the fly episode suggests a parody of tragic madness, which seems to be lurking for the rest of the play.

The book that Lavinia likes to read is in fact Ovid's *Metamorphoses*, and Titus helps her to find the Philomel passage, which leads to Marcus suggesting that she writes the name of her rapists with his staff, guided by her feet and mouth. At this point Titus speaks in Latin from *Hippolytus* ('Ruler of the great heavens, are you so slow to hear crimes, so slow to see?'), thus proclaiming himself a Senecan tragic hero (4.1.81–2). It is a passage in which Shakespeare manages to display yet again both his classical knowledge and his ingenious stagecraft. Tamora and her sons, thinking Titus to be mad, are off their guard, but Titus 'knew them all, though they supposed me mad' (5.2.142), a perception echoed in Lear's recognition of Gloucester on Dover Beach. Tamora characterizes herself as Revenge, Titus calls her sons Chiron and Demetrius, Rape and Murder and, when Tamora exits, binds and gags them. The protagonists are all now role-players, with Lavinia the handmaid of Revenge. Titus approaches with a knife and 'Lavinia 'tween her stumps doth hold / The basin that receives your guilty blood' (182–3).

> Far worse than Philomel you used my daughter,
> And worse than Progne I will be revenged.
>
> (194–5)

Both father and daughter have lost their sense of humanity in this ritual of revenge, and a form of farcical formality has now entered the play. Titus will dress as a cook, grind their bones to dust and make two pasties for Tamora's delectation. But first Lavinia must meet her appointed end, with the Emperor's approval. Titus asks Saturninus if the centurion Virginius was right to kill his daughter 'because she was enforced, stained and deflowered', and Saturninus replies, 'Because the girl should not survive her shame, / And by her presence still renew his sorrows'. Titus agrees, quoting 'precedent and lively warrant', unveils Lavinia and kills her: 'Die, die, Lavinia, and thy shame with thee, / And with thy shame thy father's sorrow die' (5.3.38, 40–1, 45–6).

Shakespeare then wraps up the killings with great economy – Titus kills Tamora, Saturninus Titus, Lucius Saturninus – and the ritual is played out. The killing of Lavinia, however, remains problematic. It may be that she welcomes death and walks towards the knife, as Sonia Ritter did in Deborah Warner's 1987 RSC production, but there is no such indication in the text. It may be a primitive belief, as Saturninus first suggests, that a raped woman is guilty and should not be allowed to 'survive her shame', but his second reply seems to carry more weight – that she is killed to extinguish her father's 'sorrows'. This can be seen either as an extreme endorsement of patriarchal status, or as an act of love – Titus has finally learnt to love another human being. The double rape of Lavinia and her mutilation does however leave us uneasy in terms of voyeurism, sexual exploitation and the titillating power of horror. Is there a certain salacious pleasure taken in the sixty lines of anticipation that leads to her rape? It can be argued that Shakespeare is merely adopting Ovid's tone when the poet describes how Philomel's severed tongue wriggled like a tail cut from a snake, and as it died tried to rejoin its bleeding mistress (*Metamorphoses*, 6.559–60). But Lavinia does seem defined solely by her suffering. When she is made to take her father's hand in her mouth, and then a stick with which to write the names of her assailants, her rape seems to be re-enacted again and again. Marcus says, in his long speech at the discovery of her torment:

> Alas, a crimson river of warm blood,
> Like to a bubbling fountain stirred with wind,
> Doth rise and fall between thy rosed lips
> Coming and going with thy honey breath.

> (2.3.22–5)

However much we may respect his 'Senecan' detachment and admire the beauty of his imagery, we cannot help feeling he should be preventing Lavinia from bleeding to death. The play, neglected for so many centuries, has attracted great interest in the past fifty years for its unwavering examination of extreme human lust, ambition and cruelty contrasted with the growth of a loving relationship within a family.

The Taming of the Shrew: Baptista, Katherine and Bianca

In *The Taming of the Shrew* Shakespeare took on a familiar story involving a father and two daughters, but gave it greater psychological complexity. On the surface his play upholds the premise that a shrewish woman should be tortured and tamed, but beneath this conventional account it can be argued that two social outsiders learn to love and respect one another. The play may be as early as 1590, certainly no later than 1592, and probably predates the anonymous *The Taming of a Shrew*, which was published in 1594 and is over a thousand lines shorter. One study has traced thirty-five literary versions of the Shrew story, and these have many features in common.[7] The shrew is usually the eldest of two or three daughters and is identified with the devil. The wealthy father warns the prospective suitor of her shrewishness, and offers a large dowry. The groom arrives late for the wedding, badly dressed, behaves boorishly and takes the bride straight off for the taming to begin: the nature and extent of the brutality varies. The test of the wife's obedience takes place after dinner at the father-in-law's house. The wife comes at once when summoned, throws her cap on the floor and steps on it, pulls off her husband's boots, places her hand under his foot, lectures the other wives and kisses her husband. This then was the required template, and Shakespeare at the start of his career was reluctant to diverge too far from it. His interest in the story seems to lie in three main areas: how to humanize the Kate-Petruccio plot; how to animate the farce of the Bianca-suitors plot; and how to examine the character of the two daughters through their relationship with their father.

It has become a commonplace of modern productions to suggest that Kate and Petruccio fall for one another on sight. Shakespeare festoons Kate with all the appropriate shrewish epithets: a 'friend of hell', 'hilding of a devilish spirit', 'curst and shrewd', 'stark mad' and 'wonderful froward'. When she and Petruccio first meet they rally and banter with one another for nearly a hundred lines, and this apparently constitutes their courtship. It is a sparring match, trading insults and puns that both clearly relish, though whether Kate is intrigued, dumbfounded or disgusted by his joke about oral sex ('with my tongue in your tail' [2.1.217]) leaves the actress a wide choice – the F stage direction is *She strikes him*. In public Kate calls Petruccio 'one half lunatic, / A madcap ruffian and a swearing Jack' (281–2), but when Petruccio interprets this as ''tis bargain'd 'twixt us twain, being alone, / That she shall still be curst in company' she seems acquiescent in her silence (298–9). Baptista joins their hands before witnesses (though as neither speak it is hardly a *sponsalia de futuro*), and they exit together. In *A Shrew* Kate is given the aside:

> But yet I will consent and marry him,
> For I methinks have lived too long a maid,
> And match him to, or else his manhood's good.

(348–50)

But Shakespeare holds back on any expression of Kate's feelings, possibly because he doesn't want to suggest that at her age she accepts that any man will do, but more probably because he wants to show a slowly developing attraction as the play progresses. *A Shrew* seeks to tidy up her motive, when Shakespeare wants with typical opacity to leave it open.

Petruccio duly turns up late for the wedding, fantastically dressed, outrages everyone in the church and carries Kate off before the feast. In the ballad *A Merry Jest of a Shrewd and Curst Wife* (c. 1550) the wife is now beaten till she bleeds, after which her battered body is wrapped in a salted horse-hide as a further torture. In other versions of the folktale her arm is broken and animals are killed in front of her. Even in *A Shrew* Ferando/Petruccio beats all his servants, and then Kate follows suit. Shakespeare eschews physical torture for a more subtle brainwashing. Kate is deprived of food, sleep and new clothes until she is prepared to say the sun is the moon and an old man is a 'young budding virgin'. Petruccio immediately denounces her as mad, insisting the virgin is a man, 'old, wrinkled, faded, wither'd', and it can be argued that Kate at last understands the rules of the game:

> Pardon, old father, my mistaking eyes,
> That have been so bedazzled with the sun
> That everything I look on seemeth green.
> Now I perceive thou art a reverend father.
> Pardon, I pray thee, for my mad mistaking.

> (4.5.44–8)

In this reading Petruccio is thereby made to appear a fool, and attempts have been made to further represent Petruccio as a psychotherapist acting for Kate's good.[8] This approach, however, cannot quite dispel the fact that, on the surface, she is tortured through deprivation until she agrees that black is white.

Kate's final speech is the ultimate conundrum. It can be interpreted as 'ironic, sincere, angry, exhibitionist, lobotomized, in love, masochistic, feminist, indulgent, threatening, or does she just have eyes on the cash?'[9] But irony would seem to undermine the whole argument of the play. Shakespeare would seem to believe, like his contemporaries, that however companionate marriage should be, in the final analysis the husband is the head of the family, the ruler of his little commonwealth – even Portia subscribes to this. Kate's attitude is much like Luciana in *The Comedy of Errors*, written at roughly the same time, that subservience to one's husband is, as Anne Barton writes, 'an in-built law of nature, not to be transgressed, and both have the force of the entire comedy behind them in their belief'.[10] The best defence of Petruccio's actions is to claim that he realizes that Kate is playing out the role of shrew as a defence against the world, and that if she is to feel free and loving within marriage she has to accept the new role of wife. Possible proof that Shakespeare endorses this view lies in the length of Kate's last speech. It could have been a dozen lines of token subservience, but instead Shakespeare writes her forty-four lines, which can hardly be carried off with an ironic wink, though it has been played as a derisive lampoon of a misogynist society, its very length enabling the actor to deliver satirical blow after blow in an attempt to humiliate the listening men (5.2.137–80). But when she speaks of love, fair looks and true obedience the attitude of her audience hardly reflects this. Nevertheless, as Fiona Shaw says, 'the play ends unresolved and out of joint, even for its own time'.[11]

In contrast to the psychological insight of the Kate–Petruccio plot, the Bianca–suitors plot is constructed, and has to be played, as farce: Gremio is described in the Folio (F) as a 'Pantelowne', and Lucentio calls him 'the old pantaloon' (3.1.36). The plot can seem overcomplicated and interminable, and the two styles often sit uneasily with one another. Just as Kate is initially 'curst', so Bianca is 'fair and virtuous'. Lucentio is first attracted by her 'mild behaviour and sobriety', then by her 'modesty', her 'sweet beauty', her coral lips and perfumed breath. When Kate binds her hands she protests, 'What you will command me will I do, / So well I know my duty to my elders' (2.1.6–7), and offers to plead for her with any of her suitors whom Kate fancies. Bianca is presented as the ideal Renaissance maiden, dutiful, chaste and humble. Shakespeare then takes great delight in slowly revealing her true self. When her tutors quarrel she begins to assert herself: 'I'll not be tied to hours nor "pointed times", / But learn my lessons as I please myself' (3.1.19–20). She leads Lucentio on ('presume not, despair not') and when she finds him reading *The Art of Love* declares, 'And may you prove, sir, master of your art' (4.2.9). It is Bianca who arranges their elopement and marriage by 'the old priest at St Luke's church', in defiance of her father. Once married, she indulges at the final banquet in some bawdy word-play with Gremio and Petruccio: 'I mean to shift my bush, / And then pursue me as you draw your bow' (5.2.46–7). When bidden to attend Lucentio she says she's too busy, and when Kate steps on her cap declares, 'Fie, what a foolish duty call you this'. Her husband protests he's lost five hundred crowns on the wager, to which she replies, 'The more fool you for laying on my duty' (126, 130). One conclusion the play emphasizes is that Bianca and Lucentio hardly know one another, while Kate and Petruccio have gained a deal of mutual understanding: Bianca's 'education' has been token, Kate's profound and lasting. Bianca has revealed herself the 'people-pleasing' younger daughter turned rebel, and Shakespeare's satirical exposé of the model maiden is complete.

In *A Shrew* Alfonso, the father, is cursorily dealt with and mainly a plot mechanism, but Shakespeare saw that a key to the very different characters of the sisters could lie in their father's treatment of them (their mother is never mentioned). Fathers in fact feature prominently in the play, the word is mentioned fifty-four times. Lucentio, Tranio and Petruccio all introduce themselves as suitors with reference to their fathers, and later in the play Lucentio will acquire both a real and a false father. Commentators often refer to Baptista as a 'weak' father, but I think Shakespeare is trying to create a more nuanced character – an averagely well-meaning, sixteenth-century father who cannot cope with a 'difficult' daughter. Hortensio, who has no axe to grind, calls him an 'affable and courteous gentleman' (1.2.97), but this is perhaps his public carapace. He is not an easy part to pin down: he can appear either indulgent, mercenary and unkind, or well meaning, generous and concerned. In production attempts have been made to turn him into a Mafia boss or a ruthless business king, though these identities sit uneasily on him. His opening gambit to Bianca's suitors is to say that Kate must be married first, and therefore anyone has his leave to court her. He may feel that with Bianca married there will be no hope for Kate, or he may simply, like a good merchant, be trying to clear his stockroom. Kate takes this, quite understandably, as a token of desperation: 'I pray you, sir, is it your will / To make a stale of me amongst these mates?' (1.1.57–8). Kate characterizes herself as either prostitute or laughing-stock, leaving Baptista speechless. She knows Bianca is his favourite:

> She is your treasure, she must have a husband,
> I must dance barefoot on her wedding-day,
> And for your love to her lead apes in hell.
>
> (2.1.32–4)

Baptista attempts no defence, just bemoans, 'Was ever gentleman thus griev'd as I?', and when Petruccio reports that he has heard of Kate's 'affability and bashful modesty', Baptista can only reply, 'She is not for your turn, the more my grief' (37, 49, 63). Is he being honest, or merely unsupportive? 'Grief' and 'quiet' are two key words in Baptista's life.

Where money is concerned Baptista is quick and business-like. Having established that Petruccio, as Antonio's son, is a man of means, he generously offers him half his lands and 20,000 crowns (well over half a million pounds in modern terms) as Kate's dowry, and in return Petruccio guarantees her widowhood. When Gremio and Tranio, disguised as Lucentio, vie for Bianca's hand, Baptista says the prize goes to 'who can assure my daughter greatest dower' (337).When Tranio makes the better offer, Baptista accepts him provided his father guarantees it, but is quick to ask for a widow's dower: if Tranio cannot guarantee this then she's Gremio's. Significantly he never mentions the need for Bianca's consent, he's willing for his favourite daughter to be married to Gremio, a 'rich old man'. He's sufficiently worried, however, about Kate's reaction to Petruccio's suit that he stipulates Petruccio has to get 'the special thing ... her love; for that is all in all' (129–30). It is hard to square these contrasting attitudes to his two daughters' happiness (Shakespeare's carelessness?). When Petruccio claims Kate is desperately in love with him, which belies Kate's 'I'll see thee hanged on Sunday first', Baptista is baffled: 'I know not what to say, but give me your hands' (312). Thus Shakespeare is at pains to describe in some detail a typical rich father's business-like approach to marriage contracts. Bianca's preference is not sought and Kate's objections are ignored, and yet Baptista is careful to see they are well provided for. Having set out these negotiations in some detail, Shakespeare never again makes the details of a financial settlement the main basis for his heroines' marriages.

Baptista shows some fatherly feelings for Kate. Petruccio's wooing clearly puzzles him: 'Now I play a merchant's part / And venture madly on a desperate mart', but 'the gain I seek is quiet in the match' (320–1, 324). When Petruccio is late for the wedding and Kate exits weeping, Baptista gives with one hand and takes with the other:

Go, girl, I cannot blame thee now to weep,
For such an injury would vex a saint,
Much more a shrew of thy impatient humour.

(3.2.27–9)

Baptista objects, rather feebly, to Petruccio's attire, but his main concern is to see them married and gain peace at any price. When Petruccio finally carries Kate off his only reaction is relief, 'Nay, let them go, a couple of quiet ones', and rather than scrap the wedding feast, 'Let Bianca take his sister's room' (239, 249). How little he knows his younger daughter is shown by his offer to take up half Lucentio's wager that Bianca will come when her husband calls. When Kate proves the more obedient he adds another 20,000 crowns as a further dowry: money is the commodity he is most comfortable with. Shakespeare does not further develop Baptista at this point: he could have spoken of how much he has misjudged his children, how happy he now is with his first-born and so on, but the opportunity is not taken up. Shakespeare has still to create a fully rounded father figure.

There is a deep ambiguity about the play, enhanced by the framing device of Christopher Sly, who in some productions turns into the wife-tamer of his fantasies. Early in his career Shakespeare is already beginning to experiment with familiar forms. Role playing is at a premium, and nothing is quite what it seems. The play is largely anti-paternalistic in its treatment of the fathers, and yet Petruccio's success as shrew-tamer would seem to uphold patriarchy in general. Or should we see Kate and Bianca as triumphing in their different ways over male supremacy? Shakespeare's career shows him much happier dealing with a single daughter (*King Lear* is the sole exception), but forced by the folktale to give Baptista at least two daughters he is ready to explore the favouritism that so often ensues. Where he is psychologically astute is in presenting Kate as the child labelled 'curst', while her younger sister, seeing the trials her elder endures, makes sure she is initially labelled 'mild and virtuous', and only allows her rebellious self-assertion to develop once she has snared her man. Shakespeare set out to write a farce, but couldn't stop himself creating something altogether more humane and complex.

1 Henry VI, *1 Henry IV* and *Henry V*

1 Henry VI is a muddled play, full of sound and fury in pedestrian verse, but it contains a father-daughter scene of some interest. The play seems to have been cobbled together in 1592, with the possible help of Nashe, Greene and even Marlowe, to exploit the success of what we now call Parts 2 and 3, which are far superior plays (I have fought my way through them).[12] In Part 1 the treatment of Joan la Pucelle, which may of course not be by Shakespeare, shows her descending from supernatural Amazonian strength to a frightened, impotent witch, summoning demons who fail to help her. It is agitprop theatre at its worst. In her final scene, before she is led away to be burnt, she meets her shepherd father, who offers to die with her. Joan, desperately claiming noble birth, will have none of it:

> Decrepit miser, base ignoble wretch,
> I am descended of a gentler blood.
> Thou art no father, not no friend of mine.

Her father is outraged:

> Dost thou deny thy father, cursed drab?
> O burn her, burn her, hanging is too good.

The English aristocrats Warwick and York comment:

> Graceless, wilt thou deny thy parentage?
> This argues what her kind of life hath been –
> Wicked and vile, and so her death concludes.

(5.3.7–9, 32–3, 14–16)

The sole purpose of the scene is to show denial of a father as the worst of female vices, a proposition the audience would presumably be expected to endorse.

In the same play an aristocratic daughter is bartered by her father without any consultation. René, Duke of Anjou and Maine and titular King of Naples and Sicily (whom Joan claimed, among others, as her true father), trades his daughter Margaret to marry Henry VI, 'upon condition I may quietly / Enjoy mine own, the country Maine and Anjou, / Free from oppression or the stroke of war' (5.2.174–6). Suffolk agrees to this, though Henry's council is later appalled at this surrender of Maine, and that Margaret is to be 'sent over at the King of England's own proper cost and charges, without having any dowry' (2 Henry VI, 1.1.59–60).

This contrasts with a later fictional scene in Henry V when Henry woos Katherine, daughter of the King of France. The marriage and dowry have already been arranged, but Shakespeare is anxious to show Henry a true English gentleman by wooing her with a mixture of military forth-rightness and egregious flattery, which reduces Katherine to observing pragmatically:

KATHERINE Dat is as it sall please *le roi mon père*.
HENRY   Nay, it will please him well, Kate; it shall please him, Kate.
KATHERINE Den it sall also content me.

(5.2.244–7)

Henry dutifully asks for her hand, and the French king demonstrates the use a marriage alliance could be put to: 'Take her, fair son, and from her blood raise up / Issue to me, that the contending kingdoms / Of France and England … may cease their hatred' (340–4). The Epilogue immediately tells us that their issue, Henry VI, 'lost France and made his England bleed', though Shakespeare omits to point out that Katherine, in her subsequent marriage to Owen Tudor, was the ancestor of Queen Elizabeth – a monarch never keen to acknowledge her Welsh Tudor connection.

The contrast between two newly married couples, rare in the canon, is demonstrated in *I Henry IV*, when Glendower meets with Hotspur, Mortimer and their wives to divide the kingdom into three. Glendower is lovingly indulgent of his Welsh-speaking daughter's passion for Mortimer – 'my daughter weeps, she'll not part with you', but this turns to an exasperated echo of Capulet (*Romeo and Juliet*, 4.2.14) – 'She is desperate here, a peevish, self-willed harlotry, one that no persuasion can do good upon' – and a fear that if Mortimer 'melt' 'then will she run mad' (3.1.188, 192–3, 205). Lady Percy, however, shows no sign of 'shedding a world of water' over her husband,but Lady Mortimer's singing of a Welsh song brings a rare sense of domestic calm to the play, only to be broken by Hotspur's desire to be 'away within these two hours'.

Love's Labours Lost

The power of an absent father, the first of several in the canon, is explored in *Love's Labours Lost*. Boyet, an attendant lord and part surrogate father to the four women (Maria calls him 'Cupid's grandfather'), reminds the Princess of France, 'held precious in the world's esteem', that the king her father has sent her to the King of Navarre to parley over possession of Acquitaine, 'a dowry for a queen' (2.1.4–8). The princess proceeds to do this extremely ably and, if Boyet had had the right papers to hand, might have wrapped up negotiations (and the play) there and then. This princess may be based on Marguerite de Valois, sister of Henry III of France, who was already the King of Navarre's estranged wife when she led an embassy of reconciliation to him in 1578. Shakespeare therefore gave his princess an altogether more important diplomatic mission. Throughout the play the women are shown to be shrewder and more able than the men, a pattern followed in most of the comedies. As Boyet comments: 'The tongues of mocking wenches are as keen / As is the razor's edge invisible' (5.2.256–7).

One of Shakespeare's most brilliant strokes of concision occurs at the end of the play when Marcade interrupts 'the merriment' with the news:

MARCADE   The King, your father –
PRINCESS   Dead, for my life.
MARCADE   Even so; my tale is told.

(5.2.716–17)

The princess, now queen, knows that for a year she must shut 'my woeful self up in a mourning house, / Raining the tears of lamentation / For the remembrance of my father's death' (804–6). It is a signal demonstration of the power a royal father wields, even in death. Whether at the end of the year the four 'Jacks' will have their 'Jills' (866) is open to doubt. It was a conclusion Shakespeare never repeated: from now on comedies would end with young heroines married, however inappropriately – Isabella must accept her 'friar' Duke, Marina the brothel frequenting Lysimachus.

A Midsummer Night's Dream: Egeus and Hermia

A Midsummer's Night Dream and *Romeo and Juliet* were apparently written in 1594/5 – it is hard to be certain which came first – but the contrast in his handling of young lovers and angry fathers is marked. In the tragedy, where Shakespeare stuck close to his source material, he wrote a very young woman fixated and loyal to her first love; in the comedy, a plot largely of his invention (with a nod towards Chaucer's *The Knight's Tale*), he suggests that partners are exchangeable during the course of a single night. He also examined a theme that recurs throughout his writing from Proteus and Valentine to Palamon and Arcite in *The Two Noble Kinsmen* – that marriages are only achieved through the severing of same-sex bonds.

Hermia's father Egeus is Shakespeare's second attempt, after the Duke of Milan, at a draconian father who even threatens his daughter with execution. If this piece of Athenian law seems a flight of fantasy on Shakespeare's part, it should be remembered that Calvin, among others, had decreed death for children who disobeyed their parents. Egeus calls Hermia his 'child' three times, and claims 'as she is mine, I may dispose of her' (1.1.42). Hermia, however, regards her 'virgin patent' as her property, not to be yielded to an 'unwished yoke'. It is a fundamental struggle for ownership of a daughter's virginity. Athenian law suggests that desire is routed through the father – Hermia's mother is again absent, indeed everyone in the play is motherless, including the Indian boy. Theseus is adamant about the father's power:

To you your father should be as a god:
One that compos'd your beauties, yea, and one

To whom you are but as a form in wax
By him imprinted, and within his power
To leave the figure, or disfigure it.

(47–51)

Both Aristotle and Aquinas had argued that the woman's role in reproduction is essentially passive; it is the father who gives shape to the life, both biologically and symbolically. Theseus, however, immediately offers an alternative to the death sentence in the shape of a nunnery, which he paints in the bleakest terms – 'chanting faint hymns to the cold fruitless moon' (73).Another of Egeus' tactics is to claim that Lysander has filched Hermia's heart through music, a list of cheap gewgaws ('bracelets of the hair, rings, gauds, conceits, / Knacks, trifles, nosegays, sweetmeats'), but above all through witchcraft, a ploy later used by Brabantio and Polixenes (334). Lysander suggests that they escape to a widow aunt who will support them, but this surrogate mother is never reached, indeed is forgotten about. Hermia seems resigned in her defiance: 'So will I grow, so live, so die, my lord / Ere I will yield my virgin patent up', and then runs away (79–80). Egeus reveals that his true partiality is for Demetrius. When Lysander suggests in that case he should marry Demetrius, Egeus agrees: 'True, he hath my love; / And what is mine my love shall render him' (95–6). Hermia is his possession, Demetrius has his love. This underlines the fact that for apparently widowed fathers with single daughters, legion in Shakespeare's plays, the son-in-law will be the heir, and to an extent master of his wife's inheritance. Egeus never explains why he favours Demetrius; it isn't for his money as with Thurio and Lucentio. He continues to champion Demetrius even when he falls for Helena. The death he then really craves is not Hermia's, but Lysander's – 'I beg the law, the law upon his head!' (4.1.154). In fact Theseus eventually overrules Egeus by declaring the three couples will all get married together.

Of the four lovers Shakespeare's interest lies more with the women than the men, just as he writes more eloquently for Juliet than for Romeo. Hermia and Helena are clearly characterized and differentiated in both text and production, while audiences often have difficulty distinguishing Lysander from Demetrius. Helena plays the victim, the masochist – 'But herein mean I to enrich my pain'; 'Use me but as your spaniel' (1.1.250, 2.1.205) – and when she finds herself being pursued by two men, she assumes it's a joke at her expense. Her paranoia about her height and her low self-esteem give the actor endless opportunities for comedy. Hermia by contrast is more practical and contained, secure in Lysander's love. She is stoical about the uneven passage of true love: 'It stands as an edict in destiny. / Then let us teach our trial patience, / Because it is a customary cross' (1.1.151–3). When Hermia finds herself abandoned by Lysander, however, and called a 'puppet' and a 'vixen', she loses her composure and wants to tear Helena's eyes out. Shakespeare's observation of adolescent female rivalry is acute (though some would argue patronizing), and he uses the magical nature of the forest as a fantasy stage where true feelings and repressed desires can be acted out. The two girls celebrate their friendship in homoerotic terms of which Lyly would have approved:

> So we grew together,
> Like to a double cherry, seeming parted,
> But yet an union in partition,
> Two lovely berries moulded on one stem.

(3.2.208–11)

The only puzzle that remains is the identity of the Master of the Revels in the last act. Q has Philostrate, who is told in the first scene to 'stir up the Athenian youth to merriments' (1.1.12), but F has Egeus. This may be a mistake, a result of some doubling necessity, or it may be that Shakespeare had second thoughts and wanted to include Egeus in the festivities as an act of reconciliation with his daughter. But the 'merry tears' that this character shed when auditioning the Pyramus and Thisbe play seems most un-Egeus-like. There is no speech repenting his hard-heartedness and wishing the lovers well. Shakespeare had experimented with putting paternal dominion in its most extreme and distasteful form, and seems content to let Egeus disappear from the play.

Romeo and Juliet: Capulet and Juliet, an actor's perspective

In 1955 I played Mercutio at school when I was fifteen, and Clifford Williams, who was running the local Marlowe Theatre at Canterbury (and from 1962 became an RSC director) picked me out as promising, and inadvertently alerted me to the possibility of my becoming an actor, and twelve years later in 1967 I finally achieved this. My generation was much influenced by Franco Zefferelli's 1960 production at the Old Vic with Judi Dench and John Stride. The emphasis was on youth, naturalism, Italian heat and speed of thought and delivery (though about a thousand lines were cut). Previous productions that I had seen suddenly seemed stilted and decorous. While at Oxford University I had been directed in 1962 as Falstaff in *1 & 2 Henry IV* by Peter Dews, and it was he who gave me my first professional job when he took over the Birmingham Rep. Dews was steeped in Shakespeare as he had directed all the history plays, *An Age of Kings*, for BBC television in 1960 (live in black and white and in hour-length instalments, with Robert Hardy as Hal/Henry V and Sean Connery as Hotspur). Dews was a very down-to-earth Yorkshireman, with an outstanding and witty gift for paraphrasing Shakespeare, which he claimed was his substitute for Stanislavskean intention and subtext. He had a great ear for Elizabethan verse and a tyrannical belief in audibility: 'They've come to *hear* a play, and your last line only a passing bat might have picked up'. I learnt a lot from him.

At Birmingham he had deliberately assembled a young company, which stayed together for more than a year. For *Romeo and Juliet* Anna Calder-Marshall (aged twenty-one) and Anthony Higgins (twenty) were the lovers, Brian Cox (twenty-one) Mercutio, Michael Gambon (twenty-seven) Prince Escalus and myself Capulet, at twenty-eight the oldest member of the company. It was a fairly traditional Elizabethan production, with an emphasis on speed and lightness. Dews saw Capulet as an essentially loving father, quite out of his depth with a rebellious daughter. This intrigued me as I had thought him a typically overbearing patriarch and, still in thrall to my academic training, I started to look at Shakespeare's source material – a habit I have followed ever since. The story of Romeo and Juliet originates in fifteenth-century Italy, though a full-scale narrative was assembled by Luigi da Porto of Vicenza, who died in 1529. Two novels, Italian and French, were drawn from this in the 1550s, and in 1562 Arthur Brooke drew on Boisteau's French narrative to form a 3,020-line poem, fourteen syllables to a line.[13] This last is undoubtedly Shakespeare's main source, and it is the changes he made to this that have the greatest significance.

Brooke moralizes that giving in to lustful desires and ignoring parental advice is bound to end in tragedy, while Shakespeare is ready to celebrate the passion, energy and commitment of young love. In Brooke there is no parental talk of Juliet's marrying till after Tybalt's death and Romeo's exile. Then Lady Capulet, thinking Juliet's tears excessive, comes up with the theory:

> The only crop and root of all my daughter's pain,
> Is grudging envy's faint disease: perhaps she doth disdain
> To see in wedlock yoke the most part of her peers,
> While only she unmarried doth lose so many years.
> And more perchance she thinks you mind to keep her so,
> Wherefore despairing doth she wear herself away with woe.

(1843–8)

Capulet admits that he's considered this, but,

> Scarce saw she yet full xvi years: too young to be a bride.
> But since her state doth stand on terms so perilous,
> And that a maiden daughter is a treasure dangerous,
> With so great speed I will endeavour to procure

A husband for our daughter young, her sickness faint to cure ...
Whom I do hold as dear, as the apple of mine eye.

(1860–4, 1871)

So Capulet confers with his friends, finds many eager suitors but settles on
Count Paris. Lady Capulet breaks this to Juliet (already married to Romeo),
who 'marvels much / As thus to yield me up, at pleasure of another, / Before
you know if I do like, or else mislike my lover' (1906–8). Lady Capulet
reports this to her husband, and 'the testy old man, wroth, disdainful
without measure' sends for Juliet, who 'grovels' weeping at his feet, but
Capulet,

With fiery eyes and scarlet cheeks, thus spake her in his rage ...
How much the Roman youth of parents stood in awe,
And eke what power upon their seed the fathers had by law?
Whom they not only might pledge, alienate, and sell,
(When so they stood in need) but more, if children did rebel,
The parents had the power of life and sudden death.

(1945, 1951–5)

Capulet threatens that if Juliet doesn't agree to marry Paris on Wednesday,
'sure thou shalt not fail / A thousand times a day to wish for sudden
death' (1980–1). Juliet later tells her mother that she asks pardon of her
father and agrees to marry Paris, and when Lady Capulet reports this
to her husband 'joyful tears ran down the cheeks of this grey-bearded
sire' (2245).

Shakespeare takes his cue from Brooke's 'grey beard' to make Capulet
elderly. After the opening quarrel where Tybalt threatens Benvolio with
death, 'Old Capulet' enters 'in his gown' and calls for his 'long sword',
which immediately marks him out as old-fashioned. His wife cuts him
down to size with 'A crutch, a crutch! Why call you for a sword' (1.1.75–6).
Capulet has two more lines, and then is silent till he exits. It is an oddly brief
but comedic introduction to a major character. We next meet him negoti-
ating Juliet's marriage to Paris, before Juliet had even met Romeo, the scene
which Brooke places much later in his poem. Three things are apparent in
Shakespeare's version. Capulet behaves like a model Renaissance father,
anxious that his daughter should not be pressed into child-bearing too early
('And too soon marr'd are those so early made'); insistent that 'my will to
her consent is but a part'; and clearly not over-impressed by Count Paris'
aristocratic status. His language is highly wrought: 'Let two more summers
wither in their pride', 'Earth-treading stars that make dark heaven light'
(1.2.10–25). I seized upon this scene to make my Capulet as affable and
caring as possible, but also adopting grandiloquent language to impress his
aristocratic suitor.

There is a comedic edge to the scene which continues in the prose dialogue between the serving men preparing for the feast, followed by Capulet's opening address to his guests, Shakespeare's first attempt at the rambling reminiscences of the elderly:

> I have seen the day
> That I have worn a visor and could tell
> A whispering tale in a fair lady's ear,
> Such as would please. 'Tis gone, 'tis gone, 'tis gone.
>
> (1.5.22–5)

This continues with his wrangle with his cousin over how long ago it was they wore a mask – this regret at the passing of time will reach its apogee in the Shallow-Silence scene in *2 Henry IV*. Learning from his nephew Tybalt that the Montague Romeo is present he counsels like the perfect host: 'I would not for the wealth of all this town / Here in my house do him disparagement' (67–8). When Tybalt objects that he'll 'not endure him', Capulet breaks into an angry, disjointed tirade, while observing the iambic pentameter, a Shakespearean trademark – both the disjoint and the regularity of the verse have to be observed:

> You are a saucy boy. Is't so indeed?
> This trick may chance to scathe you. I know what.
> You must contrary me. Marry, 'tis time –
> Well said, my hearts – You are a princox, go
> Be quiet, or – More light, More light! – For shame,
> I'll make you quiet. What, cheerly, my hearts!
>
> (83–8)

Later Capulet tries to persuade Romeo and Benvolio not to leave, but 'it waxes late', and he clearly can't wait to get to bed. It became apparent to me that Shakespeare has cleverly and economically introduced every element in Capulet that will feature as the plot unfolds: his care for his daughter's future, his desire to behave as a 'proper' gentleman, the hallmarks of old age in his language and attitudes, his sudden bursts of temper, the domestic side of his life, his use of high-flown imagery and all this spiced with a comedic edge. It is a major advance on the Duke of Milan and Baptista.

With Capulet firmly established as a benign father Shakespeare holds him back till after Juliet's marriage, Tybalt's death and Romeo's banishment. While the two lovers are enjoying their first, and only, night together, Paris arrives to press his suit. Capulet's opening speech picks up the same understanding, moralizing tone that he adopted in his earlier encounter with Paris:

Look you, she lov'd her kinsman Tybalt dearly,
And so did I. Well, we were born to die.
'Tis very late. She'll not come down tonight.

                                                              (3.4.3–5)

Capulet is still the tolerant, loving father, anxious to get to bed, when, in
the first quarto (Q1) stage direction (omitted in F), '*Paris offers to go in and
Capulet calls him again*'. Capulet performs a sudden about-turn:

Sir Paris, I will make a desperate tender
Of my child's love. I think she will be rul'd
In all respects by me; nay, more, I doubt it not.

                                                              (12–14)

Capulet, who only the day before had told Paris to wait a couple of years
and meanwhile look at other 'fresh female buds', is now desperate not to
lose him. With Prince Escalus' displeasure at his kinsman Mercutio's death
through the involvement of Tybalt, I realized Capulet's chances of bagging
an aristocrat for his daughter are in the balance. With his apparent sole
male heir Tybalt dead, Juliet's marriage is now his only hope of keeping his
estate in the family. She is both property and procreator.[14] Hence the need to
have a quiet wedding with 'a friend or two' as soon as possible, and if two
days are too soon, make it three. Lady Capulet is sent off, though it's nearly
dawn, to 'prepare' Juliet. There is no thought of consultation; Paris doesn't
need to 'get her heart'; the model parent has been jettisoned. Capulet has
violated all the normal procedures: no proper courtship, no trothplighting
or reading of the banns. His volte-face is complete, the genial, coping parent
is set aside, and this of course made him very interesting to play. There is
also no financial settlement: Paris is presumably confident Juliet will inherit
everything, and Capulet is just happy to have his daughter a countess. In a
wonderful touch Capulet reveals a slight misgiving. Knowing his daughter's
spirit he 'thinks' she will be ruled by him, and then hastily adds, in case
Paris should conclude he's not in control of his family, 'Nay more, I doubt
it not'. This last is a folio addition to Q, and one of those occasions where
I suspect it may have been prompted by the actor himself. Shakespeare
has carefully prepared a major turning point in the story. Capulet has
unwittingly precipitated the tragedy: Juliet, faced by marriage to Paris in
a few days, has to find an immediate remedy, however far-fetched and
dangerous.

Capulet is, of course, right to have misgivings. When her mother brings
the 'joyful tidings', Juliet points out, as she does in Brooke, 'I wonder at
this haste, that I must wed / Ere he that should be husband comes to woo'
(3.5.118–19). Capulet arrives to find Juliet in tears, and his opening lines
are again comedic:

When the sun sets the earth doth drizzle dew,
But for the sunset of my brother's son
It rains downright.

(126–8)

The line ends there, suggesting a pause while the father waits for his daughter to stop crying, perhaps even cheer up. Juliet clearly doesn't, and Capulet embarks on one of his highly-wrought metaphors, comparing her tears to the sea, her body 'tempest-tossed'. Whether this is played with sympathy or exasperation, it suggests a bond between father and daughter, which is cut short by the enquiry, 'How now, wife? / Have you deliver'd to her our decree?' (137–8). The formality of a 'decree delivered' indicates an ultimatum, there is to be no room for compromise. Lady Capulet's report is equally uncompromising, 'She will none, she gives you thanks' (139), and Capulet works himself up into a disproportionate loss of temper. In Brooke the diatribe develops thus:

Unless by Wednesday next, thou bend as I am bent
And at our castle called Freetown, then freely do assent
To Count Paris' suit, and promise to agree
To whatever then shall pass, twixt him, my wife, and me,
Not only will I give all that I have away
From thee, to those that shall me love, me honour and obey,
But also too so close, and to so hard a gaol.
I shall thee wed, for all thy life, that sure thou shalt not fail
A thousand times a day to wish for sudden death,
And curse the day, and hour when first thy lungs did give thee breath.
Advise thee well, and say that thou art warned now,
And think not that I speak in sport, or mind to break my vow.

(1973–84)

In Shakespeare's hands this becomes:

Hang thee young baggage, disobedient wretch!
I tell thee what – get thee to church a' Thursday,
Or never after look me in the face …
God's bread, it makes me mad! Day, night, work, play,
Alone, in company, still my care hath been
To have her match'd. And having now provided
A gentleman of noble parentage,
Of fair demesnes, youthful and nobly lign'd,
Stuff'd, as they say, with honourable parts,
Proportion'd as one's thought would wish a man –
And then to have a wretched puling fool,

A whining mammet, in her fortune's tender,
To answer 'I'll not wed, I cannot love'
I am too young, I pray you pardon me!'
But, and you will not wed, I'll pardon you!
Graze where you will, you shall not house with me.
Look to't, think on't. I do not use to jest.
Thursday is near. Lay hand on heart. Advise.
And you be mine I'll give you to my friend;
And you be not, hang! Beg! Starve! Die in the streets!

(3.5.160–2, 176–92)

This is bravura writing. Shakespeare has taken Brooke's template and, without greatly altering its argument, has turned it into highly dramatic, naturalistic, characterful verse, which I found a joy to play. To the listener it could be rhythmic prose, thought it is in regular iambics, mostly end-stopped. The Nurse's opening verse speech in 1.3.46 shares the same immediacy (and in Q1 and Q2 is actually printed as prose), just as Falstaff's prose soliloquies can sound like verse: rhythm is everything to Shakespeare, as in any great dramatist.

When the next day Juliet 'falls prostrate' to beg forgiveness, Capulet is pleased, but not affectionate: 'Why, I am glad on't. This is well. Stand up. / This is as't should be' (4.2.28–9). The 'peevish self-willed harlotry' has been 'reclaimed'. He admits that his 'heart is wondrous light', but only when Juliet has exited. Sixteenth-century fathers rarely express their love directly to their children: only when Juliet is thought to have died are these feelings allowed to surface. Capulet has recovered his good humour and playfulness: the wedding shall be next day, 'I'll not to bed tonight, let me alone. / I'll play the housewife for this once' (42–3). Then Shakespeare gives Capulet a short scene of household happiness and bustle, which was to become another of his trademarks. The Nurse calls him a 'cot-quean' to his face, his wife says he's 'been a mouse-hunt in your time', the servant quips that he has a head 'that will find out logs' and Capulet is happy to swap puns with him (4.4.3–19). His mood swings are wonderfully documented.

The family's lamentations over the supposedly dead Juliet is one of the most puzzling scenes in Shakespeare. In Brooke the Nurse summons Lady Capulet, and only *her* grief is described, not Capulet's or the Nurse's: 'Whereto live I since she is dead, except to wail and moan? / Alack, dear child, my tears for thee shall never cease ... Then gan she so to sob, it seemed her heart would brast'. In Shakespeare's hands the Nurse is given a parody of grief: 'O day, O day, O day, O hateful day', Lady Capulet echoes her repetitions: 'Alack the day! She's dead, she's dead, she's dead!', while Capulet is given one of the most beautiful couplets in the play:

Death lies on her like an untimely frost
Upon the sweetest flower of all the field.

(4.5.28–9)

And continues with a paean to death, which underlines the importance of
a son-in-law to the father of an only daughter:

Death is my son-in-law, Death is my heir.
My daughter he hath wedded. I will die,
And leave him all: life, living, all is Death's.

(38–40)

But he at last acknowledges his daughter's importance to him: 'And with my
child my joys are buried!' Friar Laurence steadies him with the conventional
advice that she's better off in heaven, though he manages to remind them,
'The most you sought was her promotion' – a statement of considerable
ambiguity. Capulet then reverts to a formal solemnity:

All things that we ordained festival,
Turn from their office to black funeral:
Our instruments to melancholy bells,
Our wedding cheer to a sad burial feast ...

(64, 71, 84–7)

They exit, and Shakespeare daringly rounds off the scene with a comedy
exchange (sadly, often cut) for Peter and the musicians over their loss of
earnings, probably included to please his chief comedian Will Kemp whom
we know played Peter, since in Q2 and Q3 Shakespeare put Kemp's name
against Peter's opening speech. If only he had named his actors more often,
we might know which apprentice played Juliet, and which actor (John
Heminges?) Capulet. This is not mere antiquarian curiosity, for if the Juliet
had been particularly successful it might be the reason Shakespeare felt able
to give such space to Portia, Beatrice and Rosalind; and if Heminges had
proved exceptional in playing idiosyncratic elderly men it might explain
why Shakespeare wrote Polonius and Pandarus at such length and invented
the part of Brabantio. Playwrights closely attached to companies are
accustomed to write for the actors at their disposal.

It is hard to know what to make of this 'death' scene. The audience
knows that Juliet is not dead, and the family's grief is therefore miscon-
ceived. We seem to be in the realm of comedy, in which the Friar's potion
appears a preposterous device, Juliet will at some point rise up, and there
will be a happy ending. From all the doom-laden premonitions of Juliet,
Romeo and Friar Laurence we know that Shakespeare was determined
to write a tragedy in the Brooke tradition, but had saddled himself with

a potentially comic plot, and this could only be turned to tragedy by a sequence of misadventures which even Thomas Hardy might have baulked at. His error lay in following his source too closely, a mistake he never made again. Yet Juliet's supposed death had to be mourned. Shakespeare could only give Lady Capulet, the Nurse and Paris stock pieces of rhetoric. His interest lay in the father's intense feeling of loss, his eloquent poetic outpouring of grief. All the love he feels for his daughter is at last, too late, unleashed. It is significant that in the final scene Capulet has only nine lines and expresses no grief at Juliet's real death: it has all been said already. Capulet is Shakespeare's most complete study of a father to date, rich in detail and understanding, but the sixteenth-century's father's inability to show his affection for his daughter face to face necessarily constrains their scenes, a limitation which I found very galling to play. With some judicious cutting I have since seen Capulet played as more of a domestic tyrant. In Trevor Nunn and Barry Kyle's 1976 RSC production, for instance, John Woodvine was 'the source and fountain of the hate and violence that runs through the play', throwing Juliet to the floor when she refuses to marry Paris and kicking Romeo's corpse in the tomb.[15]

Juliet is introduced with some care. Her father, suitor, mother and nurse tell us a good deal about her before she speaks, and when she does it is with the dutiful subservience of a child. Juliet's age is an important factor in the play. Brooke puts her age at sixteen and Painter's novel *The Palace of Pleasure* (1567) at nearly eighteen, so it would seem that Shakespeare is deliberately making his nearly fourteen-year-old Juliet as young an adolescent as possible. Despite Capulet's protest that Paris should wait two more years, Lady Capulet seems to be pressing ahead with the idea of marriage, perhaps on the grounds that she gave birth to Juliet at 'much upon these years / That you are now a maid'. Juliet replies with due humility that marriage 'is an honour that I dream not of ... but no more deep will I endart mine eye / Than your consent gives strength to make it fly' (1.3. 72–3, 66, 98–9). This scene between the three women is one of family and domestic harmony, suggestive of female autonomy, unusual in Shakespeare, and paralleled only by an altogether less harmonious scene in *Coriolanus* (1.3). It promises that the relationship between Juliet and her mother will be important, but in fact the key relationship is going to be between Juliet and her surrogate mother, the Nurse, who, unlike her mother, is certain of her ward's age. At this stage Shakespeare keeps Juliet and her father apart: they don't speak to one another at the ball, and Capulet proceeds with his plans for the Paris match without any reference to his daughter. Juliet's age is also a challenge to the actress, since in the last few decades the part is usually cast very young. Anna Calder-Marshall, my Birmingham Juliet, was a convincing teenager but felt that at twenty-one, not long out of drama school, she was too young and inexperienced to play the part, although she was fascinated by the journey from childhood to womanhood. She thought she played it better some years later with Ian McKellen on the radio, and noted that Gwen Ffrangcon-Davies spoke an excerpt at her ninetieth birthday celebrations in 1981, sounding like a young child (she had played it in 1924, aged thirty-three, with John Gielgud, aged twenty). Experience would seem to outweigh teenage veracity.

From early in the play Shakespeare introduces the death motif. Romeo, on his way to the ball, fears, 'My mind misgives / Some consequence yet hanging in the stars', which will result in 'some vile forfeit of untimely death' (1.4.106–7, 111). At the ball Juliet states that if Romeo is married 'my grave is like to be my wedding bed' (1.5.135). Shakespeare surrounds Juliet with references to classical mythology – Phaeton, Echo and, once again, Philomel. The fifteen-line 'sonnet' that leads to their first kiss still has a childish ring, but the balcony scene reveals Juliet as the more practical and determined, the more imaginative and far-sighted. It is she who decides that they have made a 'contract', though it is 'too rash, too unadvis'd, too sudden' (2.2.118), and it is she who in effect proposes marriage. She is the falconer, Romeo the bird to be caged. She seems to have grown two years in the course of the evening, and Anna Calder-Marshall found her greater maturity easier to play. For all her headlong rush Juliet maintains a sense of decorum. Shakespeare wants to distance her from Brooke's 'wily wench', who 'betwixt her teeth the bit ... now hath caught', and for whom the Nurse acts 'as bridle of her lust' (767, 721, 723), but cannot altogether banish our feeling that while Juliet may be 'in love' with Romeo and want to sleep with him, she cannot yet 'love' a man she hardly knows.

Shakespeare sees Juliet's growing maturity as a coming of age: as Thomas Morsan writes, 'Romeo and Juliet are the embodiments of the need adolescents have to differentiate themselves, and their sense of "self", from the sense of self imposed by culture and society, in this case the patriarchalist culture and society of Verona.'[16] In turn Verona's social order is reflected in the conflict between intimacy and power in Juliet's family. Shakespeare was always alive to the trials of adolescence. As the Old Shepherd in *The Winter's Tale* says, 'I would there were no age between ten and three and twenty, or that youth would sleep out the rest' (3.3.58–60). Juliet 'weeps and weeps, / And now falls on her bed', Romeo lies 'on the ground, with his own tears made drunk' and Friar Laurence denounces Romeo's 'womanish' tears as 'unseemly woman in a seeming man' (3.3.99–100, 84, 112). Both threaten to kill themselves, and of course eventually do so. In both we see all the emotional intensity and suicidal despair, the feelings of loneliness, anger and hatred pitted against the discovery of freedom, sexual release and personal commitment. Simone de Beauvoir writes of the agony for an adolescent girl in choosing 'between her original claim to be subject, active, free, and, on the other hand, her erotic urges and the social pressure to accept herself as passive object ... But if I can accomplish my destiny only as the *Other*, how shall I give up my *Ego*?'[17]

When Juliet finally meets her father again she is married, Tybalt is dead, Romeo banished and she knows that matters are out of control (3.5). While

Capulet launches into unbalanced tirades, Juliet can hardly get a word in. Her first three lines are a desperate equivocation, implying that she hates the prospect of marrying Paris, but is thankful that her father 'meant love' by it – a sophistry that he understandably identifies as 'chop-logic'. In her last two lines she begs for a hearing on her knees, calling him 'good father', but he will have none of it. Lady Capulet, usually addressed as 'madam', becomes 'sweet my mother', but to no avail. Her final scene with her father is very formal. To facilitate Friar Laurence's plan she has to accede to the Paris wedding, and to her father's rough question, 'How now, my headstrong: where have you been gadding?', she replies in textbook daughterly submission:

> Where I have learnt me to repent the sin
> Of disobedient opposition
> To you and your behests, and am enjoin'd
> By holy Laurence to fall prostrate here,
> To beg your pardon. Pardon, I beseech you.
> Henceforward I am ever rul'd by you.

(4.2.16–22)

Her divorce from her father is total, and for the rest of the play she makes no reference to him. It is hard to know what she feels about her father. She has always known him as her 'lord', just as she acknowledges Romeo as 'poor my lord'. The point Shakespeare is making, deliberately or not, is that young daughters had little connection with their fathers in apparently routine family situations. It will take the exceptional circumstances of *Much Ado About Nothing*, *Hamlet*, *King Lear* and the romances for something deeper to be revealed. What I find particular about Juliet, compared with Silvia, Bianca, Hermia and Helena, is her ordinariness. Of course Romeo finds her attractive, but otherwise Shakespeare manages to dispense with his usual encomia of 'beautiful', 'heavenly', 'fair and virtuous', which bespatter the comedies. We identify with Juliet because she comes across as a real adolescent. She is also endowed with some extraordinarily emotional and erotic verse:

> Come, civil night,
> Thou sober-suited matron all in black,
> And learn me how to lose a winning match
> Play'd for a pair of stainless maidenhoods.
> Hood my unmann'd blood, bating in my cheeks,
> With thy black mantle, till strange love grown bold
> Think true love acted simple modesty ...
> O, I have bought the mansion of a love
> But not possess'd it, and though I am sold,
> Not yet enjoy'd.

(3.2.10–16, 26–8)

This is a major advance in Shakespeare's handling of verse, an outpouring of awakening sexual desire that he never bettered. His audience may have been taken aback by an upper-class, thirteen-year-old girl using language associated with a mature 'wanton'. Even more immediate and tumultuous are the thoughts that run through her imagination before she takes the poison. What if the poison doesn't work, or it really is a poison? What if she wakes before Romeo comes and is stifled by the 'loathsome smells' and Tybalt's festering corpse? Will she not be distraught,

> And madly play with my forefathers' joints,
> And pluck the mangled Tybalt from his shroud,
> And, in this rage, with some great kinsman's bone
> As with a club dash out my desperate brains?

> (4.3.51–4)

Finally, her imagination is so inflamed by hideous phantoms that the taking of the poison is almost a relief.

Lady Capulet is the conduit through which father and daughter relate (eighteenth-century editions gave her the courtesy title 'Lady', though Q1 and F more correctly describe her as 'Capulet's Wife'). It is Shakespeare's first, and only, attempt at showing at any length the dynamic between father, mother and child. Despite the promise of their first scene, it is hard to see much empathy between mother and daughter. Lady Capulet goes on for sixteen lines about Paris's attractions, but the effect is to make her seem besotted by him, as she may well be by Tybalt, or indeed by any young man who compares favourably with her elderly husband. As she tells Juliet that she was a mother in her mid-teens, she could be under thirty, suggesting either that Capulet married late, or that she is his second, or even third, wife, but the first to bear a surviving child. Pulling herself together, she asks abruptly, 'Speak briefly, can you like of Paris' love?', to which Juliet gives her formal, modest reply. It is left to the Nurse to urge, 'Go, girl; seek happy nights to happy days', and it is the Nurse whom Juliet entrusts with arranging her marriage to Romeo and subsequent bridal night.

Lady Capulet brings the 'joyful tidings' of the Paris wedding, dutifully emphasizing 'thou hast a careful father, child', though the speed of the arrangements has taken even her by surprise. In Brooke she reports Juliet's refusal back to her husband, but Shakespeare brings Capulet on as soon as possible, leaving his wife to add the terrible disclaimer, 'I would the fool were married to her grave'. She attempts no defence of her daughter, beyond telling her husband his anger is 'mad', and when Juliet turns to 'sweet my mother', she exits with the couplet:

> Talk not to me, for I'll not speak a word.
> Do as thou wilt, for I have done with thee.

> (3.5.107, 140, 202–3)

Juliet's agreement to marry Paris mollifies her mother to the extent of asking her, as she prepares for bed, 'Need you my help?', and when this is refused she abruptly exits. When she mourns over Juliet's supposed dead body, she claims, 'One poor and loving child, / But one thing to rejoice and solace in' (4.5.46–7), but there has been little sign that Juliet has brought her solace. In the tomb Lady Capulet is given the rather anodyne couplet, at odds with her apparent age:

> O me! This sight of death is as a bell
> That warns my old age to a sepulchre.

> (5.3.206–7)

I have traced Lady Capulet's journey through the play not to suggest that she is a remote and uncaring mother – though it can be played that way – but to show that Shakespeare could not find adequate room for her in his structural scheme. Father and daughter are dealt with at length, even though they have few meetings. Lady Capulet sees more of her daughter, but no real relationship develops. In many productions the most interesting thing about her is her attachment to Tybalt, underwritten though it is. Juliet is closer to her Nurse, who has brought her up, and her father, who is the fount of authority. Henceforth Shakespeare nearly always dispenses with the mother, or at any rate a mother who has nurtured her daughter into adolescence (Marina and Perdita are unaware of their mothers' existence), and the brilliantly realized Nurse is never repeated (perhaps Pandarus is the nearest equivalent).

Just as Juliet has a surrogate mother, she shares with Romeo a surrogate father in Friar Laurence, a part that I played (again too young) in 1971 at the Oxford Playhouse, with Felicity Kendal as a particularly resourceful Juliet. The relationship between a young woman and a celibate friar, to whom anything could be confessed in safety, was useful to Shakespeare, and reaches its apogee when Duke Vincentio uses his counterfeit friar to get far enough into Isabella's confidence to propose marriage to her. It is Friar Laurence who fatally concludes that he will help the young couple 'to turn your households' rancour to pure love' (2.3.88). That Juliet feels more at home with the friar than with her own parents is shown by her outburst when Paris parts from her:

> O shut the door, and when thou hast done so,
> Come weep with me, past hope, past cure, past help!

> (4.1.44–5)

She exposes her despair by threatening suicide, just as Romeo has done, and this pushes Laurence into his desperate remedy, which she gladly accepts from her 'dear father'. When she wakes in the tomb her first words are 'O comfortable friar' (5.3.148), who might indeed have saved her if he hadn't been so afraid of arrest and disgrace – though of course it was vital to the plot that the lovers should be left alone. Shakespeare departs from Brooke in making him both a character in the play and a chorus, a moral commentator, but the result is not entirely successful. Shakespeare learnt with Falstaff, Feste, Thersites and others to integrate the commentary into the character. What Laurence does share with Capulet is the attempt to accommodate and control adolescent emotions they fear to be beyond control, and inevitably they both fail.[18]

2

Comedies

Between 1594/5 and 1599 Shakespeare wrote two tragedies, *Richard II* and *Julius Caesar*, his final four history chronicles, culminating in *Henry V*, and five comedies, sometimes termed 'romantic comedies', where the daughter's love for a partner is for a time frustrated by unforeseen events, but finally resolved by a marriage to the satisfaction of all parties – Shylock excepted. Apart from *The Merry Wives of Windsor* the Plautine template was abandoned, and the treatment of Shylock and Jessica, and of Leonato and Hero, showed a marked advance in his handling of the father-daughter relationship, introducing a greater complexity and ambiguity, while in *As You Like It* he finally felt able to write a daughter dominating both her father and the play. In *Twelfth Night* he banished fathers altogether, and the humiliation of Malvolio was to prove a turning point in a darker and more problematic examination of comedy laced with tragedy.

The Merchant of Venice: Shylock and Jessica

Shakespeare's treatment of Shylock and Jessica is so ambiguous that it turns what could be an anti-semitic melodrama into a more complex study of race, class and wealth. Shakespeare fulfils the audience's expectations – the rich Jew gets his comeuppance, the daughter steals his gold, marries a Christian and converts – but in the process the writer asks some searching questions. The story had had several contemporary treatments. In Anthony Munday's *Zelanto, or The Fountain of Fame* (1580) Truculento, 'an extorting usurer', has a daughter Brisana who tricks him into allowing her to marry Rodolpho, and after Truculento is foiled of his pound of flesh he bequeathes his fortune to his son-in-law. In *The Tragical Reign of Selinus* (1592) the 'cunning Jew' Abraham is an expert poisoner, 'a man so stout and resolute, / That he will venture anything for gold'.[1] Marlowe's *The Jew of Malta* (c. 1590) revels in a monstrous, sensuous, more than life-sized anti-hero. Barabas is in the prime of life, an epicurean, intent on his own aggrandisement, ready to 'poison wells' and kill anyone, including his much loved daughter, who stands in his way. He would rather be hated as a rich Jew than pitied as a poor Christian. His daughter Abigail by contrast is loyal, dutiful and, at the last, a keen Christian.

The Elizabethan audience must have been intrigued by what Shakespeare, only a few years after Marlowe's death, would make of this familiar story. It presumably came as a surprise that he took a radically different line. He stuck to the outline of the story, but produced a father and daughter of quite different character and motivation. Shylock is old, wears plain gaberdine, is frugal in his living and has no time for masques and revelry. His hatred is reserved for one man, Antonio, who has called him 'cut-throat dog, / And spat upon my Jewish gaberdine' (2.1.109–10). According to Jessica, 'He would rather have Antonio's flesh / Than twenty times the value of the sum / That he did owe him' (3.2.285–7). Jessica is briefly introduced as the typical daughter of a rich usurer Jew. 'Our house is hell' she proclaims in her second line, though she finds Lancelot Gobbo robbed it of 'some taste of tediousness'. Lancelot sets her up as 'most beautiful pagan, most sweet Jew'. Jessica then has a bare six lines lamenting that it is a 'heinous sin … to be ashamed to be my father's child!', that she acknowledges she is 'daughter to his blood … not to his manners' and that she will convert to Christianity and be 'a loving wife' to Lorenzo, though at no point does she show any knowledge of, or enthusiasm for, Christianity, unlike Marlowe's Abigail (2.3.2–3, 10–11, 16–21). Her letter to Lorenzo directs him how to abduct her, and 'what gold and jewels she is furnish'd with, / What page's suit she hath in readiness' (2.4.31–2).

Shylock reluctantly prepares to leave the house, orders Jessica to lock the doors and not look out of the casements at 'Christian fools with varnish'd faces', and to keep her from idleness threatens 'perhaps I will return immediately' (2.5.33, 51). Jessica ends the scene with the trite couplet: 'Farewell, – and if my fortune be not cross / I have a father, you a daughter, lost' (55–6). This cold scene establishes Shylock as the stern patriarch, determined that Jessica should abide by Jewish orthodox behaviour and share his denial of pleasure. She seems as much housekeeper as daughter. It is in marked contrast to Marlowe's much more loving opening exchange:

BARABAS   But whither wends my beauteous Abigail?
               O what has made my lovely daughter sad?
ABIGAIL   Not for myself, but aged Barabas,
               Father, for thee lamentable Abigail.

(The Jew of Malta, 1.2.226–7, 230–1)

Lorenzo, Gratiano, Salerio and the masquers arrive at the house, and Jessica appears above in boy's clothes, 'much asham'd of my exchange', though Lorenzo is evidently aroused by this 'lovely garnish'. She then withdraws to 'make fast the doors and gild myself / With some more ducats' (2.6.35, 45,

49–50). Is this to indicate greed, desire to please Lorenzo or simply to gratify the audience – the more money the Jew loses the better? Commentators have been quick to claim, in a play obsessed with money, that Lorenzo is more attracted by the ducats than the woman, but Shakespeare anticipates this. Lorenzo confides to Gratiano, the most worldly and pragmatic of men, who would be the first to agree that a fat dowry is the real enchantment:

> Beshrew me but I love her heartily,
> For she is wise, if I can judge of her,
> And fair she is, if that mine eyes be true,
> And true she is, as she hath prov'd herself:
> And therefore like herself, wise, fair, and true,
> Shall she be placed in my constant soul.

> (52–7)

Nevertheless Shakespeare makes it clear Lorenzo is in need of money. When he hears at the end of the play that he and Jessica will inherit all Shylock's possessions at his death, he observes, 'You drop manna in the way / Of starved people' (5.1.294–5). The elopement has followed the conventional pattern: the Jew shows no affection to his daughter, she finds her life 'hell' and is twice referred to as 'gentle', fit therefore to be a gentile. She escapes with as much money as possible to be a good Christian wife to a man who clearly loves her. When Shylock finds this out he seems, according to Solanio, equally concerned about the loss of his ducats as his daughter ('My daughter! O my ducats! O my daughter!'). Solanio's account that Shylock cried he had lost 'two sealed bags of ducats ... two stones, two rich and precious stones' suggests that Shylock feels himself castrated and unmanned by Jessica's flight (2.8.15, 18, 20).

Then in Act 3 Shakespeare departs from the main outline of the folktale, as he was to do so often in his later plays. First he gives Shylock his remarkable speech, 'Hath not a Jew eyes' (3.1.54–67), and Shylock gains a sympathy from the audience that never entirely deserts him. Their accustomed laughter at Jew-baiting must have become uneasy, or at any rate this seems Shakespeare's intention. Shylock continues to lament the loss of his money, and wishes his 'daughter were dead at my foot, and the jewels in her ear', but then Shakespeare produces a masterstroke. Tubal reports that 'your daughter spent in Genoa, as I heard, one night, fourscore ducats' (a few thousand pounds in modern terms). Shylock feels 'thou stick'st a dagger in me', but Tubal has worse to report: 'One of them showed me a ring that he had of your daughter for a monkey'. Shylock reveals he had this turquoise ring from his wife Leah before their marriage – 'I would not have given it for a wilderness of monkeys' (100–2, 110–15). Jessica has been throwing his money about, perhaps to impress Lorenzo, and exchanging a ring she must have known precious to her father for something as paltry (and lascivious) as a monkey. Shakespeare has made us look at father and daughter in a new light. He is realist enough to know that a girl released from 'hellish' confinement would hardly save the stolen money, but rather squander it on high living and useless baubles, as she and Lorenzo drift from Venice to Genoa to Belmont.

Shakespeare has almost finished with Jessica, without having really brought her to life. Is she sincere and loving, or shallow and self-centred, or are all these the attributes of a damaged adolescence? The Elizabethan audience might have applauded her every action, but Shakespeare seems ambivalent about her conduct. He has written her in such a way that a less anti-semitic society can find her rebellion spiteful and disloyal, and her craving for Christian acceptance at any price vain and repugnant. At Belmont Shakespeare hints at a darker future for her. First the clown Lancelot thinks that, despite her marriage and conversion, 'you are damn'd both by father and mother' (3.5.14–15), revealing a strain of Elizabethan anti-semitism that birth can never be overridden by conversion. Lorenzo, when he enters, does not refute this argument, but the scene proceeds in such an obscure way that its authenticity is doubted. It does allow Jessica a speech in praise of Portia of considerable wit and eloquence, and this is later followed by her famous exchange with Lorenzo on the subject of classical lovers, all of whom came to grief through treachery, desertion, revenge or mischance. Both see the other as a thief: Jessica has stolen from the wealthy Jew, Lorenzo has stolen her soul 'with many vows of faith, / And ne'er a true one' (5.1.15, 19–20). Portia treats Jessica with civility, but a singular lack of affectionate welcome: she is made to appear merely an adjunct to Lorenzo. It may not be coincidence that Jessica's final line in the play, as Lorenzo lauds the power and importance of music, is the deflating comment, a rebuke perhaps to Portia's aristocratic self-confidence: 'I am never merry when I hear sweet music' (5.1.69). If the father has been made to appear more sympathetic than the story would allow, the daughter has achieved the opposite. As Shakespeare becomes more confident in his handling of familiar stories his sceptical nature becomes more apparent.

Jessica and Portia mirror one another in various different ways. They are first contrasted in their relationship to their fathers, one living and one dead. Portia initially chafes under her father's ordinance: 'I may neither choose who I would, nor refuse who I dislike, so is the will of a living daughter curb'd by the will of a dead father'. Nerissa counters (rather out of character?), 'Your father was ever virtuous, and holy men at their death have good inspirations' (1.2.22–8). Shakespeare thus is careful to uphold patriarchy, for youth cannot be trusted to make sound judgements. The father's 'meaning' lies in the three caskets, and 'who chooses his meaning chooses you'. The father ensures that, even after his death, his son-in-law will be of like mind. Portia accepts this, content meanwhile to live sole mistress of her vast inheritance. She has no 'hot temper' to leap 'o'er a cold decree', for that would challenge the source of all authority and legitimacy (30–1, 18–19).

Jessica feels quite differently about patriarchal law. She may be daughter to his blood – Shylock twice reiterates she is 'my flesh and blood' – but not to his 'manners'. These are the source of 'strife' (3.1.31, 34), which she will end by becoming a Christian wife to a man of her own choosing. In doing so she is prepared to take the law into her own hands by stealing from her father. Shylock, who constantly invokes the Christian law, duly cries out, 'Justice! – find the girl' (2.8.21). In demanding his pound of flesh Shakespeare makes it clear that Shylock is primarily motivated by his 'lodg'd hate, and a certain loathing / I bear Antonio' (4.1.60–1). But he lets slip later in the scene that 'I have a daughter – / Would any of the stock of Barrabas / Had been her husband, rather than a Christian' (293–5). Shakespeare makes as strong a case as he can to explain Shylock's cruelty: his obsession to have his bond rather than twice the sum owed is fuelled by his hatred of the particular man who spat upon him and called him dog, and by the loss of his daughter to a Christian adventurer. Venetian justice and Antonio's intervention leave him with half his wealth provided he converts to Christianity, and be thus assured of salvation. This last is Shakespeare's invention, presumably intended to persuade his audience that Shylock can only be allowed to live on in some prosperity if he is a Christian. It is an unappealing compromise, and Shakespeare hustles through to a lame conclusion. Shylock is merely allowed to say, 'I am content ... I pray you give me leave to go from hence, / I am not well – send the deed after me, / And I will sign it' (392–5). The nature of his true feelings and the justice that has been meted out to him is left in the air.

Jessica hopes to find happiness by disobeying her father, Portia by obeying. They both cross-dress, but while Portia finds liberation and renown in adopting a male persona, Jessica is merely ashamed to be seen as a boy torch-bearer. Portia dutifully proclaims her submission to her husband-to-be:

Happiest of all, is that her gentle spirit
Commits itself to yours to be directed,
As from her lord, her governor, her king.

(3.2.163–5)

Jessica makes no such dedication to Lorenzo, only quipping, 'Let me praise you while I have a stomach' (3.5.85). She gives the impression that she regards herself as her husband's equal, and Lorenzo's reference to her as 'a little shrew' may suggest squalls to come. It has become a convention in recent productions to leave Jessica, like Antonio, as the excluded outsider, sometimes lamenting the loss of her religion, but this can only be achieved by some imposed business. The text suggests that she has been accepted into the idealized warmth of Belmont. How the marriage and her place in Christian society will turn out is left for the audience to decide, but if Portia is presented as the model Elizabethan wife, Jessica is seen as the disruptive force challenging family order.

The Merry Wives of Windsor: Master Page and Anne

The Merry Wives of Windsor is Shakespeare's only attempt at writing a middle-class, urban comedy-farce, the genre mined by Dekker, Jonson, Chapman and Marston. The Anne Page sub-plot – the girl in love with the romantic penniless young man rather than the rich idiotic suitors preferred by her parents – is basic stuff, but Shakespeare adds some unexpected twists. Money is as usual paramount, and in this small community the interested parties are aware of what everyone else is worth. Hugh Evans, the schoolteacher, knows that Anne has £700 (perhaps £90,000 in modern terms) from her grandfather when she reaches seventeen, and in addition that her father will make her 'a petter penny' (much more as well). Her father's choice is the booby Slender, whom Anne tartly summarizes:

> O, what a world of vile ill-favoured faults
> Looks handsome in three hundred pounds a year!
>
> (3.4.32–3)

Slender will also make her a jointure of £150 and maintain her like a gentlewoman, though he protests 'I would little or nothing with you. Your father and my uncle hath made motions' (60–2). Anne's mother favours the eccentric Frenchman, Dr Caius, whom she says is 'well moneyed, and his friends / Potent at court' (4.4.87–8). Significantly the Pages object to Fenton the penniless courtier, but are attracted to someone who has 'friends potent at court': money plus influence appear more important than social status. Anne is memorably appalled by the prospect of marriage to Caius:

> Alas, I had rather be set quick i'th' earth,
> And bowled to death with turnips.
>
> (3.4.85–6)

Anne's fancy is the impoverished gentleman Fenton who, like Falstaff, has come from London in search of provincial pickings. His attractions for Anne are obvious: as the Host says, 'He capers, he dances, he has eyes of youth, he writes verses, he speaks holiday, he smells April and May' (3.2.60–2). Master Page will have none of it, and makes his objections succinctly:

The gentleman is of no having, he kept company with the wild Prince and Poins. He is of too high a region, he knows too much ... If he take her, let him take her simply: the wealth I have waits on my consent, and my consent goes not that way.

(64–70)

So far Shakespeare has written a conventional romantic comedy, but Fenton then makes a surprising disclosure. He admits to Anne that Page dislikes his birth and his 'wild societies', and makes the objection that 'I should love thee but as a property' – a rare, but very pertinent, use of this word in relation to the marriage market. The down-to-earth Anne challenges him directly: 'Maybe he tells you true' (3.4.10–11), and this pushes Fenton into admitting:

Albeit I will confess thy father's wealth
Was the first motive that I wooed thee, Anne,
Yet, wooing thee, I found thee of more value
Than stamps in gold or sums in sealed bags
And 'tis the very riches of thyself
That now I aim at.

(13–18)

This is a striking image: the girl with a fat dowry first appears to a suitor as 'stamps in gold'. Anne is not deterred by his honesty, but rather urges him to continue to seek her father's love, because she knows Page is no tyrant. Her mother also purports to be fair and objective, telling Fenton:

I will not be your friend, nor enemy.
My daughter will I question how she loves you,
And as I find her, so am I affected.

(88–90)

Shakespeare has drawn a very average, moneyed provincial couple, of a type he must have known from Stratford, who want their daughter well married to someone of substance. The father is more adamant, the mother apparently more ready to listen to her daughter's feelings – though this seems to be hypocritical. Whether she is sincere or not, this remains one of the few plays in which Shakespeare allows the heroine a mother.

Nevertheless both parents are determined to have their way, in rivalry with one another. Page has commanded Anne 'to slip / Away with Slender, and with him at Eton / Immediately to marry', and Mistress Page, 'firm for Doctor Caius – hath appointed / That he shall likewise shuffle her away' (4.6.23–5, 27–8). Anne agrees to both marriages, arranges with Fenton that two boys will be substituted, and the two lovers are married in secret.

This rather laboured farcical plot enables Shakespeare to give Fenton an eloquent speech denouncing forced marriages:

> You would have married her, most shamefully
> Where there was no proportion held in love. ...
> Th'offence is holy that she hath committed,
> And this deceit loses the name of craft,
> Of disobedience, and unduteous title,
> Since therein she doth evitate and shun
> A thousand irreligious cursed hours
> Which forced marriage would have brought upon her.
>
> (5.5.214–15, 217–22)

The Pages, rather improbably, accept this outcome in the spirit of comedy, since 'here is no remedy', and they go home to 'laugh this sport o'er by a country fire'. Anne is given no lines beyond 'Pardon, good father. Good my mother, pardon' (225, 236, 210). In fact her part is only thirty-three lines in all – a pity, since Shakespeare shows a sympathetic understanding of an ordinary middle-class girl's determination not to marry for money. She is described as having 'brown hair' – so she is no Elizabethan beauty – but she is shrewd, forceful and resists her parents' considerable pressure to marry to their liking. What is lacking is any relationship with her father. In the first scene, when Anne fails to persuade Slender to come in to dinner and is finally joined by her father, parent and child exchange not a word.

Much Ado About Nothing: Leonato and Hero, an actor's perspective

In 1974 I played Don John at the Phoenix Theatre, Leicester, directed by Euan Smith, with Petronella Ford and Richard Moore as Beatrice and Benedick (productions always seem identified by the actors who played these parts, though their story is arguably the comic sub-plot). The setting was Edwardian, and though the image of cucumber sandwiches on the lawn worked well as soldiers and young women milled about sizing one another up, I was troubled by the ghost of the First World War: are these officers really about to return to the trenches? A recent RSC production in 2014/16 by Christopher Luscombe also made Leonato's house a temporary field hospital for soldiers presumably wounded in the trenches. The problem here is that after an introductory scene that mentions some unspecified military operation, the army and the war are never mentioned again in the text.

My introduction to the play was John Gielgud's grand and ornate production, revived a number of times in the 1950s with Peggy Ashcroft and later Diana Wynyard. Franco Zefferelli mounted a very jokey Italianate production at the National Theatre which I saw in 1965 with Maggie Smith and Robert Stephens, and to make it more 'accessible' Robert Graves allegedly replaced about sixty seemingly obscure words with clearer Elizabethan equivalents – a dangerously slippery slope. The setting was Messina, and Penelope Gilliatt wrote 'the moment the play is localised, it works as precisely as a watch ... [Hero becomes] a wretchedly believable girl trapped in a perfectly recognisable Sicily where the same ferocious code of chastity endures to this day'.[2] The play has been set in many different periods and locales, including Tuscany, Havana, Middle America and India: John Barton's 1976 RSC production with Judi Dench and Donald Sinden showed that the British Raj worked particularly well as a setting, and in 2012 the RSC followed this with a production set in modern India with Meera Syal and Paul Bhattacharjee. Shakespeare nearly always writes a recognizable and coherent society, and it is vital that, whatever the setting and period, the manners and codes described in the text can be justified.

I was therefore relieved that Nick Hytner's production at the National Theatre in 2007, with Zoë Wanamaker and Simon Russell Beale, was to be set in sixteenth-century Sicily. I approached Leonato with some caution, fearing his reputation for weakness and gullibility but encouraged by Shakespeare's decision to write the part at such length. Hytner placed great emphasis on the play's title – *Much Ado About Nothing/Noting/No Thing* (vagina or penis). He argued that the play is very much about the failure to note, to look and listen properly, and almost all the major characters are guilty. Beatrice and Benedick do finally note one another properly, and make, arguably, the best marriage in the canon. They have, of course, come to dominate the play in popular consciousness, and I feel that Shakespeare wrote them with great enjoyment and fluency. The difficult part for him, I think, lay in making the Hero plot work – what I call the 'Wrong-Woman-at-the-Window' plot, a variant of the classical tale of the unjustly slandered woman, which existed in seventeen different extant versions. This entailed putting Hero and her father Leonato at the centre of the action, and I have always felt caused Shakespeare manifold problems. His sources might have included Harrington's translation (1591) of Ludovico Ariosto's *Orlando Furioso* (1516), which ends more brutally with Polyneiso/Don John killed by Ariodante/Claudio and Dalinda/Margaret going into a nunnery. Much closer to Shakespeare's plot is the version in Belleforest's *Histoires Tragiques* (1569), where Sir Timbreo de Cardona, a courtier of the King of Aragon, falls for Fenicia, daughter of Lionato de Lionati, and withdraws his offer after the window scene, engineered by Sir Girondo Olerio Valenziano, a rejected suitor of Fenicia.

Shakespeare by this point in his career apparently felt confident enough to diverge from his sources in various key areas. First he took the risky step of not dramatizing the key scene of the wrong woman at the window. He presumably thought that it was too unlikely, too tired or too farcical to be dramatically viable. If he had seen *Fedele and Fortunio* (1585) by M.A. (Anthony Munday?), he may have remembered the bathetic lines of Pedante/Borachio as he leaves Victoria's/Margaret's:

O delicate Victoria so long as I live,
For this entertainment, great thanks will I give.
The remembrance of the sweetness of this night so well past,
Will feed me with honey while my life doeth last.[3]

Instead Borachio is made to recount the whole device to Conrad, overheard by the Watch, a not entirely happy alternative, though it does suggest to the audience that the plot will be revealed eventually. Shakespeare next decided that to make the window scam seem reliable Don John and Claudio were not sufficiently disinterested or credible as sole witnesses, and he therefore added, not the King, but his son, Don Pedro, Prince of Aragon, whose word could not be gainsaid.

Shakespeare then enhanced Leonato's status. In Belleforest Lionato came from an ancient, but impoverished, family, and was not surprised when Sir Timbreo withdrew his marriage offer as 'I am only a poor gentleman and not his equal'. Only at the end of the Belleforest story does the King of Aragon give him 'a very honourable office in Messina'. Shakespeare makes his Leonato not only governor of Messina but wealthy enough to satisfy Claudio's dowry expectations (1.1.278). Sir Girondo, the rejected suitor, is replaced by the high status Don John, a prince, albeit illegitimate, who is given no reliable motive for his plan to destroy the Claudio-Hero match. This lack has proved a considerable problem for the actor, and my solution, when I played the part, was to imagine Claudio had rejected a sexual pass I had made at him during the campaign and that I feared exposure, an idea that I passed on to Andrew Woodall, our National Theatre Don John, which appealed to both him and the director. I have found that audiences are more convinced by an actor who appears to have a strong motive for his actions, even if that motive is not revealed. Shakespeare was to repeat this apparently motiveless device with Iago, who in the Cinthio source is in love with Desdemona (Iago claims this as one of his many motives, but it hardly seems authentic). Claudio is in turn made weaker and less confident than either Sir Timbreo or Ariodante. Like Proteus he's readily disloyal to his intended bride, and mistrustful of his own feelings. Finally, the role of Hero is diminished. She is mostly silent in the company of men, is given only eight lines of defence in the church scene and then disappears from the play until the denouement. In Belleforest Fenicia is given a long rambling speech expressing her 'endless pain': 'Like a common strumpet I shall always be pointed at with the finger of scorn ... Perhaps if I married so loftily I might have waxed proud and become arrogant'.[4]

It would seem that Shakespeare made all these changes partly to make the plot more credible and interesting, but also because he perhaps realized that the main protagonist in the second half of the play had to be, not Claudio, Hero, Benedick or the two Dons, but Leonato. The rejection of Hero and the improbable plotting that follows could only be made to work if the father took over the action (Leonato has only fourteen lines fewer than Benedick). In the eighteenth and nineteenth centuries the part of Leonato was severely cut (as it is in Branagh's 1993 film and many recent productions) to make him both more sympathetic and less important. Like Capulet, Baptista and Page, Leonato is presented as a very average father, with both strengths and weaknesses fully exposed. It was a study that absorbed Shakespeare, possibly inspired by reflection on his own father, and indeed upon himself.

Shakespeare's original intention seems to have been to give Leonato a wife. In both Q and F 'Innogen his wife' enters, but never speaks and is not referred to again. It has been argued that Shakespeare realized he already had four women characters, who could not double, and that the company had run out of competent boy players, though in the Admiral's lists of c. 1602 nine boys are mentioned as playing female parts, so there seems little shortage of apprentices among the companies.[5] It is more probable that he thought Leonato and Hero would flourish more as characters if he was the customary widower and she the motherless daughter. Innogen would have certainly silenced the bawdy Margaret if she'd been present at the wedding preparations, and would have had much to say in the church scene.

Leonato has the highest status in Messina until the aristocrats in the army arrive. I was struck by the moralizing, euphuistic terms he employs at the outset: 'A victory is twice itself when the achiever brings home full numbers', and 'How much better it is to weep at joy than to joy at weeping!' (1.1.8–9, 27–8). Aragon had ruled Sicily for four centuries: Don Pedro, for all his urbanity, had absolute power and the Messina governorship lay in his gift. Once a production moves its setting out of Sicily in the sixteenth century, Don Pedro inevitably loses some of his power and status. Leonato is therefore most anxious to impress, and his euphuism is given full rein:

> Never came trouble to my house in the likeness of your Grace, for trouble being gone, comfort should remain; but when you depart from me, sorrow abides, and happiness takes his leave.

> (95–8)

Don Pedro is taken aback by this rank hyperbole, and mockingly reproves Leonato: 'You embrace your charge too willingly' (99). It sets the pattern of their relationship; Leonato is ready to follow wherever the prince leads. Claudio feels the same and Don Pedro exploits this, perhaps in order to keep the young man close to him. He suggests that he will woo Hero on Claudio's behalf, and this is overheard, though 'mis-noted', as a declaration by the prince himself, by Leonato's brother, Antonio. Leonato is exultant, though cautious:' 'We will hold it as a dream till it appear itself' (1.2.18–19). After supper he warns Hero in an abrupt, typically paternalistic way: 'Daughter, remember what I told you: if the Prince do solicit you in that kind, you know your answer' (2.1.60–2).

With his niece Beatrice, apparently orphaned with Leonato acting as a surrogate father, he is happy to banter, but pays little attention to her marriage prospects – the implication may be that she has no money of her own and acts as housekeeper (her uncle bids her, 'Niece, will you look to those things I told you of?' [2.1.318–19]). He does say, 'I hope to see you one day fitted with a husband', though only after he has advised her, 'By my troth, niece, thou wilt never get thee a husband, if thou be so shrewd of thy tongue' (52–3, 16–17). But when Don Pedro suggests 'she were an excellent wife for Benedick', Leonato is dismissive: 'O Lord, my lord, if they were but a week married, they would talk themselves mad' (331–3). With his daughter, where marriage is concerned, he is very business-like. When Don Pedro makes it clear he wooed only in Claudio's name, Leonato is immediately ready to embrace the lesser match: 'Count, take of me my daughter, and with her my fortunes' (284–5). Like Capulet he doesn't inquire of Claudio's fortune or what settlement he will make Hero – a count is a catch on any terms. It is left to Don John to point out 'she is no equal for [Don Pedro's] birth', and by implication for Count Claudio's as well (156). Shakespeare makes the trothplight between the couple an exceptionally gauche affair. Beatrice has to push Claudio into declaring, and he can only manage the very trite 'Lady, as you are mine, I am yours' (289–90). Hero says nothing, and Beatrice has to prompt her to 'stop his mouth with a kiss' (292–3). Honour is satisfied, but it has been a shy and stilted contract between a teenage couple who barely know one another. Despite this Claudio wants the marriage the next day, but Leonato insists on a week – ample time for Shakespeare to accommodate the gulling of Benedick and Beatrice, and for Margaret to be seen at the window.

Leonato's contribution to the gulling scene turns on the moment when Don Pedro asks him 'What effects of passion shows she [Beatrice]?', and he replies: 'What effects, my lord? She will sit you – you heard my daughter tell you how' (2.3.108, 110–11). The dash between the two 'yous' is in Q, while F has a comma suggesting perhaps that Leonato is quicker to recover. In any event the implication is that Leonato cannot think of any 'effects', and passes the buck. This has prompted actors to leave a long pause, and then be reduced to a stuttering wreck, which Don Pedro and Claudio take full advantage of. It fits the idea that the two officers, fresh from the army mess, are used to improvised japes, while Leonato is hopelessly out of practice. This, of course, I found a delight to play, though the rest of Leonato's utterances could suggest that he is quick to master the gulling art: 'She'll be up twenty times a night, and there will she sit in her smock till she have writ a sheet of paper ... When she had writ it, and was reading it over, she found "Benedick" and "Beatrice" between the sheets' (130–2, 135–7).

COMEDIES 57

Benedick is apparently convinced of Leonato's probity (essential to Don Pedro's plan): 'I should think this a gull, but that the white-bearded fellow speaks it' (118–19). Nevertheless Leonato's stuttering discomfiture adds a new dimension to his character, undermining his paternalistic gravity, and I gratefully seized upon it.

Shakespeare is always ready to show how well masters relate to their servants (cf. Capulet), and when Dogberry and Verges arrive to report the capture of Borachio and Conrad, Leonato, though 'in great haste' to get on with wedding preparations, is very tolerant of Dogberry's circumlocutions, allowing him to bestow 'all thy tediousness on me', and making sure they 'drink some wine ere you go' (3.5.22, 49). The placing of this aborted disclosure *before* the church scene I realized is crucial, since the audience can now be reasonably certain that the truth of the woman at the window will eventually emerge, and a comedy ending will be assured (the same is true in *Twelfth Night* where the audience are told early on that Sebastian is alive, and thus all will be well).

Shakespeare has to struggle hard to make the church scene plausible. Beatrice, who knows Borachio must be lying when he confessed he had had sex with Hero 'a thousand times in secret' (4.1.93), has to be silenced by Leonato. Benedick, who could have denounced Don John much earlier in the scene, is uncharacteristically made to say 'I am so attir'd in wonder, / I know not what to say' (143–4). Hero merely says, 'I talk'd with no man at that hour, my lord' (85), before she faints. Claudio delivers his melodramatic rant, egged on by Don John's interjections, and Leonato, desperate to get the wedding back on course, suggests that he would understand if Claudio 'have vanquish'd the resistance of her youth, / And made defeat of her virginity' (45–6). This was a bold step to take at a wedding, since the Church disapproved of consummation between contract and wedding, common though it was (see p. 169). Claudio, however, angrily refutes this and priggishly declares he has shown the 'bashful sincerity' of a brother – not perhaps a good omen for their future sexual happiness. This clears the way for Shakespeare's masterstroke. Leonato finally turns to Don Pedro: 'Sweet Prince, why speak not you?' (62). His best hope is that the prince, level-headed, incorruptible, can put a stop to this, but Don Pedro eventually replies, clearly and damningly:

> I am sorry you must hear: upon mine honour,
> Myself, my brother, and this grieved Count
> Did see her, hear her, at that hour last night,
> Talk with a ruffian at her chamber-window,
> Who hath indeed, most like a liberal villain,
> Confess'd the vile encounters they have had
> A thousand times in secret.

> (87–93)

This is hard, incontrovertible evidence, and Leonato's response is to wonder why no one has stabbed him, and wishes Hero dead. He has to face the fact that every time Don John has passed through Messina, Borachio and Hero have apparently spent their nights together (though this can be made more plausible if Borachio is cast not as an army follower of Don John's but a servant of the Messina household in his pay). Leonato's initial anger and despair is extreme, but I found it at least understandable and it left me wondering if Leonato's critics had observed Shakespeare's careful build-up to the prince's evidence. Unlike Belleforest's Lionato, who accepts Sir Timbreo's withdrawal with stoical resignation, Shakespeare's Leonato rages:

> Do not live, Hero, do not ope thine eyes;
> For did I think thou wouldst not quickly die,
> Thought I thy spirits were stronger than thy shames,
> Myself would on the rearward of reproaches
> Strike at thy life.

(122–6)

This much criticized reaction is a calculated risk on Shakespeare's part, but he had already prepared the ground for it. Borachio has anticipated the effect that the shaming of Hero will have on the protagonists when he first broaches his plan to Don John: Don Pedro will be 'misused', and Claudio 'vexed', i.e. they

Figure 1   Leonato (Oliver Ford Davies), Beatrice (Zoë Wanamaker), Hero (Susannah Fielding) and Friar Francis (Gary Pillai) in *Much Ado About Nothing* at the Olivier, National Theatre, London, 2007 (© Catherine Ashmore/National Theatre)

will be barely more than inconvenienced. But Hero will be 'undone': she will be left unmarriageable, and will either enter a convent or live on secluded in her family home, aware that she is despised by all Messina. Finally, Leonato will be 'killed', either by his own hand, or dead within the year through shame, because his emotional investment in his daughter is so intense (2.2.27–8). A remarkable thing about Leonato's speech is not just his infanticidal horror at Hero's treachery and his wish that she were some 'beggar's issue' (4.1.131), but the language in which it is couched. In its heightened imagery and rhetorical force it prefigures the great tragedies to come. Shakespeare anticipates the egotistical, manic obsession that will engulf Othello and Leontes in a play that contains so much anger and violence. Compare Leonato's:

> But mine, and mine I loved, and mine I prais'd,
> And mine that I was proud on – mine so much
> That I myself was to myself not mine,
> Valuing of her – why, she, O, she is fall'n
> Into a pit of ink, that the wide sea
> Hath drops too few to wash her clean again,
> And salt too little which may season give
> To her foul tainted flesh!

(135–42)

With Othello's rage at Desdemona's apparent infidelity:

> Like to the Pontic Sea
> Whose icy current and compulsive course
> Ne'er keeps retiring ebb, but keeps due on
> To the Propontic and the Hellespont:
> Even so my bloody thoughts with violent pace
> Shall ne'er look back, ne'er ebb to humble love,
> Till that a capable and wide revenge
> Swallow them up.

(*Othello*, 3.3.456–63)

Shakespeare has already travelled a long way from Capulet's prosey verse:

> Mistress minion you,
> Thank me no thankings nor proud me no prouds,
> But fettle your fine joints 'gainst Thursday next
> To go with Paris to Saint Peter's Church,
> Or I will drag thee on a hurdle thither.
> Out, you green-sickness carrion!
> Out, you baggage! You tallow-face!

(*Romeo and Juliet*, 3.5.151–7)

Leonato's anger is quickly and convincingly quelled. Hero speaks up for herself in language learnt from her father – if their story can be proved, 'Refuse me, hate me, torture me to death'; the Friar thinks it is 'some biting error'; and Benedick suspects Don John is at the root of it all. Leonato is partly mollified: 'If they wrong her honour, / The proudest of them shall well hear of it' (4.1.183, 169, 190–1). In his torment Leonato is at last prepared to take on Don Pedro. He accepts the Friar and Benedick's advice with the beautifully simple couplet (a parallel to Capulet's anguish at Juliet's apparent death):

> Being that I flow in grief,
> The smallest twine may lead me.
>
> (248–9)

Shakespeare could then have proceeded directly to Leonato's confrontation with Don Pedro and Claudio, but he is clearly intent on staying with Leonato's confused grief. For whatever reason Leonato feels a despair in which he seems to believe his daughter really is dead, and this proved difficult but rewarding to play when he confesses his love for her:

> Bring me a father that so lov'd his child,
> Whose joy of her is overwhelm'd like mine,
> And bid him speak of patience.
> Measure his woe the length and breadth of mine,
> And let it answer every strain for strain.
>
> (5.1.8–12)

His suffering does, however, transform him from obsequious host to a vigorous organizer bent on extracting a full apology from the prince and Claudio. Shakespeare gives him a long, heart-felt speech in the most highly wrought verse in the play, which I found challenging to negotiate. He rejects his brother's calming advice:

> men
> Can counsel and speak comfort to that grief
> Which they themselves not feel; but tasting it,
> Their counsel turns to passion, which before
> Would give preceptial medicine to rage,
> Fetter strong madness in a silken thread,
> Charm ache with air, and agony with words.
>
> (20–6)

Shakespeare takes a calculated risk with this scene, and I found it hard to determine its tone. Leonato seems more obsessed with his own suffering than with his daughter's, almost as if Shakespeare is beginning to write a different character in a different scenario. The play is veering towards tragedy when Leonato challenges Claudio to a duel: 'Thou hast kill'd my child; / If thou kill'st me, boy, thou shalt kill a man' (78–9). But Shakespeare abruptly introduces a comic element with brother Anthony's farcical tirade at these 'scambling, outfacing, fashion-monging boys' (94), and in turn their contempt for these 'two old men without teeth' (117). Dogberry is at last allowed to produce his captives, Borachio confesses all and a happy ending seems imminent. But Shakespeare has other ideas. Leonato still hangs on to the fiction of Hero's death in order that Claudio and Don Pedro can be made to play out the tomb scene prescribed by Belleforest.

> I thank you, Princes, for my daughter's death;
> Record it with your high and worthy deeds;
> 'Twas bravely done, if you bethink you of it.

> (260–2)

Grief, supposed death and rebirth are themes to which Shakespeare often returned. He had already explored Titus' despair at Lavinia's rape, the Capulet family's extreme grief over Juliet's apparently dead body and Constance's wild distraction at Arthur's loss, where she protests, 'I am not mad; I would to God I were' (*King John*, 3.4.48). Hero's supposed death is like other mock deaths and substitute brides: Juliet, Helena, Innogen and Hermione. Shakespeare saw that marriage plans in disarray gave women the power, however temporarily, to alter and control their interaction with lovers and husbands. In the tragedies this often leads to the women's deaths, but in the comedies marriages are always reconfigured – though male control is reasserted. Hero seems content with this, but Beatrice fights to the last: 'I yield upon great persuasion, and partly to save your life.' The assignation of the next line, 'Peace! I will stop your mouth', is much contested (5.4.94–7). Modern practice is to assign it to Benedick, as it naturally leads on to a kiss. Both Q and F give it to Leonato, and this makes sense. He presides over the last scene as master of ceremonies, the only man who can quell Beatrice, the assertive rebel, although, as Nick Hytner argued in rehearsal, what seems a good idea in the study can be a missed opportunity in performance. Up to this point Shakespeare has written largely uncooperative fathers, Silvia's duke, Egeus, Capulet, Shylock and Page, so Leonato is a significant advance. He is introduced as a rather insubstantial, moralizing figure, in awe of the prince, ready to accept Claudio rather than Don Pedro for his daughter, ill-equipped to play his part in the gulling and initially unable to take his daughter's part when she is denounced. Then Shakespeare shows there is another side to this apparently subservient man. He becomes the protagonist of the final two acts, is given great emotional range and shows a certain heroism in his determination, like Titus, to see his daughter righted at whatever cost to himself.

Hero remains something of an enigma. Susannah Fielding (Hero) found that 'her journey in the play is a tricky one, disjointed and hard to navigate, especially for a modern audience'. She can appear the perfect Renaissance young woman, chaste, virtuous, modest, silent. Like most of Shakespeare's young heroines she is probably no more than fifteen. She remains passive while Leonato negotiates a marriage for her, apparently content to be an object of exchange. Susannah argued that she 'doesn't want to embarrass her father ... Women had to hide their true intellect to be socially acceptable and bag a husband. Underneath she's as sharp and witty as the best of them.' Claudio, himself probably no more than sixteen or seventeen, sees her very demurely as 'the sweetest lady that ever I looked on', fit for his 'soft and delicate desires' (1.1.179–80, 286). He merely checks that she is Leonato's sole heir and 'a modest young lady' (158) – i.e. rich and chaste – and is then content for Don Pedro to woo for him. This is how a prudent young aristocrat might proceed, but it does suggest youthful insecurity and lack of self-belief. His real interest lies in sticking close to Don Pedro, and he offers to follow him to Aragon as soon as he is married, perhaps leaving his new bride in Sicily.

Silent, demure women, however, can present a problem, and give occasion to the mis-'noting' of the title. It can be argued that Hero is the 'nothing' that generates so much 'ado', and it is her very blankness that allows the masculine delusion to thrive.[6] Claudio is so uncertain of Hero that directly Don John puts forward the window test, Claudio declares, not that he will have a word with Leonato and withdraw from the marriage, but 'tomorrow, in the congregation, where I should wed, there will I shame her' (3.2.115–16). This aggressive suggestion could easily have come from Don John. By giving it to Claudio Shakespeare perhaps intends to show how little 'in love' Claudio thinks himself, how susceptible he is to betrayal. Like Proteus, Bertram and Posthumus, Claudio is one of Shakespeare's studies of doubting, half-hearted suitors and husbands. In mitigation one could argue that the silent Hero has been hard to read. When Hero blushes in church at the accusations thrown at her, Claudio interprets it as 'guiltiness, not modesty', Leonato declares, 'Could she here deny / The story that is printed in her blood?', while the Friar marks 'a thousand innocent shames / In angel whiteness beat away those blushes' (4.1.40, 120–1, 159–60).

The audience knows that Hero is quite capable of speaking for herself. When Don Pedro, masked but probably eminently identifiable, asks Hero if she will 'walk a bout with your friend?', she answers quite assertively, 'So you walk softly, and look sweetly, and say nothing, I am yours for the walk; and especially when I walk away' (2.1.79–82). This could betoken shyness and a reluctance to talk to men, but more probably a warning that she could be hard to get, following on from Beatrice's encouragement to flout her father and be her own woman:

It is my cousin's duty to make curtsy and say, 'Father, as it please you':
but yet for all that, cousin, let him be a handsome fellow, or else make
another curtsy and say, 'Father, as it please me'.

(48–51)

In the gulling of Beatrice Hero takes a firm lead, revelling in her rather
spiteful denunciation of her cousin:

Disdain and scorn ride sparkling in her eyes,
Misprising what they look on, and her wit
Values itself so highly that to her
All matter else seems weak. She cannot love,
Nor take no shape nor project of affection,
She is so self-endeared.

(3.1.51–6)

Suddenly a sophistication of language and wit are on show, whether it reflects
admiration, envy or simply an attempt to goad Beatrice into matrimony.
Susannah Fielding thought Hero 'almost a sister to Beatrice, and it shows
their closeness. Beatrice has mocked Hero many times in the past, and Hero
is enjoying getting her own back.' It is the revenge of the 'people-pleasing'
younger sister on her assertive, outspoken elder. In the preparations on the
morning of the wedding, a scene for four women rare in Shakespeare, Hero
is on edge, 'as bossy with her women', Susannah thought, 'as she is dutiful
and silent in male company'.[7] When Margaret suggests a different ruff Hero
slaps her down with 'My cousin's a fool, and thou art another.' She behaves
like a spoilt rich girl and declares, 'My heart is exceeding heavy', says
little when Beatrice takes over the scene, but does attempt a half-hearted
bawdiness with, 'There thou prick'st her with a thistle' (3.4.10, 23, 71).[8]
This is enough to suggest that the wedding and/or the wedding night are
preying on her nerves, and that Shakespeare could have written a much
fuller scene about virginal qualms, if decorum had allowed. Nevertheless
there is enough material in the balance between Hero's silences, delight
in the masked dance and the gulling and the pre-wedding nervousness to
suggest how a fifteen-year-old girl might behave in these circumstances
(Susanna Shakespeare would have been fifteen in 1598, the probable year
of composition).

Hero does not defend herself robustly in the church scene, but she
is clear in her repudiation: 'Who can blot that name / With any just
reproach? ... I talk'd with no man at that hour, my lord' (4.1.78–9, 85).
When she faints it seems very justifiable, not some stratagem of character
or dramatist, but it is a precursor to Shakespeare removing her from the
play until the denouement. This absence is a problem, and in our National
Theatre production Nick Hytner brought Hero and myself onstage to

witness secretly and 'approve' Claudio's abasement at the monument. Susannah found this particularly helpful, as 'seeing the change in Claudio, weeping, singing and hanging the epitaph helped me imagine forgiving him'. Shakespeare himself, unfortunately, gave Hero no scene to express this. Instead she dutifully pretends to be Antonio's daughter, and allows Claudio to think she is the woman he has agreed to marry, sight unseen, but Susannah argued that 'the trickery at the end really puts Claudio in the weaker spot, and allows Hero the upper hand for her line, "One Hero died defil'd, but I do live, / And surely as I live, I am a maid"' (5.4.63–4). Her virgin image, however, seems her most attractive feature to the men in her life. When Claudio discovered her innocence his first thought was, 'Now thy image doth appear / In the rare semblance that I lov'd it first' (5.1.243–4). Claudio had always apparently been in love with an image, although his Hamlet-like language in the church scene – 'She knows the heat of a luxurious bed', and 'But you are more intemperate in your blood / Than Venus, or those pamper'd animals / That rage in savage sensuality' (4.1.39, 58–60) – suggests repressed carnal fantasies. It is therefore no surprise that Hero enters into a matrimonial agreement 'masked': there has been something masked about Hero throughout the play.

Leonato is given a remarkable journey. He is paternalistic in ordering Hero to accept Don Pedro, outraged and desperate at her apparent infidelity but quickly defensive of her if it prove to be a lie, prepared to maintain the fiction that she is dead in order to right the wrong done her, ready to wallow in despair at his injured pride, but also happy, once Claudio is humbled, to oversee their marriage. It is the most complete exposition of a father taking charge throughout the play of his daughter's future happiness until Shakespeare came to write *The Tempest*. What the drama lacks is the ability to make Hero, spirited as she is with other women, more than dutiful and acquiescent in her fate. The fortunes of father and daughter are fully interlocked, but Hero seems prepared to allow Leonato to dominate at almost every turn. However, despite the care that Shakespeare lavished on the part, Leonato's destiny is always to be overshadowed by the joyful expectation the audience bring to the mating games of Beatrice and Benedick.

As You Like It: The Dukes, Rosalind and Celia

As You Like It has a slight plot by Shakespearean standards: Lesley Anne Soule argues, 'its apparent purpose being more to create performance opportunities than to involve the audience in the fictional action'. The Forest of Arden becomes a place 'for the imaginary quests of romance, but also a perfect playground for stage performers'.[9] The two consummate performers in the forest, in addition to the cross-dressed Rosalind, are both Shakespeare's creation – Jacques and Touchstone. The main plot appears at the outset to concern fathers and daughters, but this is not where Shakespeare's real interests lie. The two dukes never quite come to life, unlike their daughters who have the most intense and detailed female friendship in the canon. I played both dukes in 1967 in Birmingham and London as opposite faces of a martial upbringing, Frederick as a parade-ground martinet and Senior as an amiable old colonel. When I came to play Duke Senior for the RSC in 1977 Trevor Nunn argued that, while Frederick was often played as a nasty Roundhead and Senior as a laughing Cavalier, he'd always seen them the other way round. Frederick with his gambling, drinking and wrestling was the cavalier, Senior the puritan trying to set up an ideal community in a New World forest. Senior's opening line shows that he now regards the men who have chosen to join him as his 'brothers' and 'co-mates' (the only use of the word in the canon). It's a fascinating idea, but Shakespeare doesn't develop the community along these lines. At supper in 3.1. the Duke appears to be waited on hand and foot. When he returns to his court his co-mates will be restored 'according to the measure of their states' (5.4.173): hierarchy will be resumed. Arden proves to be no republican utopia, but a pastoral fantasy, in which Shakespeare both celebrates and debunks the idyll.

Frederick's opening remark, 'Are you crept hither to see the wrestling?' (1.2.145–6), shows his dismissive attitude to both daughter and niece. He banishes Rosalind ostensibly for treason, but lets slip his real motive with 'Thou art thy father's daughter, there's enough' (1.3.55). This sense that young women and men are defined by their fathers has already been established by Frederick's dismissal of Orlando: 'I would thou hadst told me of another father' (1.2.219). When Celia protests, her father argues that Rosalind 'robs thee of thy name' (cf. *Pericles*, p. 126), and when Celia asks for banishment he simply calls her a fool and leaves. Shakespeare therefore keeps the matter entirely personal, while his main source, Thomas Lodge's *Rosalynde* or *Euphues' Golden Legacy* (1590), adds a political dimension: 'Some of the peers will aim at [Rosalynde's] love and the marriage, and then in his wife's right attempt the kingdom.' Lodge's King Torismond is also tougher on Alinda/Celia: 'Sit you down huswife and fall to your needle; if idleness makes you so wanton, or liberty so malapert, I can quickly tie you to a sharper task.'[10] When Alinda threatens to go with Rosalynde, her father banishes her as well. Celia, however, is never banished. When Frederick hears of their escape he sends men to 'bring again these foolish runaways'. Shakespeare's reasons for toning down Lodge's tyrant are not hard to fathom. While Lodge's Torismond is killed in a battle with his nobles, Frederick is converted by an 'old religious man ... his crown bequeathing to his banish'd brother' (5.4.158–61). Shakespeare was writing a comedy, and the politics of Frederick's usurpation was an area he avoided. He gives Frederick one further humanizing touch. When Oliver reports that Orlando has fled, but that he never loved his brother, Frederick snaps, 'More villain thou!' This may be an ironic joke, but it could also imply Frederick's sense of guilt that brotherly love is a virtue he should have embraced. Perhaps a key to Frederick is Le Beau's description of him as 'humorous' – moody and unpredictable.

Celia's attitude to her father is clear from the outset. She speaks of his 'rough and envious disposition', and when Rosalind is banished she says, 'Wilt thou change fathers? I will give thee mine.' By declaring 'Let my father seek another heir!' she is prepared to forgo her inheritance, and it is her idea that they should seek Duke Senior in the Forest of Arden (1.2.230; 1.3.88, 104). Though she is careful that they should 'get our jewels and our wealth together', the whole escape plan seems to Celia a merry romp, which is quickly dispelled when she 'faints almost to death' (2.4.62) through trudging about the wintry forest. Lodge gives Alinda a more complicated journey through the story for, when she is attracted to Saladyne/Oliver, she has doubts, 'for there is nothing more precious in a woman, than to conceal love, and to die modest' – a sentiment Shakespeare never endorses, except perhaps through Viola's fabricated sister in *Twelfth Night*. Lodge also tackles the problem that Alinda is still apparently a shepherdess, while Saladyne is the son of a knight, a class disparity which Shakespeare bypasses. While Celia doesn't speak in the final denouement, even when news of her father's repentance arrives, Alinda desires Gerismond/Senior 'to be good to her father' in the battle, and after he is slain she is 'very passionate for the death of her father'. Shakespeare has no interest in Celia's relations with her father, but concentrates almost exclusively on her friendship with Rosalind.

Just as the relationship between Frederick and Celia is only examined to further the plot, so Shakespeare hardly develops Senior and Rosalind's feelings for one another. The scene that introduces Senior makes no mention of Rosalind, nor the scene where Orlando bursts in upon the feasting exiles. In 3.4 Rosalind reports that she has met her father and 'had much question with him', and when she was apparently cheeky by claiming she was of as good parentage as he, 'He laughed and let me go' (32–5). This encounter could have made a rich scene – fathers failing to recognize their daughters occur several times in later plays – but here Shakespeare was too busy with other themes. In Lodge when Rosader/Orlando first meets the King/Senior he tells him of the girls' banishment, and 'this news drives the King into a great melancholy, that presently he arose from all the company, and went into his privy chamber'. Later when Saladyne arrives and has no news of the two girls, the King exclaims, '"Injurious Fortune that to double the father's misery, wrought the daughter with misfortunes". And with that (surcharged with sorrows) he went into his cell.' When Rosalynde finally reveals herself, 'Gerismond, seeing his daughter, rose from his seat and fell upon her neck, uttering the passions of his joy in watery plaints driven into such an ecstasy of content, that he could not utter a word.' Senior's reunion with Rosalind is a more sedate affair. He readily agrees to Orlando marrying her, 'had I kingdoms to give with her';

agrees with him that he's spotted something of his daughter in Ganymede; when Rosalind reveals herself declares only 'If there be truth in sight, you are my daughter'; and finally welcomes his niece as his daughter's equal (5.4.8, 26–7, 116). It's one of the coolest reunions of father and daughter in the canon. Shakespeare's interest in Senior lies almost entirely in debunking his living in the forest like 'the old Robin Hood of England', fleeting 'the time carelessly, as they did in the golden world' (1.1.113–15). Exile, an important factor in the Elizabethan political scene, intrigued Shakespeare, but Senior, unlike Bolingbroke, Hamlet and Prospero, seems to take it in his stride.

Shakespeare, well acquainted with the harsh rural life in the forests surrounding Stratford, sets the second act in winter, where 'the icy fang and churlish chiding of the winter's wind ... bites and blows upon [the Duke's] body'. Senior doesn't merely conclude that this will toughen him up, but acknowledges the 'adversity' and twice uses the word 'sweet' about the lessons to be drawn: that they are 'free from peril', 'painted pomp', and courtiers' flattery. Deprived of all his palatial accoutrements, he finds that nature provides discourse, books and sermons (2.1.2–17). Amiens commends this translation of the 'stubbornness of fortune / Into so quiet and so sweet a style' (19–20), but 'style' seems the appropriate word. The Duke protests overmuch. It's hard not to feel that Shakespeare is having fun at his expense, characterizing him as Robin Hood in a golden world, but knowing full well that if circumstances changed he would hot foot it back to court – as indeed he does.

Rosalind dominates the play, and at 685 lines it is the longest woman's part in the canon, though still shorter than the male tragic heroes. It was a major experiment on Shakespeare's part to put a woman at the centre of a romantic comedy, and then to examine her feelings about love in such a complex and realistic way. He must have had an exceptional boy at his disposal, one who might have played Portia and Beatrice, and he makes full use of the gender permutations. A boy plays a girl who dresses as a man, and then presents herself as the imagined adored object of a man in love. To add to the confusion she chooses the name Ganymede, Jupiter's boy-lover. In the epilogue, the only one given to the female lead, the distinction between male and female becomes even more blurred. Shakespeare takes the opportunity to allow the boy player to speak to men as a woman, and to women as a boy.

The opening three scenes illustrate and question the dominance of fathers; the word is mentioned thirty-six times. Celia chides Rosalind for falling, not for Orlando, but for 'old Sir Rowland's youngest son'. When Rosalind defends herself by arguing, 'the Duke my father loved his father dearly', Celia reasonably points out, 'Doth it therefore ensue that you should love his son dearly? By this kind of chase, I should hate him, for my father hated his father dearly ...' (1.3.28–31). In fact though Rosalind is initially sad, 'unless you could teach me to forget a banished father' (1.2.4), once she has seen Orlando her concern is no longer for her father, but 'some of it is for my child's father' (1.3.11). Fathers and husbands are often linked in the minds of Shakespeare's heroines, not only because the father is the first man in a child's early life, but also because daughters have grown up knowing that they will have to submit to the patriarchal status of both men. Though Celia takes the lead in planning their escape, it is Rosalind who suggests that she dresses as a man. Male attire will liberate her in so many ways, not least from being defined as her father's daughter. At court family connection and status is paramount, in the forest it counts for little. When she assumes the role of Ganymede many actors have found that she becomes a significantly different character from the diffident Rosalind of the court.

Though they have gone into the forest ostensibly to join Duke Senior, Rosalind's thoughts are now elsewhere: 'What talk we of fathers, when there is such a man as Orlando?' (3.4.35–6). No attempt is made by either girl to declare themselves to the duke: Rosalind resents the time Orlando spends with her father, and the fact that her supposed lover is courting him as well. She dominates Orlando's courting of her, though she is honest in warning him that 'maids are May when they are maids, but the sky changes when they are wives' (4.1.141–2). His Rosalind will be jealous, clamorous, giddy and changeable – certainly no model Renaissance wife. Male attire has afforded a double function, enabling her to be more frank and open than would be customary, but proving an obstacle that has fanned the flames of her desire. Like Portia and Olivia she knows she has chosen someone beneath her in status and wealth, but to whom she will have to submit (a fantasy to appeal to an upwardly mobile Elizabethan male audience). But first she has to 'educate' Orlando, whose only idea of love is to moon about the forest pinning terrible verses to trees. Their scenes together form the centrepiece of the play, where Orlando learns that he must understand and respect a woman on her own terms. What the Globe audience made of this revolutionary talk we have no idea, nor how popular the play was (it was not published till F).[11] Rosalind even arranges her own wedding, though she has not entirely forgotten her daughterly duties. She checks whether her father will 'bestow her on Orlando here?', and when she reveals herself her first address is to her father: 'To you I give myself, for I am yours / [to Orlando] To you I give myself, for I am yours' (5.4.7, 114–15). Desdemona and Cordelia will assert the same divided loyalty. In allowing Rosalind to choose her own husband Senior shows himself a liberal, or possibly lazy, parent.

In its breadth and complexity Rosalind is a great role, to which most actors, female and occasionally male, aspire. Like Juliet she is fathoms deep in love, but never loses a sense of reality. Like Isabella and Helena she is determined, energetic and imaginative. In her male disguise she holds a balance between the masculine and feminine: her androgyny gives her the ability to reconcile warring opposites. Like Innogen she never loses her emotional sensitivity, and faints at the sight of her lover's blood; she is Prospero-like in her magical ordering of the marriages at the end of the play. She is as witty as Beatrice in her speeches to Orlando. Shakespeare had already perfected his rhythmical prose speeches in Falstaff's great soliloquies, and Rosalind speaks in a rhythmic prose which can be transposed into free verse iambics:

> No, no, Orlando, men are April when they woo,
> December when they wed. Maids are May
> When they are maids, but the sky changes
> When they are wives. I will be more jealous
> Of thee than a Barbary cock-pigeon
> Over his hen, more clamorous than a parrot
> Against rain, more new-fangled than an ape,
> More giddy in my desires than a monkey.

(4.1.139–46)

The part and the play stand at a turning point in Shakespeare's development. The comedies that follow will all have dark undersides, and their heroines, Viola, Olivia, Isabella and Helena, will have no living fathers to guide or hobble them. But the great female roles to come will never equal Rosalind's reckless assault on life, and will never again, with the exception of Cleopatra, dominate the play. In *As You Like It* Shakespeare finds little room for the relationship between father and daughter: the two young women dominate, and it is the fathers' turn to be under-examined.

Twelfth Night: Viola, Olivia and absent fathers

Twelfth Night occupies a darker world than *As You Like It*: a carnival madness reigns and the norms of society are turned upside down. Shakespeare virtually banishes the two fathers from the second half of *As You Like It*, and in *Twelfth Night* they are removed altogether, though they never feel entirely absent. *Gl'Ingannati* (*The Deceived*, acted 1531) is the seedbed for all the later treatments of the story. Shakespeare might have read the versions in Belleforest, Barnaby Riche (1581) or even *Gl'Inganni* (1592) where the disguised girl calls herself Cesare. Common to most versions is that 'Viola' first meets 'Orsino' in the house of her father, and later pursues him. 'Olivia' has a father who, in the original *Gl'Ingannati*, falls in love with 'Viola' when he discovers she is a girl. Shakespeare therefore alters this basic plot quite considerably. His Viola's father died on her thirteenth birthday, probably no more than a year or two before. Olivia's father died 'some twelvemonth since'. This frees Shakespeare to concentrate on a different theme, the two young women's relationship with their brothers.

Olivia's brother died 'shortly' after their father, and so Olivia unexpectedly inherited both title and fortune, apparently, unlike Portia, without strings attached. She is in mourning, not for her father as one might expect, but for her brother, and intends to remain 'veiled' for seven years, though the fact that she reveals her face so readily to Cesario suggests that this is a melodramatic ploy. Her father and brother are never mentioned again. Viola's father is invoked more often. In her first scene she comments of Orsino, 'I have heard my father name him. / He was a bachelor then' (1.2.289). Sebastian tells Antonio, 'My father was that Sebastian of Messaline whom I know you have heard of' (2.1.16–17). Their father firmly established as important and well-known, Shakespeare can concentrate on sister and brother. In *Gl'Ingannati* they look very like one another, but it is Shakespeare's innovation to make them twins. The fact that Judith and Hamnet, had he lived, would have been fifteen at the time of writing has been much commented on, and it is not entirely fanciful to suggest that in Sebastian Shakespeare is conjuring up the shadow of his lost son. Certainly he gives considerable space (thirty-two lines) to their reunion and makes it the climax of the story – a fact unfortunately played down in many productions. Their father is again a real presence in their dawning recognition. They agree that his name was Sebastian, that he 'had a mole upon his brow', and that he 'finished indeed his mortal act' on their thirteenth birthday. Sebastian recalls this in the most emotional terms: 'O, that record is lively in my soul!' (5.1.228–42). Of their mother there is no mention.

Viola and Olivia are therefore united in their grief for a lost brother. Shakespeare might have held Sebastian's survival back, as *Gl'Ingannati* does, but, perhaps obeying the rules of comedy, he tells the audience early in the play that he is alive. By dressing as Sebastian Viola in a sense becomes her twin (perhaps as Judith tried to make up for the loss of Hamnet), and his supposed loss permeates her passage through the play. Viola is no Portia or Rosalind, relishing and exploiting her male role. She is more like the troubled women of the tragicomedies and the late romances. Orsino spots immediately that 'all is semblative a woman's part' (1.4.34). Viola quickly realizes that 'Disguise, I see thou art a wickedness', and concludes, 'O time, thou must untangle this, not I, / It is too hard a knot for me t'untie' (2.2.27, 40–1). She finds herself quite unable and unwilling to control the situation, and is tossed hither and thither as each farcical situation arises. She also knows that Time will make her youth and beauty pass 'even when they to perfection grow', particularly as she is swaddled in her male disguise, and Feste will echo this pessimism at the end of the play. The nearest she can get to declaring her love for Orsino is to conjure up her lost family:

My father had a daughter lov'd a man,
As it might be perhaps, were I a woman,
I should your lordship.

(2.4.108–10)

Father and lover are again linked. Orsino often comes across as a father figure, taking the place of both her lost father and brother, and in production this is often enhanced by casting Orsino as a forty-year-old. This is mirrored in comedic fashion by Malvolio's assumption of a paternal role with Olivia, who finds herself in need of an older man's service and advice, and this enables him to think that Olivia's passion for him is plausible. Shakespeare may have banished the real fathers from the play, but they hover over the young women in many guises. That the part of Malvolio has come to dominate the play in so many ways is no coincidence, for it marks the final permutation of Shakespeare's examination of romantic comedy, and ushers in the surrogate fathers of the tragicomedies.

3

Tragedies and tragicomedies

The term 'problem plays' has been current for over a century to describe *Hamlet, Troilus and Cressida, Measure for Measure* and *All's Well That Ends Well*, though F1 grouped the first two under Tragedy and the second two under Comedy. F. R. Boas wrote in 1896 that 'we are excited, fascinated, perplexed, for the issues raised preclude a completely satisfactory outcome', and critics have ever since sought to develop this cautious definition. Paul Edmondson, for example, writes that 'each play presents its audience with a morally complex and frustrated universe through which no direct course of action can be taken and in which no satisfying choices can be made'.[1] But this perceptive analysis could equally well apply to *Timon of Athens, King Lear, Coriolanus* and several others: in the second half of Shakespeare's career 'problem' is a broad church. The tragedies of *Hamlet* and *King Lear*, which both feature freshly conceived father-daughter relationships, break new ground in so many ways, not least in defying the spectator to comprehend a 'meaning'. In the three tragicomedies that follow *Hamlet* Shakespeare devotes himself to a new genre, the complexities of orphaned daughters and manipulative surrogate fathers.

Hamlet: Polonius and Ophelia, an actor's perspective

I played Polonius in 2008 for the RSC in a production by Gregory Doran at the temporary Courtyard Theatre in Stratford-upon-Avon (it later transferred to the Novello Theatre in London in 2009 and was filmed for BBC television). David Tennant played Hamlet, Patrick Stewart and Penny Downie Claudius and Gertrude, and Mariah Gale Ophelia. I had previously played Horatio to Ian Charleson's first Hamlet for the Cambridge Theatre Company in 1974; and the Player King to Daniel Day-Lewis – and subsequently Ian Charleson and Jeremy Northam – at the National Theatre in 1989. I had also seen at least a dozen stage Hamlets, including Richard Burton, Paul Scofield, Peter O'Toole, David Warner, Ian McKellen, Michael

Pennington, Alex Jennings and Simon Russell Beale. I therefore thought I knew the play very well, but as always found a host of new questions.

On Polonius my two greatest influences were Michael Bryant (National Theatre 1989) and Tony Church (RSC 1965 and 1980). Michael, who was a consummate actor from whom I learnt a great deal in many productions, played Polonius entirely seriously as a secretary of state of bureaucratic, almost military, precision, unperceptive and intolerant as a father, and the comedy arose from his blind earnestness. Michael Ratcliffe in the *Observer* found him 'sharp, prurient and thoroughly unpleasant, a meddler with, and hater of, other people's love'.[2] Tony Church played the part twice in quite different interpretations, both of which I saw and discussed with Tony when we acted together at the RSC in 1981.[3] In 1965 the director Peter Hall saw Polonius as a knave and manipulator, the epitome of the Establishment and an oppressive Victorian-style paterfamilias with an abiding sexual curiosity. Tony found this robbed the part of much of its humour (which is surely intended?), until he doubled his speaking-rate – always a good note for playing comedy. In 1980 John Barton emphasized the personal over the political. He saw the play as the breakdown of an essentially happy family, in which Polonius' pedantries and eccentricities could be endearing rather than oppressive. When Polonius is killed, Ophelia breaks down and Laertes leads a rebellion, he argued that this surely meant there had been a great love between father and children? Ophelia was overpowered not by patriarchal tyranny but by too much love. I could see that for me it was not a case of choosing between polar opposite interpretations, for all these elements are present in the text. The problem lay in finding a balance between the varied, often contradictory, aspects of a surprisingly complex character. Gregory Doran was in general agreement that Polonius was both a concerned father and a politically manipulative courtier, and he embraced my potentially comic exploration of his tortuous pedantry. He then sat back to observe what I made of this strange mix, before stepping in to report what was working and what wasn't. A director is hopefully the best audience an actor will ever have.

As usual, after reading the entire play several times and noting what every character says about Polonius, I started with Shakespeare's sources. The royal counsellor and the girl set to ensnare the prince exist in most versions of the Hamlet story, but Shakespeare has made significant changes by linking them as father and daughter. A late Elizabethan writer's main source would be Belleforest's *Histoires Tragiques* (1564–82), a reworking of Saxo 'Grammaticus', a twelfth-century writer, first published in 1514. Saxo initially says that 'some people' came up with a plan to trap Amleth into revealing his sanity with a 'fair woman', and later added that it was Amleth's uncle's idea and that Amleth and the woman 'had been under the same fostering in their childhood; and this early rearing in common had brought [them] into great intimacy'.[4] Amleth's foster-brother warned him not to show any sign of sound reason or to do 'the act of love openly'.

Amleth duly drags the woman off to a secret place and they make love. She agrees to deny this, so that when Amleth admits to their union it is taken as a sign of madness. Belleforest says that the girl loved Hamlet from childhood, and adds that she would have been sorry not to enjoy the man who she loved more than herself, and it may well be that Shakespeare had this childhood scenario in mind, which he later developed with Helena and Bertram, and Innogen and Posthumus. Whether the two are lovers or not, they are clearly in league against the scheming king. A 'friend' of the king then comes up with a plan to trap Amleth in conversation with his mother. This friend then hides under the bed quilt, but is discovered by Amleth, killed and chopped into pieces, which are stuffed down a sewer and eaten by pigs.

It was probably Shakespeare's idea to turn the 'friend' into the father of the young woman and the deviser of both plans, though it may have been the author, probably Thomas Kyd, of the lost *Ur-Hamlet*. All we know of the earlier play is that it had a ghost and, according to Thomas Nashe, 'handfuls of tragical speeches'. Belleforest has no ghost, nor players, play, gravedigger or soliloquies, and in all previous versions it is Hamlet, not the 'woman's' brother, who fights with the king. Belleforest calls the king's 'friend' Corambis, and this is taken up in Q1 (1603) and in the much later *Fratricide Punished* (first published in 1781), a version which toured in Germany and made considerable changes to the plot. At some stage in his conception of the play Shakespeare changed the name to Polonius (though he was to use the name Corambus in *All's Well That Ends Well*, 4.3.160), and the actor(s) who presumably cobbled together Q1 may be referring back to different versions of the story, including the *Ur-Hamlet*. It might seem odd that the King of Denmark had a Polish counsellor, but the other characters share a strange ragbag of classical and European names. The name may well have been chosen in reference to the Polish statesman Grimaldus Goslicius, whose book *The Counsellor* was published in translation in 1598, in which he comes across as verbose and sententious, imagining that his 'art … is rather to be termed the science of prating', a word which Shakespeare picked up on when Hamlet calls the dead Polonius 'a foolish prating knave' (3.4.217).[5] It may also have been a way of deflecting the censor and the audience's attention away from a connection with Elizabeth's counsellor Lord Burleigh, nicknamed 'Ponderosus', who was known to have sent a servant, Winderbank, to spy on his son in Paris, and aspired to marry his granddaughter Anne to Shakespeare's sometime patron, the Earl of Southampton. Though Burleigh had died in 1598, Shakespeare may have felt it unwise to antagonize the powerful Cecil family.

Shakespeare evidently relished writing the character of Polonius; it is the third longest part in the play, some 340 lines, over twice the length of Gertrude. Corambis, to judge by *Fratricide Punished*, was an outright comic part, but Shakespeare introduces Polonius more judiciously. In the first court scene (1.2) he speaks only a few lines, but they are already over-elaborate and self-regarding, a tiny prologue to the prolixity that is to come:

> He hath, my lord, wrung from me my slow leave
> By laboursome petition, and at last
> Upon his will I seal'd my hard consent.

> (1.2.58–60)

Our production was modern, but for most of the play I wore a form of black morning coat with an ostentatious chain of office that would have served for any period in the past 150 years. In my next scene in my house (1.3) I wore a cardigan, that great signifier of family and domestic repose. Whatever period or ambiance a director chooses to set his/her production in it is vital to create a coherent society in which it is clear that Polonius is both a domestic patriarch and Claudius' chief counsellor (he has no rival in the text). His first two family scenes (1.3 and 2.1) concern his relationship first with his son and then with his daughter, an introduction unique in the canon, and I realized a great deal hangs on these scenes in terms of establishing character and family relationships. His advice to his son is concise, well thought out, if platitudinous. The speech is an exercise in rhetoric, which any Elizabethan grammar school boy would pick up. Polonius is obsessed with hendiadys ('words or talk', 'flash and outbreak', 'lecture and advice'), and his children have caught it from him ('sanity and health', 'steep and thorny').[6] When compared with Burleigh and Walter Raleigh's advice to their sons, five points emerge as common: be familiar but not vulgar; choose friends wisely; avoid quarrels but give a good account of yourself; clothe yourself well but not gaudily; don't borrow or lend.[7] Polonius omits the admonitions to serve God, choose a good wife and trustworthy servants and educate children well – he certainly doesn't want Laertes to choose a wife for himself in Paris. What he puts in their place is significant:

> Give every man thy ear, but few thy voice;
> Take each man's censure, but reserve thy judgment.

> (1.3.68–9)

This is the credo of a politician and spymaster. The final admonition is more riddling. 'To thine own self be true' could mean either practise noble integrity, or pursue ignoble self-interest – in any event 'be constant'. Perhaps in Polonius' mind they are one and the same: to survive at court you need continually to further your own interests without appearing to do so. It may even be that he hopes his son will adopt an honourable course that he is only too aware he himself has failed to achieve. The point of the advice is surely to establish Polonius as a caring, if domineering, father, and prepare for Laertes' passion as avenger of his death.

As soon as Laertes departs the father's habitual inquisitiveness cannot be contained: 'What is't, Ophelia, he hath said to you?' (88). This is both sinister and comic (i.e. it usually gets a laugh), a duality that Shakespeare extends throughout the part. Finding that it is 'something touching the Lord Hamlet' he immediately criticizes her 'free and bounteous' behaviour, as it ''tis told me' – the theme of spying is reiterated throughout the play. He 'pooh-poohs' her notion of Hamlet's 'tenders of affection' on the grounds she is a 'green girl, / Unsifted in such perilous circumstances' (101–2). In his view Ophelia is not only naive but has foolishly dabbled in the dangerous politics of the court. His command to 'tender yourself more dearly / Or … you'll tender me a fool' indicates that he wants her to behave more circumspectly, because if she gives away her chastity the court will think he's been duped. His instructions are contradictory. On the one hand he orders her not to 'give words or talk with the Lord Hamlet'; on the other he reiterates: 'Set your entreatments at a higher rate / Than a command to parley' (107–9, 122–3, 134). There is a suggestion here that she should play 'hard to get', which gives support to the idea that Polonius has not ruled out a possible marriage, which would clearly be in his interests. This mixture of genuine concern for his children, desire to enhance his status and determination not to be fooled runs consistently through his actions. I found this scene showed that Polonius is both dominating and caring towards his children, but hardly 'loving' – there is certainly no expression of affection.

Figure 2 Polonius (Oliver Ford Davies) and Ophelia (Mariah Gales) in *Hamlet* at the Royal Shakespeare Theatre, Stratford-upon-Avon, 2008. Photo by Ellie Kurttz (© Royal Shakespeare Company)

We next see the different attitudes he has towards his son and daughter, in a scene that must be some weeks later. He sends Reynaldo, who may well be the servant who has 'told' him of Ophelia's 'free and bounteous' behaviour to Hamlet, to spy on Laertes. Reynaldo is not to stop him wallowing in the fleshpots of Paris, but to put on him 'what forgeries you please', though restricted to such 'wanton, wild, and usual slips ... most known / To youth and liberty' (2.1.20, 22–4). Polonius is apparently quite complaisant with gambling, quarrelling, drinking and brothel visiting, because this is what aristocrats do. Nevertheless he is extremely pedantic in trying to define how far Reynaldo may go, and his efforts must leave Reynaldo confused:

> You must not put another scandal on him,
> That he is open to incontinency –
> That's not my meaning; but breathe his faults so quaintly
> That they may seem the taints of liberty,
> The flash and outbreak of a fiery mind.

> (29–33)

Is Laertes, therefore, to visit a brothel but not have sex with a prostitute? As always the more Polonius tries to define his position the more unclear he becomes. Shakespeare then shows him slipping further into his dotage by the way he loses his drift with Reynaldo: 'And then, sir, does a this – a does – / What was I about to say? (50–1). It is a daring naturalistic device, both comic and moving: the audience is temporarily tricked into confusing actor and character. I had watched Michael Bryant many times play this so truthfully in 1989 (most of the audience were convinced he had dried) that I knew I might copy but never rival his apparent authenticity. The point of the exercise, however, becomes clear: Reynaldo's 'bait of falsehood' will take 'this carp of truth', and 'by indirections find directions out' (63, 66). Indirection becomes a key to the play. Much of the scene is also about role-playing: Polonius acts out how Reynaldo is to act, as he observes the roles Laertes adopts.

Then Ophelia bursts in with her account of Hamlet's extraordinary visit, though it is hard to interpret his state of undress. Is it his trial run for an 'antic disposition', the conventional disarray of a love-sick suitor, or is it there to suggest possible madness? The account of this visit takes Polonius by surprise, but the trained politician in him comes up immediately with an explanation: 'Mad for thy love?' Ophelia replies that she fears so, and this makes Polonius triumphantly declare that it is 'the very ecstasy of love' (85, 102). This may be a wishful misinterpretation, but it is not fundamentally mistaken – Hamlet will later say he'd 'loved Ophelia' more than forty-thousand brothers (5.1.269–71), though it may be that she appeared a more romantic object dead than alive. Polonius makes a rare admission of humility ('beshrew my jealousy'), that in fearing Hamlet 'did but trifle / And meant to wrack thee ... it as proper to our age to cast beyond ourselves in our opinions' (112–15).

Without consulting her he plans to hustle her off to see the king: if Hamlet's love is genuine, however eccentric, it is in Polonius' interests to have it out in the open. These two scenes establish so much about the Polonius family, while remaining somewhat peripheral to the plot – we never, for example, meet Reynaldo again, discover what he found out or hear Laertes' reaction to it all. It is a rare instance in Shakespeare of a family interacting with one another, and indeed the words father, daughter, brother, sister, mother echo through the play. It also demonstrates the different codes of conduct a father expects of a son and a daughter. Polonius wants Laertes to have a degree of licence abroad, Ophelia to adopt a modest, retiring conformity at home.

With Polonius established as a concerned but manipulative and despotic father, Shakespeare now shows another, comedic side of him. It is a device that he had already honed with the Duke of York in *Richard II*: I found that in playing York for the Almeida Theatre in 2000 and the RSC in 2015/16 in London and New York that his first scene, at the death of Gaunt, is entirely 'straight', while his second scene when he bewails his inability to respond to the arrival of the exiled Bolingbroke is clearly comedic. When Polonius arrives to see the king, Q1 has Ophelia in his company as he had proposed, though all later editions have her entering only in the following scene. We, however, seized upon the opportunity to have her present, which our Ophelia, Mariah Gale, found particularly humiliating. From the outset Polonius is careful to ingratiate himself with Claudius:

> I assure my good liege
> I hold my duty as I hold my soul,
> Both to my God and to my gracious King.

> (2.2.43–5)

A few minutes later he risks asking Claudius 'What do you think of me?', and the king replies, 'As of a man faithful and honourable' (129–30). In fact Claudius is a consistent champion of Polonius, presumably because he values his statecraft and knowledge of the court, possibly because he owes to him the smooth passage of his election as king.

After the ambassadors' exit, Polonius embarks on sixty-five lines of what I can only term 'stand-up comedy', though attempts have been made to claim he is merely uneasy at talking about his daughter's love life. In it he attempts to prove 'your noble son is mad' (92), that he is in love with Ophelia, which Polonius has forbidden her to reciprocate, and that this has driven him 'into the madness wherein now he raves / And all we mourn for' (149–50). All this Polonius delivers with a wealth of rambling parentheses and pedantic circumlocutions:

> My liege and madam, to expostulate
> What majesty should be, what duty is,

Why day is day, night night, and time is time,
Were nothing but to waste night, day and time.

(86–9)

Gertrude is quickly on to Polonius' pedantries: 'More matter with less art', but Claudius remains remarkably tolerant, perhaps intent on discovering how dangerous Hamlet's instability might prove to him. I then found the reading of Hamlet's strange love letter (is he satirizing the genre?) gave particular scope for comedy, the line 'in her excellent white bosom, these etc.' (112) causing him extreme embarrassment (the 'etc.' could well refer to further allusions to her bodily perfection). Mariah Gale, however, found Hamlet's doubt of everything except 'Never doubt I love' very poignant. Polonius' obfuscation is very funny, but at the same time chilling in the way he is prepared to sacrifice his daughter to ingratiate himself with Claudius. His solution is to 'loose my daughter' to Hamlet (162), while he and Claudius hide behind an arras. Despite this barnyard image of making the female available for copulation, their hidden presence will ensure that Ophelia's 'chaste treasure' will be preserved, while establishing, Polonius hopes, that Hamlet really is in love. The comedy continues with Polonius' meeting with Hamlet, where Hamlet runs rings round him but leaves him with the impression that he is both mad and 'still harping on my daughter' (187). Polonius has by this stage been made a figure of fun, but Shakespeare gives him several rather endearing asides to the audience, which I found very helpful. He finds Hamlet's madness fascinating – 'How pregnant sometimes his replies are – a happiness that often madness hits on' (208–10) – and his confession that 'truly in my youth I suffered much extremity for love, very near this' is strangely touching (189–90). The audience may agree with Hamlet that Polonius is a 'tedious old fool', but Shakespeare makes his tediousness the acme of comedy. It can be argued that Polonius' apparent stupidity is a mask to cover his real thoughts and feelings, but his asides would belie this – and this would also be very difficult to play. Hamlet calls him Jephthah, with a daughter 'he loved passing well' (413), and this leaves us with the sense that Hamlet realizes Polonius is prepared, like Jephthah, to sacrifice his daughter to keep in with his lord and master.

In 3.1 Claudius sets up the meeting between Hamlet and Ophelia, while 'her father and myself, lawful espials' bestow themselves (32). This theme of 'lawful espials' runs through the play, and would have been very familiar to an Elizabethan audience steeped in Walsingham and Burleigh's espionage plots to root out Catholic assassins and supporters of a Spanish invasion. On a domestic level many fathers would have agreed it permissible to go to any lengths to find out a young man's intentions towards their daughter. Polonius gives Ophelia a prayer book to read to 'colour / Your loneliness' (a young woman could hardly roam the court unattended), and then makes the surprising admission (though it is unclear whether he counts himself among the general 'we'):

We are oft to blame in this,
'Tis too much prov'd, that with devotion's visage
And pious action we do sugar o'er
The devil himself.

This goads Claudius into picking up the half-line (as an aside in F):

O 'tis too true.
How smart a lash that speech doth give my conscience.

(3.1.46–50)

Shakespeare, having established Polonius as an arch-manipulator, and Claudius as a guilty villain, then softens and humanizes these images, while telling the audience that the Ghost's accusations are to be believed. Claudius has a guilty conscience, and Polonius is aware how reprehensible are his tactics: suddenly both characters take on a further dimension. Patrick Stewart unfortunately cut his aside in order not to pre-empt the prayer scene confession, as so many Claudiuses do. Their interpretations of Hamlet's denunciation of Ophelia differ significantly. Claudius believes Hamlet is not in love, but so dangerous he needs to be sent away (to his death, though this plan may come after Polonius' murder); Polonius clings on to the 'neglected love' idea and proposes his overhearing of Hamlet's 'showing of his grief' to his mother. Despite their momentary guilty reservations, Claudius remains a murderer and Polonius a spymaster: neither can shed their identities. Polonius' only interchange with his daughter, his last as it will turn out, is brusque:

How now, Ophelia?
You need not tell us what Lord Hamlet said,
We heard it all.

(179–81)

This has been called one of the cruellest lines in Shakespeare. And yet it could be kindly meant: Polonius is trying to save his daughter humiliation and distress, however crassly he phrases it. Polonius' conduct and intentions, as with all the three-dimensional parts in Shakespeare, are open to interpretation and debate. Having agreed that 'yonder cloud' is 'like a camel', and 'backed like a weasel', should 'very like a whale' be played as submissive, sarcastic or angry (I chose anger)? His attachment to wordplay is a comic mirror of Hamlet's: they duel throughout the play until 'word-murder' turns to physical murder and Polonius finds 'to be too busy is some danger' (3.4.33). After working on the part I understood more clearly that his death is the turning point in the play. After this murder, whether intended or not, there is no going back for Hamlet, Claudius or Gertrude, and it will finally seal their fates. My favourite commendation of my performance came from a woman in the audience who, when I was killed, cried out 'Oh, not him!', a reminder that to some the plot is an entirely novel thriller.

Shakespeare has a great deal of fun in making Polonius claim authority on a multiplicity of subjects, and these pomposities I found a joy to play: Love ('I suffered much extremity'); Espionage ('we of wisdom and of reach'); Insanity ('a happiness that often madness hits on'); Literature ('"beautified" is a vile phrase'); Drama ('this is too long'); and general judgement ('Hath there been such a time ... That I have positively said 'tis so / When it proved otherwise?'). In nearly every instance Polonius is shown to be wrong. He is a great comic creation, yet shares with Falstaff a side that is dangerous, manipulative and amoral.

Ophelia has been characterized as childlike, timid, ineffectual, 'a doll without intellect'.[8] But this is not the Ophelia we first meet. As Mariah Gale writes, 'She runs rings round Laertes' rhetoric', first hearing out her brother's warnings against opening her 'chaste treasure' to Hamlet's 'unmastered importunity', but then gives as good as she gets:

Do not as some ungracious pastors do,
Show me the steep and thorny way to heaven,
Whiles like a puff'd and reckless libertine
Himself the primrose path of dalliance treads
And recks not his own rede.

(1.3.47–51)

This is witty, well expressed and very much to the point, and suggests a good sibling relationship. When her father then demands, in a much more peremptory fashion, to know what is between her and Hamlet, she puts up a strong case for the 'honourable' nature of Hamlet's love for her, but is browbeaten both by her father's claims to know all about the 'blazes' of lust, and by his strict orders to end the affair. Her brother's advice has been largely practical – that Hamlet is 'subject to his birth' and cannot 'carve for himself' – while her father's is more personal and scathing: 'When the blood burns, how prodigal the soul / Lends the tongue vows' (116–17). There is a growing assumption in recent productions in a modern setting that Hamlet and Ophelia have slept together (Branagh's 1996 film shows them in bed), but in our production Mariah thought this unlikely. It would mean that the apparently truthful Ophelia is lying from the outset about Hamlet's 'honour'. When asked if she believes the 'tenders of his affection' she replies, 'I do not know, my lord, what I should think' (104). This line of apparent simplicity yields a number of interpretations. Is she 'a doll without intellect'; is she beginning to doubt Hamlet's intentions under this double family onslaught; is she preserving her own thoughts and feelings from her father's intrusiveness; or is she simply, perhaps ironically, resigned to being told yet again by her father what to think?

Hamlet's strange, wordless visit to her, doublet unbraced and stockings fouled, understandably 'affrights' her and, with her brother gone, she has no one to turn to, in the absence of any female companion, but her father. Polonius seems very certain that this is 'the very ecstasy of love', a prognosis that must be both alarming and reassuring to Ophelia, but he goes on to pronounce that Hamlet is mad, that she is responsible for 'denying his access' to her and that the whole affair must be made public to the king. Shakespeare catches wonderfully the seasoned politician's snap reaction to a crisis, which proves to be totally misplaced. Small wonder that Ophelia feels totally out of her depth, having innocently triggered a family and national crisis. Recent suggestions that a rape has taken place again seem at odds with claims of 'honour' and 'honesty'. It seems more likely that Hamlet himself had no set plan when he came to her room, apart from a desire to see her, and, finding himself tongue-tied (unable to end their relationship?), left without a word. Ophelia also apparently said nothing, suggesting perhaps that, in addition to 'fright', her faith in Hamlet has been crushed by her family.

She is forced to agree to being 'loosed' upon Hamlet, and Claudius makes it clear that she will be spied upon. Gertrude seems to condone, even encourage, her relationship with Hamlet – 'I do wish / That your good beauties be the happy cause / Of Hamlet's wildness' (3.1.38–40) – and hopes she will be responsible for bringing him to his senses. A terrifying pressure is being put upon her: she is, after all, more a 'prisoner' in Denmark than Hamlet. If she overhears 'To be or not to be' – there is no stage direction that she exits – it must be hard for her to know what construction to put upon it (the speech is of course often placed earlier, before the arrival of the Players, but Hamlet's contemplation of 'self-slaughter' could arguably occur at any point in the play). She sticks to her script, which is to redeliver the 'remembrances of yours' (3.1.93). If this is her idea it shows how seriously she is taking her mission, however painful; if it is her father's it shows how thoroughly he wants her to appear to reject Hamlet, but Hamlet says nothing of this rejection, so obsessed is he with her sexual and breeding potential. She doesn't wilt under Hamlet's aggressive questioning. In answer to aspersions on her beauty and chastity, she robustly replies, 'Could beauty, my lord, have better commerce than with honesty?' (109–10), but her hopes are then destroyed by one of Shakespeare's trademark stark, almost monosyllabic, exchanges:

HAMLET   I did love you once.
OPHELIA Indeed, my lord, you made me believe so.
HAMLET   You should not have believed me ... I loved you not.
OPHELIA I was the more deceived.
HAMLET   Get thee to a nunnery. Why, wouldst thou be a breeder of
         sinners?

(115–21)

There is much argument about the double meaning of 'nunnery', but though Hamlet is clearly referring to a convent the image of the brothel still persists. If Gertrude has become in Hamlet's eyes a whore, will Ophelia also be corrupted and in turn corrupt men, and is sexual abstinence in a convent therefore her best retreat? In his paranoia he projects on to Ophelia the threat he feels from his mother's sexuality.[9] His following misogynistic and misanthropic tirade, full of self-loathing, only confirms to her his madness.

Shakespeare then gives her a soliloquy, an expression of inner thoughts denied to Gertrude, Laertes and, to an extent, Polonius. Her first thought is that this model Renaissance prince, 'th'expectancy and rose of the fair state', whom she so admired, is 'here o'erthrown' and 'blasted with ecstasy', as her father had prophesied. Only after this generous summation of his 'noble mind' does she think briefly about herself:

And I, of ladies most deject and wretched,
That suck'd the honey of his music vows ...
                    O woe is me,
T'have seen what I have seen, see what I see.

(151–62)

Mariah Gale argues that 'this is love, isn't it, when the other person comes first no matter how hurtful their behaviour?', but Ophelia has now lost both her lover and the respect of the king and her father.

She next loses the respect of the court. Hamlet prefers to sit by her rather than his mother, for 'here's metal more attractive', and this is noted by her father – 'O ho, do you mark that' – and presumably by the entire court. Hamlet then openly taunts her sexually in a coarse and brutal way, leaving the court to surmise she has become a whore ('It would cost you a groaning to take off mine edge'). Ophelia manages to retain some dignity – 'You are merry, my lord', and she calls him 'keen' (bitter) – but at great cost to herself (3.2 *passim*). Later that night her sometime lover kills her father and is hustled abroad. Ophelia's isolation is complete, and it is this loneliness that Shakespeare now explores. Juliet had her nurse and Friar Laurence, Jessica had Lorenzo and his friends, Hero had Beatrice and Ursula, Rosalind had Celia. Ophelia is the first of Shakespeare's figures of innocence who are caught up in a corrupt society, and forced by men to become implicated in this corruption. It is the first study of the relationship between the pressures of the public world and the survival of love, which is taken up in *Troilus and Cressida* and all the great tragedies that follow. Ophelia has become the puppet of the patriarchs of the state, repressed her own feelings and lost her newly emerging identity, her real subjective self. But is she mad? Horatio (F)/A Gentleman (Q2) says 'she is importunate, / Indeed distract' (4.5.1–2), and Claudius comments she is 'divided from herself and her fair judgment' (85). It is as if Shakespeare is trying to avoid the term 'mad', and the word is not finally used until Laertes' reference to her dispensing of herbs – 'a document in madness' (176). Mariah was baffled by people's unthinking reference to 'the mad scene', and felt rather that Ophelia experienced 'grief, confusion, guilt ... perhaps she is torn asunder by two opposing loves? What if you love the man who kills your other love? It would tear you in two.'

Her condition was much copied by other dramatists. Lucibella in Henry Chettle's *Hoffman, or Revenge for a Father* (c. 1602) talks wildly but abandons suicide, recovers her wits and revenges the deaths of her father and fiancée (perhaps suggesting that Ophelia should have done the same). Aspatia in Beaumont and Fletcher's *The Maid's Tragedy* (1610–11) wears a willow garland, sings a pathetic song and foresees her death. She ends playing both Ophelia and Laertes, disguised as her brother and fatally challenging Amintor to a duel. Fletcher in *The Two Noble Kinsmen* (1613) makes the Jailer's Daughter sing and contemplate a watery death (see p. 152). Her 'afterlife' in succeeding centuries has been considerable. As Kaara L. Petersen and Deanne Williams argue: 'She has become an endlessly adaptable symbol for the universality of the feminine and, more broadly, the human psychic condition in any era, across cultures ... analysed by structuralism, deconstruction, poststructuralism, psychoanalysis and new historicism.'[10] A list worthy of Polonius himself.

Is her 'distraction' Shakespeare's invention? In his original source the girl makes love with Hamlet, promises not to betray his sanity and is never heard of again. No references to the *Ur-Hamlet* mention a mad scene. It is possible that Shakespeare included not one, but two, such scenes because they were good box-office, but he also saw that 'madness' was a way of liberating Ophelia, now bereft of the three men who had controlled her life. Horatio/A Gentleman, who introduces her, says 'she speaks much of her father, says she hears / There's tricks i'th' world', but she initially finds it difficult to articulate her thoughts, but 'hems, and beats her heart ... speaks things in doubt / That carry but half sense. Her speech is nothing' (4.5.4–7). Mariah, however, thought that her speech and actions were quite purposeful. She enters singing a ballad of a woman betrayed and forsaken by her lover, then moves to a song about her father 'dead and gone' and finally to a scurrilous rhyme about a maid losing her virginity to a man who refuses to marry her as she is no longer chaste (her fear perhaps in relation to Hamlet). Her repressed sexuality is now released. She has lucid and purposeful moments: first in the gnomic challenge to Claudius, 'We know what we are but know not what we may be', and then in the lament for her father, 'I cannot choose but weep to think they would lay him i'th' cold ground. My brother shall know of it.' (42–3, 69–70).

In fact Laertes has already heard of it, and arrives to witness Ophelia's re-appearance laden with flowers, which include daisies for unrequited love, fennel for flattery, columbines for infidelity and violets for fidelity which 'withered all when my father died'. Cold and whiteness, symbols of death, plague her remembrance of her father – 'white his shroud as the mountain snow', 'his beard was as white as snow, / All flaxen was his poll' (35, 192–3). Her brief life has been dominated by her father's ascendancy over her (in recent productions she often entered wearing a piece of her father's clothing, as Glenda Jackson did for the RSC in 1965, Carol Royle in 1980 and Joanne Pearce in 1992); the affection given and withdrawn by Hamlet; her desired loss of her chastity; and the corruption and hypocrisy she has perceived surrounding her. In a play where most of the characters are playing out a role, Ophelia is one of the few people *not* acting: she and Horatio can be seen as the only figures of integrity in the court. R. D. Laing wrote of her: 'There is no one there. She is not a person. There is no integral selfhood expressed through her actions or utterances ... She has already died,'[11] but Shakespeare's intention is to show that however confused she may be in her divided self, she knows all too well what matters to her and what has been taken away. Mariah thinks her 'a whistle-blower who goes out in a blaze of glory', though David Leverenz argues that Ophelia 'through her impossible attempt to obey contradictory voices ... mirrors in her madness the [same] tensions that Hamlet perceives ... Her history is another instance of how someone could be driven mad by having her inner feelings misrepresented, not responded to, or acknowledged only through chastisement [by father, brother and lover] and repression.'[12] Hamlet's own thoughts of madness and suicide are in a sense realized in his rejected lover's downfall. Her subsequent drowning lies on the borders of heedless depression and suicide, perhaps as Katherine Hamlett's had when she drowned in the Avon in 1579, an event which the fifteen-year-old Shakespeare was probably aware of.

Hamlet is a significant departure for Shakespeare in many ways, most clearly in his discovery that plot and action can be subsidiary to the dramatic inwardness of his protagonist's thinking, but he experiments in so many areas, not least in Polonius and Ophelia's identities and relationship. Polonius is a *senex,* caring but tyrannical, in the Capulet mould, but he is also both a brilliant comic tour-de-force and a psychologically complex figure, in a way that Capulet, Baptista and Leonato are not. Most fathers in Shakespeare are shown to use their daughters to further their dynastic and financial ambitions, but he is the first to play perhaps a double game, forbidding his daughter to encourage a prince's suit, which would clearly be the ultimate prize, in the hope that this may force a successful issue. It is the work of an ambitious, though finally over-sophisticated, operator. Ophelia is introduced as a girl of spirit who knows that she has to submit to her father's dictates, that she needs him to guide her through the tangle of court politics and that she is a commodity to be traded. She is alone in a man's world, with no woman to turn to. Father and daughter's dependence on one another, once Hamlet has begun his suit, is total. Polonius is also the only living father in the play, though Hamlet has a ghostly father. The Ghost spies on Hamlet, as Polonius does on Laertes. The Ghost urges Hamlet to revenge, Polonius urges his daughter to reject Hamlet, and this double intervention leads to both their children's deaths. Ophelia is unique in the canon in having to deal with the killing of her father, and it destroys her 'fair judgement'. Daughters are very seldom given space to comment on their fathers at the end of Elizabethan plays, and, although Ophelia may be delusional, she leaves the clear impression that her unfulfilled sexual longings vie with horror at the loss of her father.

Troilus and Cressida: Calchas, Pandarus and Cressida

Troilus and Cressida was possibly written soon after *Hamlet* in 1601 (though not registered till February 1603), and its performance history is in doubt. It was finally published in 1609 in two states with two different title pages, one claiming that it was 'never staled with the stage, never clapper-clawed with the palms of the vulgar', the other affirming that it was acted at the Globe. It is structurally odd, beginning with ten long scenes and then speeding up in a helter-skelter of sudden action. Degree, reputation, honour and love are examined, mocked and found wanting. The Trojan War is seen as absurd, corrupt and meaningless, a tragic waste of men and women in their prime. Vows are only there to be broken; irony, scepticism and disillusionment reign supreme. It presents enormous problems for any production, perhaps because Shakespeare has crowded too many themes, genres and structures into one three-hour play.

Cressida has a Trojan father, Calchas, who has defected to the Greeks because as a soothsayer he has predicted the outcome of the war 'through the sight I bear in things to come' (3.3.4). The historical Calchas was always a Greek, and Cressida, who is not mentioned in Homer, is almost certainly a mythical construct of Boccaccio, Chaucer and Caxton, based on a fourth-century Latin account of the war by Dictys the Cretan. She has accordingly passed into legend as 'the faithless woman', and Shakespeare, whose young heroines had been up to this point uniformly faithful, however much slandered, was undoubtedly attracted to examining the nature and circumstances of Cressida's 'faithlessness'. She is paired with Helen, both are figures of exchange, both, as Diomedes says, the occasion for 'a hell of pain and world of charge' (4.1.59). All we know of her relations with Calchas is that she says, when refusing to leave Troy, 'I have forgot my father. / I know no touch of consanguinity; / No kin, no love, no blood, no soul, so near me / As the sweet Troilus' (4.2.97–100). It is an extreme variant of Rosalind's 'What talk we of fathers when there is such a man as Orlando?' Calchas had in fact tried in the past to persuade Troy to let Cressida go, but it is not until the capture of Antenor that the Greeks have a sufficiently valuable figure to exchange. Agamemnon deputes the exchange to Diomedes, who when he arrives in Troy is quick to say: 'To Diomed /

You shall be mistress and command him wholly' (4.4.118–19). Cressida arrives in the Greek camp and is sheltered in her father's tent. Diomedes calls by, and the briefest of exchanges takes place:

DIOMEDES   What, are you up here, ho? Speak.
CALCHAS   Who calls?
DIOMEDES   Diomed. Calchas, I think? Where's your daughter?
CALCHAS   She comes to you.

(5.2.1–5)

Calchas has clearly accepted that his daughter will need a protector/lover – young women are in short supply in the Greek camp – and Diomedes will do as well as any. This is the sum total of this father's responsibilities, and we hear no more of Calchas.

Cressida has no living mother, but she has an uncle, presumably her mother's brother, who acts as her guardian, Pandarus. Cressida seems to have no female friends, is only ever seen in the company of men and Pandarus therefore fulfils the role not only of surrogate father but of a lady-in-waiting as well. They both enjoy the gossip, banter and abuse of this interdependence, but it's clear from the start that Cressida's interests are not foremost in her uncle's mind. Shakespeare owes much to Chaucer's long poem *Troilus and Criseyde*, but Chaucer's Pandare is a considerate and concerned friend and father figure. Shakespeare decided, perhaps through long observation of the London scene, to make his Pandarus a selfish voyeur, and directors and actors have gone to town on making him a mincing, syphilitic wreck. He is principally interested in Troilus – 'I could live and die i'th' eyes of Troilus' (1.2.237–8) – and in delivering his niece up to him. His relish in imagining them pressing the bed 'to death' is both voyeuristic and, in a sense, incestuous. He compares the art of love to cake-making: grinding, bolting, leavening, kneading, heating, baking, cooling (1.1.15–26). He sells Troilus remorselessly in a revealing catalogue of masculine virtues – 'birth, beauty, good shape, discourse, manhood, learning, gentleness, virtue, youth, liberality' (1.2.246–7). Cressida resists this hard sell, though she is not above trading bawdiness with her uncle, lying 'upon my back to defend my belly' from taking 'the blow' which may 'swell past hiding' (253, 262). In fact she is already deeply in love with Troilus, though she explains in soliloquy why 'I hold off':

> Women are angels, wooing;
> Things won are done; joy's soul lies in the doing.
> That she beloved knows naught that knows not this:
> Men prize the thing ungained more than it is.
> That she was never yet that ever knew
> Love got so sweet as when desire did sue.

Therefore this maxim out of love I teach:
'Achievement is command; ungained, beseech'.

(279–86)

This is a more bitter and cynical extension of Rosalind's teaching, but it
reveals a pragmatic acceptance of a woman's position that will lead to
her yielding to Diomedes' 'demand'. When later she declares her love for
Troilus she admits she was won 'at first glance', in a more mature version
of Juliet's thoughts:

Why have I blabbed? Who shall be true to us
When we are so unsecret to ourselves?
But though I loved you well, I wooed you not;
And yet, good faith, I wished myself a man,
Or that we women had men's privilege
Of speaking first.

(3.2.121–6)

Juliet regrets admitting her love, but simply because 'I would it were to
give again.' Cressida knows she needs an intimate and a protector other
than Pandarus, and she feels she can trust Troilus. But from the outset
she is 'offended' by her own 'company'. She sees herself as two persons: a
'kind of self' that loves Troilus, and an 'unkind self' that 'itself will leave /
To be another's fool' (144–6). Jan Kott writes: 'She is passionate, afraid of
her passion and ashamed to admit it. She is even more afraid of feelings.
She distrusts herself. She is our contemporary because of this self-distrust,
reserve, and need of self-analysis.'[13]

Troilus is if anything more confused than Cressida, and Shakespeare seems
to pour himself into this confusion. Troilus, so steeped in martial training,
feels love makes him 'womanish', 'less valiant than the virgin in the night'
(1.1.11). He eulogizes Cressida – 'Her bed is India; there she lies, a pearl'
(99). Waiting for Cressida to appear he characterizes himself to Pandarus
as 'a strange soul upon the Stygian banks / Staying for waftage' (3.2.8–9),
with Pandarus as Charon and Cressida as either hell or Elysium. He sees the
sexual act as 'Death, I fear me, / Swooning destruction, or some joy too fine'
(20–1). The spectre of inconstancy hangs over their union. Troilus worries:

O, that I thought it could be in a woman –
As, if it can, I will presume in you –
To feed for aye her lamp and flames of love,
To keep her constancy in plight and youth,
Outliving beauty's outward, with a mind
That doth renew swifter then blood decays!

(154–9)

Troilus is revealed as an amalgam of lust, self-pity, serious self-examination and notions of high romance, and Cressida, sensing his indecision, tries to help – 'for to be wise and love / Exceeds men's might' (152–3). Shakespeare captures wonderfully the ebb and flow of her confidence, her trust in Troilus and herself, and her doubts of their future. It is a far cry from Juliet and Rosalind. Pandarus sees Cressida as a bird to be tamed, and if 'you draw backward, we'll put you i'th' thills' (43–4), yoked like an errant farm animal. He sees his niece not just as a property to be traded, like so many fathers, but as a body to give satisfaction. He then tries to make light of the threat of falsehood: 'Let all constant men be Troiluses, all false women Cressids, and all brokers-between panders' (198–200): he is in no doubt that the woman is the more likely to break promise. Nevertheless he ends by turning to the audience and upholding the rights of women to sexual fulfilment – and a pander's right to voyeuristic satisfaction:

> And Cupid grant all tongue-tied maidens here
> Bed, chamber, pander to provide this gear!
>
> (206–7)

The next morning both men are condescending to Cressida. Troilus is anxious to leave, and Cressida mourns, 'I might have still held off, / And then you would have tarried!' (4.2.18–19). Troilus treats her like a child – 'Sleep kill those pretty eyes / And give as soft attachment to thy senses / As infants' empty of all thought!' (4–6). Cressida cannot bear to be mocked by her uncle, for 'you bring me to do – and then you flout me too' (27), but Pandarus is unrelenting: 'Would he not – ah, naughty man – let it sleep?' (33–4). While Chaucer gives them three years together, Shakespeare allows them this one night. When the news arrives of the Antenor exchange, Pandarus' thoughts are all for Troilus and himself: ''Twill be his death, 'twill be his bane; he cannot bear it' (93–4). Pandarus immediately blames Cressida: 'I knew thou wouldst be his death' (87). The conquest of his niece accomplished, he loses interest in her fate. In Chaucer Troilus begs her to steal away with him, and wonders if he can appeal to Priam. When Pandare suggests, like Juliet's Nurse, that 'if she be lost, we shall recover another' (*Troilus and Criseyde*, 4.406), Troilus is appalled: 'Thou biddest me I should love another / All freshly new, and let Criseyde go! / It lieth not in my power, leave brother' (456–8). But Shakespeare's Troilus immediately accepts the situation, and tells Paris, 'I'll bring her to the Grecian presently', and likens himself to a priest at the altar (4.3.6–9). He might have saved Cressida by declaring her his betrothed, but this seems never to have entered his mind, perhaps because there is too great a gulf in their status: he is a prince, she a daughter of a priest who has defected. Cressida reacts quite differently. Four times she asks if she must go, and four times Troilus confirms she must. What envelops them is the fear of inconstancy. Troilus is the first to raise it: 'Hear me, my love. Be thou but true of heart', and Cressida angrily rejoins, 'I true? How now, what wicked deem is this?' (4.4.57–8), but it is Cressida who ends their scene with 'My lord, will you be true?' (100). She is left feeling deserted by both guardian and lover.

The arrival in the Greek camp, where the generals line up to kiss her as if she were an upmarket courtesan rather than an honoured guest, has been interpreted in many ways. Shakespeare gives Cressida no explanation of her conduct. Two things emerge: Cressida accepts the role that is thrust upon her; and she enjoys the power she wields over these men and particularly, as her confidence grows, over Menelaus and Ulysses. Ulysses' opinion is that she is a 'daughter of the game', 'her wanton spirits look out / At every joint and motive of her body' (4.5.57–8, 64), but this may be mere misogyny (never trust that Shakespeare endorses what one character says about another). It was Ulysses who suggested ''Twere better she were kiss'd in general', but then goes on to denounce her. Diomedes demands no kiss but simply 'Lady, a word', and it is clear to everyone that she is designated his 'charge'; she twice uses the word 'guardian' about him. It is the universal story of sex in time of war (in 1945 German women in Berlin attached themselves to a particular Russian soldier in the hope that it would save them from being gang-raped). Diomedes claims later that she had made promises to him, she falters and begs for time, he threatens to abandon her, and she answers desperately, 'Ay, come. – O Jove! – Do come – I shall be plagued' (5.2.111). He exits, contented, and Cressida is at last allowed a little soliloquy:

> Troilus, farewell! One eye yet looks on thee,
> But with my heart the other eye doth see.
> Ah, poor our sex! This fault in us I find:
> The error of our eye directs our mind.
> What error leads must err. O, then conclude:
> Minds swayed by eyes are full of turpitude.

> (113–18)

It is a kind of epitaph: the vagaries, or 'errors' (the word is much on her mind), of passion are full of wickedness.

Troilus has, of course, witnessed all this, and accepts that she is now 'Diomed's Cressida' (144). He speaks at length, but one feels that he, and perhaps Shakespeare, is flailing about for meaning. His most telling remark is 'This is and is not Cressid' (153). As a sexual being her future lies, at any rate for a time, with Diomedes, who shows no sign of caring for her, nor she for him. The Cressida that loved Troilus, understood him, was a comfort, even a mother figure, to him is not lost: 'Cressid is mine, tied with the bonds of heaven' (161). Nevertheless when, later, Pandarus brings him a letter from Cressida, presumably affirming her love and trying to explain her conduct, he reads it and tears it up: 'My love with words and errors still she feeds, / But edifies another with her deeds' (5.3.111–12). His confusion is still unresolved; what is now uppermost in his mind is revenge, first on Diomedes, and then, when Hector is slain, revenge on all the Greeks' 'vile abominable tents'. To Troilus martial values take precedence over love. The final line in F is 'Hope of revenge shall hide our inward woe' (5.11.31).

Shakespeare's first thought for an ending (which most productions embrace) may be contained in the 1609 Quarto. Troilus turns on Pandarus, who has never been more than a pander to lead him to Cressida:

> Hence, broker-lackey! Ignomy and shame
> Pursue thy life, and live aye with thy name!
>
> (33–4)

Pandarus, who has lost both his protégés, now admits to a 'whoreson phthisic', a rheum in his eyes and 'such an ache in my bones', and turning to the audience begs the 'good traders in the flesh' and the 'brethren and sisters of the hold-door trade' (who, of course, surrounded the Globe stage and theatre) to 'weep at Pandar's fall' (45–51). This last was omitted in F, too strong meat perhaps for both the censor and the theatre's more puritanical patrons.

Troilus and Cressida is only seven or eight years on from *Romeo and Juliet*, but it demonstrates a very different sensibility. Shakespeare now perceives that two young people can be instantly attracted to one another and want to make love, but that they are confused about their feelings, intentions, how much they want to invest in this relationship and what they think it will lead to. The fear of inconstancy threatens their faith in one another, and the chance of war destroys their getting to know each other. Like Ophelia and Hamlet they are sacrificed to the politics of the time. Cressida has no father or uncle who really cares for her. She is flirtatious but hardly promiscuous, and knows that she has to use her sexuality to survive and submit to the realpolitik of the enforced change of sides. Troilus feels bereft but does nothing to try and save her, and his jealousy of Diomedes leads only to thoughts of revenge. Shakespeare seems on the track of a complex understanding of the chaotic effect outside forces have on brief love, and nearly brings it off, defeated perhaps by the over-ambition of his sprawling, all-embracing concept.

Measure for Measure: Duke Vincentio and Isabella

In *Measure for Measure* Shakespeare develops the theme of surrogate father by turning him into a prospective husband. It can appear a play of two halves, the first the careful assembling of a potential tragedy, and the second a somewhat unconvincing farce. Philip Sidney had denounced this genre as 'mongrel tragi-comedy'. By combining the themes of Disguised Ruler and Corrupt Magistrate Shakespeare sets himself a structural challenge he cannot quite meet – he becomes so interested in Duke Vincentio that Angelo is not present on stage for all of Act 3 and most of Act 4, and his crucial decision to execute Claudio, despite having slept with, as he thinks, Isabella, is consigned to a brief soliloquy (4.4.21–35). This examination of Vincentio's internal state follows on from the experiment with Hamlet and, perhaps playing to Burbage's strengths, continues on through the great tragedies to Antony and Coriolanus.

The character of Isabella bridges the two themes. Her brother Claudio says that 'in her youth / There is a prone and speechless dialect / Such as move men' (1.2.179–81), suggesting perhaps her attractive body language. They are both orphans, as Escalus reports to Angelo (2.1.7). Isabella's desire to enter a nunnery with 'a more strict restraint' suggests a strong sense of moral purpose, if not an adolescent masochism; and this strong connection to religion is unusual among the heroines of the period. She has to be coaxed/bullied by Lucio into pressing her brother's cause with Angelo, but as her confidence grows she shows a sophisticated grasp not only of her ethical dilemma but also of the rules of balanced rhetoric:

> There is a vice that most I do abhor,
> And most desire should meet the blow of justice;
> For which I would not plead, but that I must;
> For which I must not plead, but that I am
> At war 'twixt will and will not.

> (2.2.29–33)

In pleading mercy and compassion she reveals a mature grasp of psychology. She presses Angelo:

> Because authority, though it err like others,
> Hath yet a kind of medicine in itself
> That skins the vice o'th' top.

> (135–7)

It is small wonder that Angelo says in an aside, 'She speaks, and 'tis such sense / That my sense breeds with it' (142–3). He is attracted as much by her intelligence as her youth and beauty, though the sexual imagery which she lets slip – 'Th'impression of keen whips I'd wear as rubies, / And strip myself to death as to a bed / That longing have been sick for' (2.4.101–3) – presumably excites him. Shakespeare has immediately found an individual voice for Isabella. In another context, as Adrian Noble argued in rehearsals for a 1983 RSC production, the scene could be between a law tutor and a star pupil.

The cardinal importance to Isabella of her chastity troubles many modern actors, and some have mentally substituted the word 'integrity'. There is some justification for this doubt, as the Church would probably have condoned the surrender of chastity to save the life of a brother condemned by a corrupt justice. Isabella may abhor the idea of physical violation, but she is especially keen to defend her 'honourable reputation', as she finds 'shamed life a hateful' (3.1.116). Shakespeare here departs from his two main sources, Cinthio's *Hecatommithi* (1565) and Whetstone's *Promos and Cassandra* (1578), where the heroines are prepared to surrender their chastity on the promise of marriage. Isabella's marriage to Angelo was not part of the complicated resolution Shakespeare had in mind. One does sense in her encounter with Claudio, however, the influence on both of them of their 'most noble father'. When Claudio says, 'If I must die, / I will encounter darkness as a bride / And hug it in mine arms', Isabella replies, 'There spake my brother: there my father's grave / Did utter forth a voice' (82–6).

At this point a new father appears, both a pretend friar and a surrogate parent. The theme of disguised ruler was much in vogue in 1604/5, witness Dekker's *The Honest Whore*, Middleton's *The London Prodigal* and Marston's *The Fawn*. Most of these spies were, however, fathers checking on their offspring, while Vincentio, like Marston's Malcontent, intends wholesale surveillance of his subjects. This would have appealed a good deal to James I, who had himself attempted a secret visit to observe the Stock Exchange. In his *Basilicon Doron* he promoted the idea of the king as 'nourishe-father' to his subjects. Vincentio disguised as a friar would have been for James 'the ultimate fantasy of the father-ruler'.[14] From the outset the Duke likens himself to 'fond fathers' who threaten but do not punish, so that 'Liberty plucks Justice by the nose' (1.3.23, 29). He tries out his new father role with the pregnant Juliet. If the sin of fornication with Claudio was 'mutually committed ... then was your sin of heavier kind than his' (2.3.27–8), and Juliet accepts this very male condemnation of women's supposed innate lustfulness. In this world of male authority Angelo refers to Juliet as the 'fornicatress', while Claudio is called 'your brother', never the fornicator. The Duke/Friar may seem to Isabella a reincarnation of her noble father, but when they first meet in private he speaks in most un-parentlike terms: 'The hand that hath made you fair hath made you good. The goodness that is cheap in beauty makes beauty brief in goodness; but grace, being the soul of your complexion, shall keep the body of it ever fair' (3.1.180–2).

Vincentio, like Angelo, cannot stop himself from referring to Isabella's 'beauty' and her 'body', and this could imply that he is immediately attracted to her. He plunges at once into proposing the bed-trick with Mariana, claiming that 'by this is your brother saved, your honour untainted' for 'the doubleness of the benefit defends the deceit from reproof' (252–3, 256–7). Isabella is naturally ready to clutch at any straw, however dodgy the proposal and its justification, and is happy to call him 'good father'. The Duke has just persuaded Claudio to 'Reason thus with life: / If I do lose thee, I do lose a thing / That none but fools would keep' (6–8), in a speech that is stoic but arguably unChristian. One possible interpretation of this is that the Duke is near to breakdown, and it is the attraction of Isabella and the prospect of unmasking Angelo that pulls him out of despair. His move into prose for the first time in the play is a sign perhaps of a new practical resolution.

The audience knows from this moment that Claudio can be saved at the Duke's instigation, but both writer and character need to hold this back to facilitate the outing of Angelo. When Isabella later arrives in the prison to know if her brother's pardon has arrived, the Duke speaks in the most riddling terms:

But I will keep her ignorant of her good,
To make her heavenly comforts of despair
When it is least expected.

(4.3.109–11)

On the face of it this is callous and unwarranted withholding of information. If he intends to test Isabella's moral character in the depths of her grief he doesn't say so. If one theme of the play is intended to be the education of both Isabella and Vincentio, Shakespeare has left it opaque. Does Vincentio plan to play the magician and produce a happy ending at the very last minute, in the hope that Isabella's gratitude and joy will translate into affection for him? Is he treating her as a teacher would a pupil, a trait he would seem to share with Angelo? The playwright aspect of the central character is much to the fore, supporting the fanciful notion that Shakespeare himself played the part: both seem to be making up the plot as they go along. He makes the Duke and Isabella already on close, if formal, terms:

DUKE   Good morning to you, fair and gracious daughter.
ISABELLA The better, given me by so holy a man.

(112–13)

The Duke gives the bad news, Isabella cries and the Duke tells her of his imminent return.

DUKE   If you can pace your wisdom
         In that good path that I would wish it go,
         And you shall have your bosom on this wretch,
         Grace of the Duke, revenges to your heart,
         And general honour.
ISABELLA I am directed by you.

(133–7)

Isabella has lost all autonomy, and become the Duke's creation. The plot, which seemed to set Isabella up at the outset as the chief protagonist (rather as Helena is in *All's Well That Ends Well*), has allowed the part to dwindle into subservience in order to accommodate the Duke's machinations. The Duke behaves like a god, but whether he is benevolent or simply meddling is left open (a window perhaps into Shakespeare's own religious convictions?).

In the final scene the Duke puts Isabella through test after test. He declares her mad, suborned against Angelo's honour 'in hateful practice', and has her arrested. Having forced Angelo to marry Mariana, he then condemns him to death. Does he expect Isabella to plead for Angelo's life? When Mariana asks her to 'take my part' he derides the request: 'Should she kneel down in mercy of this fact, / Her brother's ghost his paved bed would break, / And take her hence in horror' (5.1.431–3). Despite the fact that Isabella's 'Most bounteous sir' (440) is picking up a half-line after the Duke's 'He dies for Claudio's death' (two separate lines in F) her lengthy pause has become part of theatrical tradition – Peter Brook at Stratford in 1950 encouraged Barbara Jefford to hold it longer than she thought safe. She finally speaks and proceeds to argue that Angelo's 'bad intent' was not consummated (since Mariana was his wife on a pre-contract), while Claudio did technically commit fornication. It is not a convincing plea: that evil actions are harmless, when carried out under mistaken circumstances, is a lame argument. She has lost the voice of the alpha law student, but she has managed, against the odds, to uphold the principle of compassion, and the Duke knows that Claudio can be produced. Whether the Duke had intended this final test, and whether Mariana's plea was a lucky intervention or a pre-arranged ploy, the text does not reveal.

The Duke then makes his marriage proposal, wavers – 'but fitter time for that' – and forty-two lines (2 ½ minutes?) later tries again (489, 531). Isabella says nothing. The fact that Shakespeare could not provide her with even a couplet of acceptance has caused much heart-searching in modern productions. The Jacobean audience would have assumed her compliance – there is no historical record of a commoner refusing a ruler's marriage offer – and in 1604 they would undoubtedly have walked off hand in hand, and the dukedom's need for an heir would be fulfilled. Isabella's silence is, however, eloquent. The Friar has been a man of God and a celibate father figure. He has suddenly turned himself into a would-be lover, and Shakespeare is too good a psychologist to think that Isabella could immediately acquiesce to this sudden transition. A few years earlier he might happily have written her a speech; now it seems he can't truthfully imagine what she might say. But then Isabella has not just remained silent for the last eighty lines of the play, she hasn't really opened her mind to us since she asked the Duke to 'show me how, good father' in the prison.

If the outcome of the Duke's proposal is left uncertain – and in recent productions Isabella is often left alone on stage at the end – it is perhaps because the whole tenor of this comic ending is suspect. Mariana may want to be a respectable married woman, but the pardoned criminal Angelo is not a good prospect. Lucio presumably has no intention of remaining faithful to Kate Keepdown. Isabella has no option but finally to accept the Duke. Only Claudio and Juliet have a true, loving union, and they are kept firmly in the background. Comic closure has been achieved, but without really answering the intellectual issues of virtue, chastity, mercy and the rule of law which the play has set in motion. Perhaps Shakespeare's growing interest in opacity of motive is responsible for this sense of uncertainty. The hurried resolution of the Duke's final speech is indicative of Shakespeare's frustration. This play, together with *All's Well That Ends Well*, marks the end of his attempts to engineer a conventional happy ending from a plot that seems destined to end tragically. The surrogate father turned lover, to the 'daughter's' speechless surprise, is not an experiment Shakespeare ever repeated.

All's Well That Ends Well: The King of France and Helena

There are no living fathers in *All's Well That Ends Well*, as in *Measure for Measure*, but although dead they exert an influence at the outset. The two plays have been grouped together in the period 1602–5, though some metrical tests have suggested, not altogether convincingly, a later date for *All's Well That Ends Well*, perhaps 1606–8.[15] The play opens with Bertram, the Countess, Helena and Lafeu 'all in black' mourning the death of Bertram's father, and within fifteen lines the Countess is talking of Helena's physician father, whom, Lafeu says, 'the King very lately spoke of him admiringly – and mourningly' (1.1.27–8). The Countess hopes that Bertram will 'succeed thy father / In manners, as in shape!' (60–1), and Lafeu instructs Helena 'You must hold the credit of your father' (78–9). When the King meets Bertram he talks obsessively of his father; 'Youth, thou bear'st thy father's face ... Thy father's moral parts / Mayest thou inherit too!' (1.2.19–22), but Bertram's filial devotion is markedly reticent. He will come to prefer as a surrogate father the 'braggart soldier' Parolles to the aged, moralizing king. Paternal dominance is thus proclaimed by the older generation, but we soon discover that Bertram and Helena's thoughts lie elsewhere. Helena, an only child, has been brought up by her father as a surrogate son:

> On's bed of death
> Many receipts he gave me; chiefly one,
> Which ... he bade me store up as a triple eye,
> Safer than mine own two; more dear I have so.

> (2.1.103–5, 107–8)

She is in many ways the most modern of Shakespeare's heroines in that she thinks she can create her own destiny:

> Our remedies oft in ourselves do lie,
> Which we ascribe to heaven; the fated sky
> Gives us free scope; only doth backward pull
> Our slow designs when we ourselves are dull.

(1.1.216–19)

'Dull' Helena does not intend to be. She is in love with Bertram, who is probably only fifteen as he is considered too young to go to war, and far above her in social station. She proclaims, Rosalind-like, that this transcends any thoughts of her dead father:

> I think not on my father,
> And these great tears grace his remembrance more
> Than those I shed for him. What was he like?
> I have forgot him; my imagination
> Carries no favour in't but Bertram's.

(80–4)

Shakespeare is intrigued by making the woman the sexual initiator, hence the very racy discussion with Parolles, the other social climber, on virginity: 'Is there no military policy how virgins might blow up men? ... How might one do, sir, to lose it to her own liking?' (122–3, 151–2). We are already far from the world of Rosalind and Viola, with a woman who would be totally at odds with Isabella. Helena is in love with Bertram's beauty, 'his arched brows, his hawking eye, his curls'. She says nothing of his character, beyond the fact that his superior status gives him 'bright radiance and collateral light' (95, 89). She has placed him on a pedestal, aware that it is 'idolatrous fancy', and objectified him in a way more associated with Shakespeare's male lovers – 'Juliet is the sun. / Arise, fair sun, and kill the envious moon' (*Romeo and Juliet*, 2.1.45–6). It is a good thing she makes no claims for his character because Shakespeare has stuffed him full of faults, far in excess of Beltramo in his main source, William Painter's *The Palace of Pleasure* (1575). Bertram is insensitive, self-indulgent, lecherous and a liar, quite prepared in the last act to marry Lafeu's daughter, Maudlin, to keep in with the King: Shakespeare may be slyly claiming him as a typical aristocratic adolescent. He had never risked writing such a sexually assertive heroine before; all his previous heroines know, or at any rate think, they are beloved. Julia reads that Proteus is 'love-wounded'; Helena knows that Demetrius was once in love with her; Portia lets Bassanio take the lead; Rosalind knows Orlando is littering the forest with verses to her; while poor Viola 'never told her love'.

Helena is given no such encouragement by Bertram, who sees her as 'a poor physician's daughter' and, after his enforced marriage, a 'detested wife'. This gives Shakespeare a considerable problem. It is possible to see Helena as the tamer, bringing Bertram to heel as a responsible husband, or as the healer, first of the King's body and then of Bertram's adolescent selfishness, but Shakespeare is too acute to make Helena so Olympian. She swings between passive and active. She can be shy, modest and respectful. When Bertram tells the King he 'cannot love her', she loses heart: 'That you are well restor'd, my lord, I'm glad. / Let the rest go' (2.3.146–9). At other times she is blazingly reckless. When the King asks how much she will risk on her cure, her reply is near-hysterical:

> Tax of impudence,
> A strumpet's boldness, a divulged shame,
> Traduc'd by odious ballads; my maiden's name
> Sear'd otherwise, nay worse of worst, extended
> With vildest torture, let my life be ended.

> (2.1.169–73)

Even allowing for the fairy-tale nature of the scene with its grandiloquent imagery and rhyming couplets this is extraordinarily tortured writing. There is also a strong sexual undertow in the scene. In Painter Helena simply says, 'If I do not heal you within these eight days let me be burnt.' Shakespeare cannot quite control these pendulum swings between fairytale and the naturalistic. She dominates the wonderful first half of the play, but then gets somewhat lost in the necessary convolutions of plot, including the desperate device of the bed-trick. Nor is Shakespeare's heart in the happy ending. As in *Measure* what started out in tragic mode becomes an ill-at-ease comedy. When Helena asks 'Will you be mine, now you are doubly won?' Bertram's reply should be a long speech generously acknowledging his errors. Instead he remains terse and conditional, though the repetition of 'ever' suggests he is at least making an effort to be generous:

> If she, my liege, can make me know this clearly
> I'll love her dearly, ever, ever dearly.

And Helena replies, with ominous foreboding:

> If it appear not plain, and prove untrue
> Deadly divorce step between me and you!

> (5.3.314–17)

Shakespeare's view of their marriage prospects seems a world away from Painter's resolution: 'From that time forth he loved and honoured her as his dear spouse and wife.' One reason for Shakespeare's reluctance to honour the comedic ending is the lack of a proper courtship. Silvia, Juliet, Portia, Rosalind, even Kate and Viola come to a shared understanding with their lovers. Hero, Ophelia and Helena all fail in establishing a proper courtship and the results are, for a time at least, tragic. Nevertheless Helena remains 'a radical experiment – a bold effort to place on the comic stage women who show sexual desire, pursue consummation, have intercourse during the five acts, and are celebrated at the end'.[16]

Shakespeare also makes the King of France a more complex and less sympathetic figure than Painter's original. In the first court scene he speaks of a vanished world of honour and integrity, in contrast to present society where younger spirits 'all but new things disdain; whose judgments are / Mere fathers of their garments; whose constancies / Expire before their fashions' (1.2.61–3). Levity and jest are all pervasive, language is a false substitute for deeds. Much of this is expressed in abstract, compressed and sometimes obscure verse:

> So like a courtier, contempt nor bitterness
> Were in his pride or sharpness; if they were,
> His equal had awak'd them, and his honour,
> Clock to itself, knew the true minute when
> Exception bid him speak, and at this time
> His tongue obey'd his hand.

> (36–41)

This language would tax any audience, Jacobean or modern. The King takes Bertram under his wing, but is even more captivated by Helena, partly seeing her as a heavenly intervention – 'Methinks in thee some blessed spirit doth speak' – and partly through her personal allure – 'youth, beauty, wisdom, courage – all / That happiness and prime can happy call' (2.1.174, 180–1). When, after the successful cure, she chooses Bertram for husband the King is peremptory: 'Why, then, young Bertram, take her; she's thy wife' (2.3.106), whereas in Painter, 'the King was very loath to grant him unto her. But for that he had made a promise, which he was loath to break ...'

One reason why Shakespeare makes his king so despotic is that the writer relished the opportunity to argue that virtue is more important than title:

> From lowest place when virtuous things proceed,
> The place is dignified by th' doers deed.
> Where great additions swell's and virtue none,
> It is a dropsied honour. Good alone
> Is good, without a name; vileness is so:
> The property by what it is should go,

Not by the title.

(126–32)

He goes on to argue that the 'mere word' Honour is 'a slave / Debosh'd on every tomb, on every grave / A lying trophy' (137–9). This is strong stuff, probably much to the taste of the bulk of his audience, but not surely to his aristocratic patrons. But then we know so little about the play's history, its date of composition or its contemporary stage appearances. While Painter's king is very conciliatory – 'thinking verily you shall lead a more joyful life with her than with a lady of a greater house' – Shakespeare's monarch is angry and tyrannical, in the same racing, fluent verse one finds in *Othello*:

> Proud, scornful boy, unworthy this good gift,
> That dost in vile misprision shackle up
> My love and her desert ... Check thy contempt;
> Obey our will which travails in thy good; ...
> Or I will throw thee from my care for ever
> Into the staggers and the careless lapse
> Of youth and ignorance; both my revenge and hate
> Loosing upon thee in the name of justice,
> Without all terms of pity.

(152–4, 158–9, 163–7)

Figure 3 King of France (Oliver Ford Davies), Helena (Michelle Terry) and Bertram (George Rainsford) in *All's Well That Ends Well* at the Olivier, National Theatre, London, 2009 (© Simon Annand/National Theatre)

This forcing of a ward to marry against his will to a person of lower status was of course indefensible, though Shakespeare was well aware of the many abuses of wardship. It can be argued therefore that this King is not a good father to his people, something that James I laid great store by – at least in theory. Not only does he abuse his position as a guardian of wards, he proceeds in the last act to accuse Bertram of killing Helena, to threaten Diana with death and then encourage her to choose an aristocratic husband. This abuse of his power sits uneasily in the necessary comic resolution of the play. But though Shakespeare is as usual critical of arbitrary power, his real interest lies in surrogate parents – the Countess is his invention and the King's participation is greatly increased. As with Vincentio, if arbitrary power is to be exercised for the ultimate good of the people then Shakespeare appears to celebrate that. He also asks us to celebrate the influence of a mother, albeit a surrogate mother, on his heroine. The scenes between the Countess and Helena give us a tantalizing glimpse of how well he could have written for mothers and daughters throughout the canon.

In her mixture of assertiveness and self-deprecation Helena is a hard character to pin down. She is poor and isolated, an outsider in a male hierarchy. Sheldon P. Zitner writes: 'The critical response to Helena is an anthology of (largely) male thinking about the status of women', and Robert S. Miola characterizes her as 'untitled virgo, wondrous woman, part simple serving maid, part religious sermonizer, part incantatory folk-tale sorceress ... determined schemer.[17] I feel Shakespeare pours himself into Helena's obsessive, humiliating and apparently hopeless love, but is never quite certain where he or his character are going. Much has been made of the connection with the sonnets. Shakespeare, like Helena, was a provincial outsider, gaining entry to the Court through a particular skill, and seeking an attachment to a cold-hearted aristocrat 'beyond his sphere'. They both might echo: 'Farewell, thou art too dear for my possessing / And like enough thou know'st thy estimate' (*Sonnet* 87.1–2). Helena does of course, through trickery, possess Bertram, and muses, sonnet-like: 'But, O strange men! / That can such sweet use make of what they hate' (4.4.21–2).

Othello: Brabantio and Desdemona

Othello is the nearest Shakespeare came to writing a domestic tragedy, in the vein of *Arden of Faversham* (1592), *A Warning for Fair Women* (before 1599) and *A Woman Killed with Kindness* (1603). The handker-chief and the marital bed take over from the 'big wars'.[18] Shakespeare's experiment is to turn the conventional triangle on its head: Othello is not a cuckold, Desdemona is not adulterous and Cassio is not the lover wanting Othello dead. Desdemona presents a particular challenge to the modern actor: why does such an assertive young woman turn into such a submissive wife? The solution to this is part of yet another experiment by Shakespeare on the role of women in contemporary society. The Boito/ Verdi opera leaves out Shakespeare's Act 1, as many other critics, including Samuel Johnson, have desired. Shakespeare, however, wants to show how the marriage came about, how the father tried to prevent it and what Venetian society thought about it all: it is a rare example of his filling out a detailed backstory. Brabantio, for example, is Shakespeare's invention. He doesn't exist in his chief source, Giraldi Cinthio's *Gli Hecatommithi* (1565), which merely says, 'The lady's relatives did all they could to make her take another husband.' After Disdemona's murder the Moor was 'condemned to perpetual exile, in which he was finally slain by Disdemona's relatives, as he richly deserved'. Although Shakespeare doesn't follow Cinthio in allowing the couple to live together 'in such concord and tranquillity' for some time in Venice, he wants to show them calm, determined, loving and in charge of their destiny.[19]

Brabantio is another of Shakespeare's over-protective, apparently loving, single parents. Desdemona keeps his house – 'But still the house affairs would draw her thence' – much as Jessica and Beatrice did. Brabantio thinks her obedient, docile, and contented with her lot; 'a maiden never bold, / Of spirit so still and quiet that her motion / Blushed at herself' (1.3.95–7); 'So opposite to marriage that she shunned / The wealthy, curled darlings of our nation' (1.2.67–8). According to Othello, 'Her father loved me, oft invited me, / Still questioned me the story of my life' (1.3.129–30), and Brabantio must have left Desdemona and him alone together when she 'bade me, if I had a friend that loved her, / I should but teach him how to tell my story / And that would woo her. Upon this hint I spake' (165–7). Brabantio may have unwittingly allowed his daughter this degree of licence, not thinking of the Moor as a potential suitor, confident that he had her secured in both body and mind. On hearing of their marriage he rants, 'O heaven, how got she out? O treason of the blood! / Fathers, from hence trust not your daughters' minds / By what you see them act' (1.1.167–9). In Shakespeare's canon locking up daughters – Silvia, Jessica, Hermia, Celia, Innogen – is always a recipe for their escape.

Brabantio first learns of his daughter's elopement from the sexually and racially explicit Iago: 'An old black ram / Is tupping your white ewe! … You'll have your daughter covered with a Barbary horse' (1.1.87–8, 109–10). Brabantio calls him a 'profane wretch', but turns out to be a complete racist himself. He insists, like Egeus, that his daughter is 'corrupted / By spells and medicines bought of mountebanks', else how could she 'fall in love with what she feared to look on?' (1.3.61–2, 99), or 'run from her guardage to the sooty bosom / Of such a thing as thou?' (1.2.70–1) The state, however, needs Othello's military prowess, and the Duke declares 'your son-in-law is far more fair than black' (1.3.292). Othello has become, in the state's eyes, an honorary white.

Despite the marriage Brabantio remains confident of his daughter's allegiance: 'Do you perceive, in all this noble company, / Where most you owe obedience?' (1.3.178–9). When she explains her 'divided duty', his response is, like Leonato's, 'I had rather to adopt a child than get it', and, like Capulet's, 'I am glad at soul I have no other child', and he continues, 'for thy escape would teach me tyranny / To hang clogs on them' (192,197–9): in other words a second daughter would have been manacled at the neck or legs, one of the harshest threats any of Shakespeare's patriarchs make. When the Duke suggests Desdemona should live at her father's house, Brabantio is the first to say 'I'll not have it so' (242), and the others agree. His final words to his daughter show no sign of softening: he remains frank, if bitter, to the end:

> Look to her, Moor, if thou hast eyes to see:
> She has deceived her father, and may thee.
>
> (294–5)

In fact, though the time sequences in the play are notoriously awry, his heartbreak is such that he survives only a few days. Graziano reports later in censorious vein:

> Poor Desdemona, I am glad thy father's dead;
> Thy match was mortal to him, and pure grief
> Shore his old thread in twain.
>
> (5.2.204–6)

Shakespeare, who was often so careless in tying up loose ends, is determined to mark how a daughter who takes her life into her own hands could be deemed by the world to have destroyed her father's life.

Desdemona comes across as very young: 'I am a child to chiding'; 'she that so young could give out such a seeming'; 'she reserves it [the handkerchief] evermore about her / To kiss and talk to'. She may be another of Shakespeare's fifteen-year-olds, immured in her father's house, and innocent of sex, marriage and the ways of the world. She has, however, 'shunned / The wealthy, curled darlings of our nation', presumably proposed by her father, so she seems to be looking for someone more exciting, more interesting, more substantial – and Othello certainly fits the bill. His tales produce in her 'a world of kisses' ('sighs' in Q, so someone had upped the emotional temperature by F); 'She swore in faith 'twas strange, 'twas passing strange, / 'Twas pitiful, 'twas wondrous pitiful' (1.3.161–2), and her hint that she wished heaven had made her such a man was so elephantine that even Othello, who thinks he has not 'those soft parts of conversation / That chamberers have' (3.3.268–9), could not miss it. His summary of why they were attracted to one another is instructive:

She loved me for the dangers I had passed
And I loved her that she did pity them.

(1.3.168–9)

The Duke might think 'this tale would win my daughter too' (172), but despite its reciprocity it seems hardly a sound basis for a marriage. It plays into Othello's sense of self-regard, that he can be the protective male, but also makes him fatally dependent on her love for him.

Once she has manoeuvred Othello into proposing, she is clear, honest and determined, and, like Juliet, her adolescent innocence is a source of strength. She pushes ahead with the elopement, is presumably the instigator of the secret marriage and is not afraid to address the senate, the epitome of patriarchy. Her father cannot believe 'she was half the wooer' (176), but she is direct and simple about her 'divided duty':

To you I am bound for life and education:
My life and education both do learn me
How to respect you; you are the lord of duty,
I am hitherto your daughter. But here's my husband:
And so much duty as my mother showed
To you, preferring you before her father,
So much I challenge that I may profess
Due to the Moor my lord.

(182–9)

It is a classic statement of the 'duty' a woman knows she owes to the two 'lords' in her life. Shakespeare gives Brabantio no counter-argument: 'God be with you, I have done.' He 'gives' her to Othello, though 'with all my heart / I would keep from thee' (190, 195–6). This is important because *Othello* is the play where Shakespeare most fully examines a young woman's relation to both her father and her husband: *Cymbeline* attempts the same, but is less convincing.

Desdemona is clear how much she has affronted conventional behaviour: 'That I did love the Moor to live with him / My downright violence and storm of fortunes / May trumpet to the world' (250–2). She asks to go with him, though she can have no idea what living in a military garrison in Cyprus will entail, just as Othello has no grasp of a woman's place in such constricting quarters. She follows him presumably out of love, thinking it would be preferable to a single life among gossiping and censorious Venetians. As Iago shrewdly comments, 'It was a violent commencement in her, and thou shalt see an answerable sequestration' (345–7). He can see that she is 'framed as fruitful / As the free elements' (2.3.330–1), but knows that this very openness and generosity of spirit can be twisted to appear a mask for baser appetites. Her father has already seen that it is possible 'perfection so could err / Against all rules of nature' (1.3.101–2). Once Iago has worked on his credulity Othello concurs: 'O curse of marriage / That we can call these delicate creatures ours / And not their appetites!' (3.3.272–4). Shakespeare knew how misogynist male society could be (Iago calls all three women in the play 'whores'), how easily young women could be demonized for admitting their sexual appetites and how frequently their chastity could be questioned.[20] Desdemona plays into this by her constant pressing of Cassio's suit.

Actors may experience the difficulty of equating the strong-willed Desdemona of the first half of the play with the compliant and self-abnegating wife of the second, but Shakespeare is using Cinthio's plot to examine the realities of marriage. Desdemona was determined to have Othello, but she is also determined to be a good and conventional wife, and not to 'suckle fools, and chronicle small beer' (2.1.160). Once she has cast her lot with Othello in a distant country she has no one to turn to but Emilia, who acts as a kind of nurse-cum-lady-in-waiting. Like Juliet's nurse Emilia is not totally to be trusted, because she is in turn dependent on Iago, to whom she fatally gives the handkerchief. Shakespeare uses Emilia, however, to give his most outspoken speech on the equality of man and wife:

> But I do think it is their husbands' faults
> If wives do fall ... Let husbands know
> Their wives have sense like them: they see, and smell,
> And have their palates both for sweet and sour
> As husbands have. What is it that they do
> When they change us for others? Is it sport?
> I think it is. And doth affection breed it?
> I think it doth. Is't frailty that thus errs?
> It is so too. And have we not affections?
> Desires for sport? and frailty, as men have?
> Then let them use us well: else let them know,
> The ills we do, their ills instruct us so.
>
> (4.3.85–6, 92–102)

Desdemona's image of marriage is essentially domestic, she has been brought up to be the mistress of a Venetian palace, married to some conventional young aristocrat. In her urging of Cassio's suit she declares, 'I'll watch him tame and talk him out of patience, / His bed shall seem a school, his board a shrift' (3.3.23–4). But Othello has no concept of the domestic, no understanding of what taking a wife might entail and certainly no desire to experience his bed a school. After the comic fantasies of a Rosalind, a Viola, even a Hero, Shakespeare is examining the realities of a marriage that needed time to establish an understanding, which Iago brutally denies them.

As Othello begins to lose confidence in her, Desdemona knows she must play out the wifely role: 'Be as your fancies teach you: / Whate'er you be, I am obedient' (3.3.88–9), but she is not entirely passive. When Othello strikes her, she defends herself with the simple, 'I have not deserved this' (4.1.240), and later retaliates 'By heaven, you do me wrong' (4.2.82), but nevertheless affirms 'His unkindness may defeat my life / But never taint my love' (4.2.162–3). She fights against being murdered, but even when dying, and Emilia asks who has done this, she replies 'Nobody. I myself. Farewell. / Commend me to my kind lord' (5.2.124–5). She remains to the end convinced that she is in some way responsible, an acute observation by Shakespeare of a Jacobean woman's inbred sense of guilt. He is not claiming Desdemona as a saint (though she has elements of patient Griselda), he is commenting on the power of patriarchy. Patriarchal absolutism and wifely submission are put under the spotlight, and both are found wanting. Irene Dash sees the play as 'the tragedy of a woman, of women, pummelled into shape by the conventions that bind'.[21] Othello's tragic status is more questionable, suggesting that Shakespeare, as he had done with Hamlet, is reinventing the notion of the tragic hero. He never examines marriage in his comedies, with the questionable exception of *The Taming of the Shrew*, but in his tragedies wives are nearly always broken by the experience of marriage. Juliet and Desdemona elope, attain their freedom and are destroyed, but by what? The chance intervention of an undelivered letter and a sadistic psychopath; a male-dominated and misogynist society; or by their own impetuous assertiveness? Shakespeare holds all three up for question.

King Lear: Lear, Goneril, Regan and Cordelia, an actor's perspective

The part of King Lear has given rise to the widest variety of interpretations: at one extreme an old bull tyrant who should never have abdicated, at the other a frail dementia sufferer. At these extremes R. A. Foakes argues that 'King' is primarily a play about what Lear does, 'Old Man' is a play about what is done to him,[22] and Alan Howard, who played the part at the Old Vic in 1997, suggested to me that you are more likely to play 'King' in a large theatre, 'Old Man' in a chamber theatre. Peter Brook saw the role as 'a mountain whose summit has never been reached, the way up strewn with the shattered bodies of earlier visitors – Olivier here, Laughton there: it's frightening'.[23] In 2002 David Hare, who directed Anthony Hopkins at the National Theatre in 1986, tried to encourage me as I approached the part at the Almeida Theatre: 'There are eleven scenes, and no one can do them all. You are bound to be able to do some.' I approached the part with trepidation.

The first Lear I saw was Donald Wolfit in 1953 when I was thirteen. The set was Stonehenge and so was his performance, very powerful in the first half, less convincing in the second (only later did I realize Harold Pinter was one of the knights). I followed this with John Gielgud's fourth Lear in 1955. His director, George Devine, wrote: 'Our object has been to find a setting and costumes which would be free of historical and decorative associations, so that the timeless, universal and mythical quality of the story may be clear.'[24] Amen to that, but I could see that Isamu Noguchi's 'timeless' costumes were a disaster. Kent's stocks were a form of Barbara Hepworth sculpture, and Gielgud was trapped in a huge horsehair beard and an immense cloak full of holes which grew larger as his mind disintegrated. In 1959 at Stratford Charles Laughton, who had wanted to play the part for thirty years, lacked, in Michael Blakemore's words, 'the machinery for the huge rhetorical passages', and his Fool, Ian Holm, observed 'there was no madness, no struggle against the elements, nothing'.[25] Laughton wrote that he was mainly interested in the last two acts, 'the terrible journey of Lear to his death',[26] and I found him intensely moving in the reconciliation with Cordelia.

These three productions presented to me by the age of twenty some of the basic problems of playing the part. How much does the setting and period affect the entire production? What is the nature of Lear's madness? Do you need great reserves of energy and a powerful voice to cope with the anger and the storm? Is it possible to convince in both halves of the play; are size and subtlety possible bedfellows? Are the first three acts the real challenge of playing the part, for as Michael Pennington recently wrote: 'The second half, if you're any good as an actor, you ought to be able to do in your sleep ... They're a beautiful piece of writing, and just heaven to play. You can't fail'?[27]

These questions were largely answered by Peter Brook's 1962 RSC production with Paul Scofield. The set of tall, grey, rusty metal screens opening out to a black cyclorama did suggest universality, the production had a hard, though sometimes unrelenting, temperament and pace, and Scofield's arrogant, despotic, gravel-voiced descent into frailty was a great achievement. I did not, however, find it a final answer, a template to be copied. His iron implacability left him too little room for manoeuvre as setbacks multiplied, and his relationship with his daughters was under-examined. In the 1971 film Scofield, robbed of half his lines, seems even more entrapped within a character who has no developing journey, and it is not, alas, an accurate reflection of his stage performance.

I have, of course, seen many other Lears over the years, from strong despots like Eric Porter, Anthony Hopkins, Ian Holm, Ian McKellen and Simon Russell Beale, to manic intellectuals like John Wood, Alzheimer's victims like Michael Hordern, genial cavaliers like Robert Stephens and child-like pranksters like Brian Cox. When in 1998 Jonathan Kent asked me to play the part at the Almeida in 2002 I had over three years to research and think about it, and these musings were eventually published as *Playing*

Lear (Nick Hern Books, 2003). Jonathan Kent and I agreed on a basic approach, vital in the case of Lear, that he abdicates because he fears his mind is going, that uncontrollable anger is his undoing and that he is authoritarian, foolish and largely unsympathetic in at least the first two acts. I was both intrigued and alarmed by this emphasis on his anger. The approach is entirely justifiable: throughout the play 'anger', 'wrath' and 'madness' seem almost interchangeable terms. I remembered how Richard Burton wrote in his *The Anatomy of Melancholy*, published in 1621, that monarchs are 'most encumbered with cares in perpetual fear, agony, suspicion, jealousy ... Sovereignty is a tempest of the soul; Sylla-like they have brave titles, but terrible fits ... Anger is a cruel tempest of the mind.'[28] Actors, however, have time and again found ways of bypassing Lear's anger – it is tiring to play, hard to find variety and audiences find it unsympathetic, so it has seemed to some much easier to concentrate on the second half of the play. Our setting was to be largely twentieth century. We started in a panelled room, perhaps Sandringham, which disintegrated as the play went on. *King Lear* has been set in many periods, but I feel it works best modern, Elizabethan or primitive pagan: periods in between always seem to raise problems at variance with the tone of the text – Judi Dench, for example, told me she found it very hard in 1976 to play Regan's wildness in an elaborate nineteenth-century costume.

I am particularly interested in Lear's relationship with his three daughters, a major leap from Shakespeare's preference for the single daughter. I am aware that there is a strong element of folktale here, which Shakespeare's treatment has turned on its head. Cinderella and her sisters are usually seen from the women's point of view; the father is little more than a cipher, a *senex*. Shakespeare's play sees the story largely from the father's point of view, and the motivations and inner life of the sisters suffer accordingly. It is Lear's love test which sets in motion the civil war and the deaths of all but Edgar and Albany: they are all victims of a loveless and dysfunctional family structure. The three sisters presented Shakespeare with particular challenges: he had never before written a daughter, or in this case daughters, bent on destroying, or at least bringing to heel, a father; nor by contrast had he attempted to breathe life into a daughterly paragon of integrity. The results are mixed.

Shakespeare must have been familiar with the old play, *The True Chronicle Historie of King Leir and his Three Daughters*, which was performed at the Rose in 1594 (and was clearly not by Shakespeare), and it may be that its eventual publication in 1605 spurred him into writing his own treatment, though it seems more likely that the publication was trying to cash in on the success of Shakespeare's play, perhaps even fool the purchaser into thinking this 'True Chronicle' *was* the new play. He also knew the story in the Holinshed version, and seems to have read it in John Higgins' *The Mirror for Magistrates* (1574). The outline is fairly consistent in most sources: the love test, the division of the kingdom, Cordelia's banishment, Goneril and Regan's cruelty, Cordelia and the King of France's victory and Lear's restoration. Some versions continued to Lear's death after two years, Cordelia's reign of five years, her overthrow by her sisters' sons and her suicide by hanging (a form of death that Shakespeare seems to have imported). He may also have been inspired by the Annesley case (1603–4), in which Cordell, the youngest daughter, appealed successfully against her eldest sister's attempt to have their father declared a lunatic in order to take over control of his estate – Lear's madness is, after all, Shakespeare's invention. For all its ancient, cosmic dimensions he could see that the Lear story had the material for a family tragedy, and once he had added the story of Gloucester and his two sons he had a pattern that had proved so successful in *Hamlet*, the interwoven destruction of a pair of families.

Shakespeare plunges straight into the love test and its aftermath, whose ramifications occupied 742 lines, out of 2,663, in the old *King Leir*. Shakespeare's 308 lines leave a lot of questions unanswered, and have proved a major problem in production. Why is Lear abdicating and dividing the kingdom when Goneril and Albany would be the expected heirs; how enfeebled or demented is he; when did his wife die; how long have Goneril and Regan been married; did they choose their husbands; are they children of his first marriage and Cordelia of his second; why the love test when the portions have already been decided? *King Leir* supplies answers to some of these questions (Lear's wife's death and the marriages to Albany and Cornwall, at Lear's behest, are both very recent, and have left Lear unused to the management of his children), and explains Goneril and Regan's envy of Cordelia's 'mounting fame' at Court, and the need to flatter their father, 'who dotes as if he were a child again' (181). So Goneril declares, 'To do you good I would ascend / The highest turret in all Brittany, / And from the top leap headlong to the ground' (245–7). Regan agrees, and Leir then urges Cordelia to 'drop down nectar from thy honey lips' (276), and she replies:

> I cannot paint my duty forth in words,
> I hope my deeds shall make report for me.
> But look what love the child doth owe the father,
> The same to you, I bear, my gracious lord.

(277–80)

This is a variant on the more usual folk-tale version, where Cordelia, after declaring her love for him as a father, declares, 'So much as you have, so much you are worth, and so much I love you, and no more' (Holinshed and Geoffrey of Monmouth).

Shakespeare chooses to open the play with Kent's reported rumour that Lear 'had more affected the Duke of Albany than Cornwall' (1.1.1–2). The division of the kingdom, and one that included the unmarried Cordelia, may therefore be Lear's surprise – he refers to his plan as his 'darker purpose' – though Burgundy has clearly anticipatied a major dowry. The love test could be a last-minute addition, a paternalistic joke played on his daughters – Goneril later refers to 'other your new pranks' (1.4.229). I

Figure 4 Lear (Oliver Ford Davies) and Goneril (Suzanne Burden) in *King Lear* at the Almeida Theatre, 2002 (© Ivan Kyncl)

found his opening speech, though open to ambiguity, surprisingly lucid. It has authority, monomania, humour and even a hint of vulnerability. Lear is not deep into dementia. I particularly enjoyed characterizing France and Burgundy's long stay at court as their 'amorous sojourn', as if contemptuous of a competition in love – a derision that will come back to haunt Lear. It seems that Shakespeare realized that the 1608 Quarto text gave insufficient explanation of his purpose in abdicating, and the lines 'while we / Unburdened crawl toward death'; 'that future strife / May be prevented now'; and 'we will divest us both of rule, / Interest of territory, cares of state' are all folio additions (1.1.40–50). All three daughters are forced to improvise. Goneril and Regan speak in extravagant, but quite plausible, Jacobean mode – there is no leaping from the highest Breton turret. When Goneril says, 'Sir, I do love you more than word can wield the matter, / Dearer than eyesight, space, and liberty', and Regan agrees, 'I find she names my very deed of love: / Only she comes too short', a cheeky improvization which makes Lear and the audience laugh (1.1.55–6, 71–2), these sentiments are a match for Princess Elizabeth's letter to her father, James I, in 1613, where she writes that her heart ' now permits my eyes to weep their privation of the sight of the most precious object, which they could have beheld in this world'.[30] As Peter Brook has pointed out, these speeches can sound sincere, if fulsome: a Jacobean audience could certainly have accepted them as such. It is with Cordelia that Shakespeare makes his biggest change. She has already voiced her dilemma (in '*asides*' as marked in F): 'What shall Cordelia speak?

Love, and be silent … I am sure my love's / More ponderous [weighty] than my tongue' (62, 77–8). Invited to speak, she answers 'Nothing', and then repeats it – and these two 'nothings' are Shakespeare's addition to Cordelia's accustomed folktale replies, and considerably enhance her sense of defiance. Nancy Carroll (Cordelia) found that her asides gave her an immediate relationship with the audience, and that her 'Nothing' was the prelude to her wanting 'no thing' from her father throughout the play. Lear is terse: 'Nothing will come of nothing', and 'Mend your speech a little, / Lest you may mar your fortunes' (90, 94–5). I found it difficult to interpret the tone of these lines: they could be menacing, angry, reasonable or encouraging. Has he devised the love test merely as a cover for giving 'our joy' Cordelia (and her intended husband, Burgundy) the best third? She has only to come up with the formulaic response that Lear has been accustomed to hearing all his life. Only later will he realize that 'To say "ay" and "no" to everything I said "ay" and "no" to was no good divinity' (4.6.98–100). Cordelia finally manages, like Desdemona, a dutiful response, emphasizing their mutuality:

> You have begot me, bred me, loved me. I
> Return these duties back as are right fit,
> Obey you, love you and most honour you.
>
> (96–8)

Obedience and honour are equated with love as a fit 'duty'. She then continues, truthfully if fatally: 'Why have my sisters husbands, if they say / They love you all? … Sure I shall never marry like my sisters / To love my father all' (99–100, 103–4).

Lear finds this 'untender', and his melodramatic, pagan language (dragons and the cannibalistic Scythian are invoked) implies that he loses his temper, which seems to continue, more or less unabated, for the rest of the scene. This I found a major problem: does he seethe with uncontrollable rage, become coldly implacable or does the anger come and go, mixed with differing emotions? He first disclaims 'all my paternal care, / Propinquity and property of blood', and divides her inheritance between her sisters. It seems, therefore, that Lear wants more from his daughters than obedience and submission. With his wife dead he needs to appear a loved father, even if he doesn't know how to return this love, and the youngest, his favourite, is singled out to fulfil the role of wife-mother. Though he has disclaimed all his paternal care, I found that he continues to talk about Cordelia, hoping perhaps for an apology and reconciliation, for the next 150 lines. There is a degree here of incestuous desire, rare in Shakespeare. Indeed, Lear goes on to say, 'I loved her most, and thought to set my rest / On her kind nursery' (123–4). Goneril regards Lear as a helpless, demanding child: 'Now by my life / Old fools are babes again' (1.3.18–19). The Fool is not only the one person to criticize Lear's division of the kingdom, but shrewdly observes,

'Thou mad'st thy daughters thy mothers.' If Lear 'gav'st them the rod and puttest down thine own breeches' (1.4.163–5), then patriarchy is destroyed and matriarchal power takes over. As Coppelia Kahn argues, Lear wants 'two mutually exclusive things at once: to have absolute control over those closest to him and to be absolutely dependent on them'[31] He is, in Freud's phrase, 'His Majesty, the baby'. Robbed of Cordelia's nurturing love, Lear tries to banish 'my sometime daughter' from his family: 'Unfriended, new adopted to our hate, / Dowered with our curse, and strangered with our oath ... for we / Have no such daughter' (1.1.204–5, 264–5). His 'better thou / Hadst not been born than not to have pleased me better' (235–6) is an extreme variant on Capulet and Leonato's feelings about their errant daughters. When Kent begs him to 'check / This hideous rashness' (150–1), and calls him mad, Lear has already warned him 'Come not between the dragon and his wrath' (123). These are key images, for Lear sees himself as a dragon, an unloved creature of destructive power and fire, and admits to 'wrath', since in our production uncontrollable anger was to prove his undoing and drive him to madness. The now dowerless Cordelia, confronted by Burgundy and France, boldly speaks up for herself and beseeches her father to make it clear that her only fault in his eyes is the 'want of that for which I am richer, / A still soliciting eye and such a tongue / That I am glad I have not' (232–4). Nancy Carroll found her as stubborn as her sisters, and indeed her father. I find Shakespeare an expert on family quarrels: both Lear and Cordelia say rash and unnecessary things that once said cannot be unsaid.

The scene ends with a short but important scene between the three daughters. Goneril and Regan have been careful not to criticize Cordelia, perhaps confident she can be left to ruin her chances by herself. Cordelia now tells them what hypocrites she knows them to be, and Goneril counters acidly, 'Let your study / Be to content your lord, who hath received you / At fortune's alms' (278–80), hypocritical advice since Goneril will prove far from 'contenting' her own lord, Albany. Suzanne Burden (Goneril) argued that 'a loveless marriage, an extremely fraught relationship with a parent, and a lack of offspring might send anybody over the edge'. Left alone, Goneril and Regan analyse Lear's wayward character and the likely degeneration of his great age with considerable insight:

GONERIL You see how full of changes his age is ... He always loved our sister most, and with what poor judgement he hath now cast her off appears too grossly.
REGAN 'Tis the infirmity of his age; yet he hath ever but slenderly known himself.
GONERIL The best and soundest of his time hath been but rash; then must we look from his age to receive ... the unruly waywardness that infirm and choleric years bring with them ... We must do something, and i'the heat.

(290–309)

This is a rare instance in Shakespeare of a daughter commenting on her father's character, and it proves a particularly shrewd assessment. Regan's observation is the most telling – 'he hath ever but slenderly known himself'. The key to Lear, in the first two acts at least, seems to me his lack of self-knowledge. *King Lear* was written at much the same time as *Macbeth*, and it is as if Shakespeare is experimenting with the contrast. Macbeth has many soliloquies and a great deal of self-understanding, even if it doesn't prevent his descent into bloody tyranny. Lear has no outright soliloquies laying out his thoughts, though speeches like 'Poor naked wretches' can of course be addressed to the audience. This lack of self-awareness makes him in a sense unknowable, which for the actor is both perplexing and liberating, giving rise to the huge spectrum of interpretation.

By the end of the first scene Shakespeare has upset a number of his audience's expectations. Lear has appeared not just weak and foolish, but rash, angry, changeable and childish. Goneril and Regan are revealed as more intelligent, sympathetic and complex than the traditional sisters. The sophisticated rhetoric of their speeches are the best they can dutifully improvise in response to a surprise test of loyalty. Nancy Carroll found Cordelia's 'I cannot heave my heart into my mouth' an indication that she thinks true love is expressed through actions rather than words, despite Lear's dismissing it as 'pride'. The actions of all three daughters can be interpreted as protecting themselves from their father's impossible demands. Goneril and Regan realize that Lear cannot 'retain / The name and all th'addition to a king' (1.1.91–2), and at the same time abdicate all his responsibilities for government and parenthood. Dividing up his kingdom might be the action of a doting parent, or a misguided attempt to stop squabbling, but it's not that of a wise king. James I would certainly have disapproved: he might insist in *Basilikon Doron* that he is both a good king and loving father, but absolute power, divinely approved, sits uneasily with the compromises a fond parent has to make. Lear may think that, just as he can give away his lands, so he can disclaim 'paternal care, / Propinquity and property of blood' (114–15), but as a father he cannot. He rails at the blood connection, but knows it cannot be broken. He will later attack Goneril, 'But yet thou art my flesh, my blood, my daughter, / Or rather a disease that's in my flesh, / Which I must needs call mine' (2.2.413–15). 'Filial ingratitude' beats at his senses, but he acknowledges that his daughters remain part of him – 'Is it not as this mouth should tear this hand / For lifting food to't?' (3.4.15–16). It is an extremely difficult opening scene, perhaps the most perplexing for the actor in the canon, though Leontes' sudden jealousy would vie with it. There is such an absence of backstory, so little opportunity for Lear and Cordelia to show their love for one another, and no clue as to Lear's mental and physical state that results in such rash anger. The actor has to invent explanations for all these, while accepting that he has little hope of conveying these to the audience.

Finally we are driven back, as John Barton argued to me, to the folktale premise – this is how the story must start.

Goneril has decided that she and Regan must 'do something, and i'the heat', while Lear anticipates no problems. When his knight ventures that Lear 'is not entertained with that ceremonious affection as you were wont', Lear acknowledges mildly that he had 'perceived a most faint neglect of late, which I have rather blamed as mine own jealous curiosity than as a very pretence and purpose of unkindness' (1.4.56–7, 66–9). The Fool's arrival clearly puts him in a good mood, but this is then shaken by Oswald's insolence and by the Fool's warning that 'thou hadst little wit in thy bald crown when thou gav'st thy golden one away' (155–6), so that when Goneril appears he chides her for being 'too much of late i'the frown' (1.4.181). Goneril, however, has a purposed intent, and sails into not only a criticism of his retinue's behaviour but an accusation 'that you protect this course and put it on / By your allowance' (198–9). Both realize this is a turning point: Goneril is reneging on 'all th'additions to a king'. Lear is dumbfounded and can only express his bewilderment at his new kingless identity in a series of ironic questions:

Does any here know me? Why, this is not Lear.
Does Lear walk thus, speak thus? Where are his eyes?
Either his notion weakens, or his discernings are lethargied – Ha!
    sleeping or waking? Sure 'tis not so. Who is it that can tell me who
    I am?

(217–21)

In F the Fool answers, 'Lear's shadow'; in Q Lear makes it a further question, 'Lear's shadow?' Assigning the line to the Fool gives it greater ambiguity, but perhaps Shakespeare's first thoughts were simpler and more revealing – is he now a shadow of his former self? Lear's journey, baffled and blind about himself as he is, is to come to terms with this.

Goneril is inexorable: 'Be then desired, / By her that else will take the thing she begs, / A little to disquantity your train' (238–40). Suzanne Burden felt that Lear had always been hardest on his first-born, perhaps for not being a son, and that, after years of navigating a careful course, she is at last freed to wield power over him. His reaction is immediate. Calling her 'degenerate bastard' and 'detested kite' he determines to move on to Regan, and shows for the first time some understanding of what his rashness has brought about:

O most small fault,
How ugly didst thou in Cordelia show,
Which like an engine wrenched my frame of nature
From the fixed place, drew from my heart all love

And added to the gall. O Lear, Lear, Lear!
Beat at this gate that let thy folly in
And thy dear judgement out.

(258–64)

This moment of clarity is immediately swamped by a return to rash anger, and he curses his 'thankless child' with sterility, or 'if she must teem, / Create her child of spleen' (273–4), thus ensuring that Goneril will be unwavering in her determination to destroy his authority, lest he 'hold our lives in mercy' (320), though it may be significant that F's omission of Goneril's reference to 'idle old man', 'old fool' and 'babe' make her less dismissive of her father, and more anxious to keep the peace. I was initially puzzled by Lear's immediate return after storming out, until I realized that he is now, perhaps for the first time, very frightened: he has lost two daughters, and has only Regan left to be 'kind and comfortable' (298). The evils of procreation come to obsess Lear: 'Turn all her mother's pains and benefits / To laughter and contempt' (278–9). In the storm he doesn't simply want the thunder and lightning to singe his head and flatten the earth, but 'Crack nature's moulds, all germens spill at once / That make ingrateful man!' (3.2.8–9). Images of cannibalism, of parent and child devouring each other recur throughout the play: ''Twas this flesh begot / Those pelican daughters' (3.4.73–4); the pelican being a bird who, in legend, loves her children too much, allows them to attack her, kills them and then sheds her own blood to revive them. As Albany observes of Goneril's treatment of her father, 'Humanity must perforce prey on itself, / Like monsters of the deep' (4.2.50–1).

Left alone with the Fool, Lear's mood changes again. I have retained a strong image of Scofield and Alec McCowen quietly sitting on a bench, but Jonathan Kent will have none of it (beware grafting on moments from other productions). He wants me still angry, furiously packing up my belongings, when I suddenly stop and say, 'I did her wrong' (1.5.24). With a differently conceived Lear Shakespeare might have written him a fifteen-line speech, explaining what he feels about Cordelia's wrongful banishment, but Shakespeare knows that 'I did her wrong' is the limit of Lear's ability to express himself. A minute later he suddenly says:

O, let me not be mad, not mad, sweet heaven! I would not be mad.
Keep me in temper, I would not be mad.

(43–5)

A gentleman enters to say the horses are ready, and the scene ends. The placing of these two brief acknowledgements of the wrong done to Cordelia and the first intimation of the madness to come is, I realize, a supreme example of Shakespeare's stagecraft.

Lear storms out of Goneril's house, thinking that 'beloved Regan' is his last chance. The long scene that follows shows Shakespeare at his most psychologically acute, as Lear stumbles from mood to mood. It starts strangely with an altercation between Lear and the bestocked Kent:

LEAR What's he that hath so much thy place mistook To set thee here?
KENT It is both he and she, Your son and daughter.
LEAR No.
KENT Yes.
LEAR No, I say.
KENT I say, yea.
LEAR No, no, they would not.
KENT Yes, they have.
LEAR By Jupiter, I swear no.
KENT By Juno, I swear ay.

(2.2.205–14)

This exchange raises the question of how much comedy there is in the play. Olivier in his 1946 production found a good deal, and Jonathan Miller, according to his Lear Michael Hordern, thought 'that if you don't approach it as a funny play about people going gaga you missed a dimension'.[32] My director was firmly against this, and reluctantly I acceded (though Shakespeare always seems to realize that a little laughter in a tragedy never comes amiss). The stocking of Kent leads to the first of Lear's seizures, '*hysterica passio*', a choking and giddiness associated with the womb, which he refers to as 'this mother', thus setting off a riot of interpretation about Lear's anima and the suppressed presence of the mother of his daughters. This is on Lear's mind when Regan finally appears and obeys the formality of saying she is glad to see him.

If thou shouldst not be glad,
I would divorce me from thy mother's tomb,
Sepulchring an adulteress.

(322–4)

Like Leonato he toys with the fantasy idea of his daughter's illegitimacy. Despite the fact that Regan tells him, 'O, sir, you are old: / Nature in you stands on the very verge / Of her confine', and begs him to return to Goneril and 'say you have wronged her' (338–40, 344), Lear temporizes because he realizes how much he needs Regan's love. He lacerates Goneril's ingratitude but assures Regan 'thou shalt never have my curse ... Her eyes are fierce, but thine / Do comfort and not burn' (362–5). Lear is hopeful that he can appeal to her to show 'the offices of nature, bond of childhood, / Effects of courtesy, dues of gratitude' that any father could expect from a daughter. His uncertainty of her gratitude makes him continue, 'Thy half o'the kingdom hast thou not forgot, / Wherein I thee endowed' (370–3). If natural family bonds and courtesy fail, then it's all down to gratitude for wealth and estate. It is likely that Lear has always felt closer to 'our dearest Regan' than to Goneril, 'our eldest born', but only because Regan has always been more circumspect in declaring her hand. Lizzy McInnerny (Regan) commented that as the middle daughter in her own family she felt she lacked the power of the eldest and the favoured position of the youngest, and therefore had to fight her corner more diplomatically, and Suzanne Burden agreed that Regan was 'cannily manipulative in a way she [Goneril] could never be'. The three daughters are clear examples of the modern concept of 'Birth Order': the assertive eldest, the 'people-pleasing/ rebel' second and the favoured youngest. It is shrewd psychology on Shakespeare's part, and may reflect his observation of his own child Judith, sandwiched between Susanna and the favoured twin Hamnet. As Lear's mind begins to crack I found myself scrabbling round on the floor in a parody of subservience:

> Dear daughter, I confess that I am old;
> Age is unnecessary. On my knees I beg
> That you'll vouchsafe me raiment, bed and food.

(346–8)

This Regan understandably finds 'unsightly tricks' (349). Then, in my desire to get closer to her, I clutch her from behind, pinioning her arms and whispering in her ear, though I worry that this will seem abusive behaviour (and many spectators duly took it as such). I am not alone in this – many Lears have felt the impulse to make desperate, and perhaps inappropriate, physical contact with their daughters (see p. 6) Regan manages to remain largely noncommittal, until Goneril's arrival stiffens her resistance and she immediately takes her sister by the hand. It is this united front that makes Lear's body rebel – 'O sides, you are too tough! / Will you yet hold?' (389–90). At the same time his mind keeps wandering to the question of who stocked his servant: this desire to maintain a kingly authority runs like a crazed refrain through the scene. He tries to parley with Goneril – 'We'll no more meet, no more see one another ... I can stay with Regan, / I and my hundred knights' (412, 422–3). But Regan, bolstered by her sister, proposes cutting his knights down to twenty-five, arguing, very reasonably, that 'How in one house / Should many people, under two commands, / Hold amity?' (432–4), but when Lear cries 'I gave you all', she counters sourly, picking up the half-line, 'And in good time you gave it' (442). Lear decides to return to Goneril, who has offered fifty knights, for 'thou art twice her love': love is a commodity to be counted and bartered. But Goneril is inexorable: 'What need you five and twenty? Ten? Or five?', and Regan, growing in competitiveness, chips in, 'What need one?' (451–5). This triggers in Lear, though close to tears and madness, the revelation that man is distinguished from beasts only by living beyond the bare 'needs' for survival, something that will soon be tested in the storm. He uses his daughter as example:

O, reason not the need! Our basest beggars
Are in the poorest things superfluous;
Allow not nature more than nature needs,
Man's life is cheap as beast's. Thou art a lady;
If only to go warm were gorgeous,
Why, nature needs not what thou gorgeous wear'st,
Which scarcely keeps thee warm.

(456–62)

His anger is almost spent, but in one final flurry Shakespeare wonderfully defines the tumult in his mind (partly a paraphrase of Atreus in Seneca's *Thyestes*, but then Shakespeare was a talented thief):

No, you unnatural hags,
I will have such revenges on you both
That all the world shall – I will do such things –
What they are yet I know not, but they shall be
The terrors of the earth!

(470–4)

I found it very difficult to determine the degree of irony and introspection in this speech. Lear's mind is breaking down, but also unlocking to new perceptions of the human condition. When he staggers out into the storm, declaring that he will go mad, Regan reverts to a defensive excuse that her 'house is little', but Goneril feels no contrition: ''Tis his own blame; hath put himself from rest / And must needs taste his folly' (480, 482–3). They speak of him as a troublesome old man rather than any relation. It is an extraordinary examination of family discord written, I feel, at white heat, since it flays about intuitively, without regard to logical progression. Shakespeare is unflinching in portraying the anger and hatred between father and daughters, perhaps at great cost to himself, and it is a theme he never returned to. Lear and his elder daughters never meet again. I found it the most difficult and painful scene in the play, the one I 'couldn't do'.

Having shown the sisters challenging and browbeating their father, Shakespeare now presents them at their cruellest in their scene with Gloucester. Regan is for hanging him instantly, Goneril for plucking out his eyes (3.7.4–5). Regan then vies with her husband in demanding that Gloucester lose both eyes, in stabbing in the back the servant who intervenes and in ordering Gloucester to be thrust 'out at gates, and let him smell / His way to Dover' (92–3). Her rebellious need for power, long suppressed, is at last satisfied. This scene marks a turning point. Shakespeare has examined Goneril and Regan as victims of their father's tyrannical and arbitrary anger; now he has to concentrate on Lear and Gloucester as victims, and the sisters have to become the fiends of folktale. In *King Leir* Regan says, 'I feel a hell of conscience in my breast' (2357), but Shakespeare allows her no such remorse.

Act 3 presents two particular problems: how to evoke the storm, and what is the nature of Lear's 'madness'. It is possible to dispense with thunder and lightning altogether. In 2010 Michael Grandage decided that Derek Jacobi should, as Laughton would have wished, 'whisper the storm, as if it was coming from inside his head, and was more a vocalization of his thought than a man railing against the elements', and Jacobi agreed that 'this time the audience heard every one of those fabulous words'.[33] There are benefits in this approach, but I was left with the feeling that if Shakespeare had wanted Burbage to whisper the storm he would have written the scenes quite differently. Since Jonathan Kent presented me with rain, a collapsing set and eighty-seven thunder claps, there was no opportunity to whisper. Fortunately I have a very strong voice (a Russian conductor once told me I should be singing Alberich in *The Ring*). I found that, to avoid generalized rant, it was vital to be specific about treating the elements individually, sometimes as friends ('horrible pleasures'), sometimes as enemies ('servile ministers'). Lear wants the rain to inundate the world, lightning to singe him and thunder to destroy procreation, but all the while he's shaking a fist at the gods as some form of mania sets in. Lear is aware that railing at Goneril and Regan 'that way madness lies, let me shun that' (3.4.21), and his realization that he has taken too little care of the 'poor naked wretches' in his kingdom (28–36) shows a lucid sanity, while his treatment of Poor Tom as his philosopher king shows a mind descending into turmoil. John Barton has always maintained to me that Lear becomes confused and delusional rather than properly mad, and Jonathan Miller told me he thinks it 'an extreme sense of dislocation'. Renaissance thought, moreover, held madness to be a sign of genius, discerning the 'truth' of knowledge.[34] I am much persuaded by the psychiatrist Dorothy Rowe's view that 'madness' is a defence people use when they feel themselves to be under immense threat and have to do something to hold themselves together. I think that approach fits Lear better than analyses of dementia and Alzheimer's. Throughout the storm his daughters feature constantly in his mind:

> This tempest in my mind
> Doth from my sense take all feeling else,
> Save what beats there, filial ingratitude. ...
>   O, Regan, Goneril,
> Your old, kind father, whose frank heart gave you all –
> O, that way madness lies, let me shun that.

(3.4.12–14, 19–21)

Lear is at last talking about his confusion/madness, and I found this very releasing. Filial ingratitude is a stepping stone to a much wider understanding of humankind as a 'poor, bare, fork'd animal'. When, in the hovel, Edgar/Poor Tom begins to rave, Lear asks, 'Have his daughters brought him to this pass?', and later he puts Goneril and Regan on trial for 'kicking the poor King' (a passage absent in F, suggesting perhaps that Shakespeare wanted to play down the severity of Lear's 'madness'). In fact all three imagined dogs/daughters, Trey, Blanch and Sweetheart, begin to bark at him. 'Is there any cause in nature that make these hard hearts?' he asks (3.6.61, 75–6). When, weeks later, he meets the blinded Gloucester, though he initially takes him for 'Goneril with a white beard', his concerns have broadened into thoughts of female lust – 'there's hell, there's darkness, there is the sulphurous pit, burning, scalding, stench, consumption' (consummation in Q) (4.6.123–5). He sees women's lust as the source of corruption in society, rather as Hamlet had with Gertrude and Ophelia:

> Behold yon simp'ring dame,
> Whose face between her forks presages snow,
> That minces virtue and does shake the head
> To hear of pleasure's name –
> The fitchew nor the soiled horse goes to't with a more riotous appetite.
>
> (116–21)

Lear may hate women's lust because he's disgusted by his own; he may rail against women because he cannot come to terms with the female side, the anima, of his nature. He struggles throughout the play with 'unmanly' tears: 'Let not women's weapons, water-drops, / Stain my man's cheeks' (2.4.469–70). Tears represent feminine weakness, vulnerability, perhaps at root mortality; they 'scald like molten lead' (4.7.48). Ironically, Goneril and Regan's refusal to mother him brings out his 'womanish' tears. His railings turn to society's hypocrisy – 'which is the justice, which is the thief?' – and to existential lamentation – 'When we are born we cry that we are come / To this great stage of fools' (149–50, 178–9). Shakespeare has begun to depart radically from his template. The first two acts follow more or less the accepted version of the story, but the storm, Poor Tom and Lear's descent into madness/dislocation are entirely Shakespeare's invention. I am not convinced that he knew where he was going or what he was trying to achieve, but then one aspect of genius is letting your subconscious run riot. Goneril and Regan's part in the plot is enhanced by the introduction of Edmund, enabling the sisters to compete fatally for his sexual favours. All three believe that in a natural society personal appetite is everything, human preys on human, unless checked by authority: Thomas Hobbes is anticipated. But Shakespeare is at his most radical in his treatment of Lear and Cordelia. As A. D. Nuttall observes, Cordelia lives in a curious way outside the play. She appears in the first scene 'as a socially awkward, deeply moral young woman, but she is also haloed by a certain light that never leaves her'.[35] The scene where the Gentleman says she shook 'the holy water from her heavenly eyes' (4.3.31) is absent in F, but the later Christ-like echo (Luke 2.49) of 'O dear father, / It is thy business that I go about' (4.4.23–4) is unmistakeable. Her husband, the King of France, has already echoed the Sermon on the Mount in 'Fairest Cordelia, thou art most rich being poor, / Most choice forsaken and most loved despised' (1.1.252–3). After Lear has eluded his attendants at Dover, the Gentleman remarks: 'Thou hast one daughter / Who redeems nature from the general curse / Which twain have brought her to' (4.6.201–3) – the twain being both Goneril and Regan, but also Adam and Eve who caused the 'general curse' by their expulsion from Eden. In a play that is ostensibly pagan Cordelia appears in this very Christian light, the only young woman Shakespeare ever endowed with this almost supernatural aura. Nancy Carroll, however, argued that to personify goodness is unplayable, and that Cordelia is more exemplified by the strength, anger and drive that caused her to raise and lead an army.

When they finally meet, Lear first takes his daughter for 'a soul in bliss', and she kneels to him asking for his hands 'in benediction o'er me' (4.7.46, 58). But I found the scene far from serene, and needing, as Diana Rigg (Scofield's Cordelia) counselled me, a lot of energy. Lear is on 'a wheel of fire', and his mind is racing: 'I am a very foolish, fond old man, / Fourscore and upward ... and to deal plainly, / I fear I am not in my perfect mind' (60–3). Shakespeare finally reveals Lear's age – could it be that he deliberately held this back so that the actor (the thirty-six-year-old Burbage) would not feel burdened by playing great age till he was a demonstrably broken man? Lear then recognizes the weeping Cordelia, but his first thought is devastating:

> If you have poison for me, I will drink it.
> I know you do not love me, for your sisters
> Have, as I do remember, done me wrong.
> You have some cause; they have not.
>
> (72–5)

Cordelia has amply demonstrated her love in her earlier tirade against her sisters' treatment of their father – 'Mine enemy's dog / Though he had bit me should have stood that night / Against my fire' (36–8) – yet her reply to Lear, 'No cause, no cause', is puzzling. It may be extreme Christian charity, a refusal to rake over past wrongs, or a motherly reaction to pacify the child. Her husband, who in every previous version leads her army, has been omitted from the play and she is left, the childless, to Lear almost virginal, daughter, to soothe him as a 'foster nurse of nature' (4.4.12). Lear has got what he wanted, the 'kind nursery' of his favourite daughter with him as the 'smug bridegroom' (4.6.194), but I feel they can't really communicate their love for one another – forgiveness and benediction, but not expressed love – and their relationship is to have no future. The battle is lost, but Lear has no sense of this. Cordelia, desperate at her defeat and thus failing her father, wants to confront 'these daughters and these sisters' (5.3.7), but Lear has no desire for Goneril and Regan to force him back to reality (and Shakespeare presumably has no desire to write such a scene). Lear thinks he can live in a fantasy prison world with Cordelia, where 'we two alone will sing like birds i'the cage ... And pray, and sing, and tell old tales' (9, 12), and Cordelia says nothing to disabuse him, just as we never really get to hear what she thinks of her family in the second half of the play. Nancy Carroll felt she says little at the end of the play because her journey is complete, and that her love ultimately expresses itself through actions not words. She cannot heave her heart into her mouth.

These short scenes contain some wonderful writing, but elsewhere Shakespeare is having great structural difficulties in bringing all the different strands of the play to a conclusion. Goneril and Regan, such complex and interesting characters in the first half of the play, are reduced to something close to pantomime sisters, though Suzanne Burden contests this, claiming that Goneril 'is a (possibly unfinished) portrait of a woman on the edge; the very edge'. Competing with her over Edmund, Regan says, 'I never shall endure her. Dear my lord, / Be not familiar with her', and Goneril has an aside, 'I had rather lose the battle than that sister / Should loosen him and me' (5.1.15–16, 18–19). When Goneril has poisoned Regan (offstage) and she cries, 'Sick, O sick', Goneril has another melodramatic, or possibly manic, aside, 'If not, I'll ne'er trust medicine (5.3.96–7). Shakespeare has lost interest in them to the extent that neither is allowed a death scene and they expire offstage, Goneril presumably feeling remorse for killing her sister, or possibly realizing her future holds neither Edmund nor political domination – but Shakespeare has neither time nor inclination to enlarge on this. Edgar and Edmund, however, are allowed interminable exchanges (usually heavily cut) and fight the regulation duel: it's as if Shakespeare suddenly remembered he had to please the audience with a fight before his surprise ending.

The final scene is difficult to interpret. Cordelia in Lear's arms carries the unmistakeable image of a *pietà*, but what is this meant to signify? A more conventional ending to a tragedy would be Lear in Cordelia's arms. Indeed, Freud thought Cordelia was Death, bearing away the dead hero from the place of battle, like the Valkyr in German mythology, but this seems a perverse reading, typical of Freud's floundering on the subject of fathers and daughters.[36] Lear is certainly gentle and nurturing with the dead Cordelia, in a way that he never was in life. He seems to have gained in perception, acknowledging his faults and asking forgiveness, although, despite the fact he knows she's 'dead as earth', he continues to play with the notion she may be alive. As Cordelia referred to him as 'child-changed', it would appear that he has exchanged the childishness of the angry, unperceptive father for a child-like dependence on a daughter's 'nursery'. Does fatherhood

Figure 5 Lear (Oliver Ford Davies) and Cordelia (Nancy Carroll) in *King Lear* at the Almeida Theatre, 2002 (© Ivan Kyncl)

have no middle way? Family love may have been reasserted, but who has been responsible for its destruction? Is it patriarchal blindness to children's needs, or the lust and ambition of rebellious daughters?

As the play opens up after the first two, largely chamber, acts, Shakespeare is writing something totally original, and other issues, other questions assert themselves. Howard Felperin argues that the play doesn't comment on or tie up its themes; it only presents them: the play is 'the very negation of the possibility of unity, coherence, and resolution, of the accommodation that all our systems of explanations provide.'[37] The characters continually look to Nature for meaning, but the play provides no answers. Does it present an absurdist, existential universe, where only the Fool and Edmund can see that the world is driven by brute force, cruelty and lust? Is the play about suffering, as the bad triumph and reduce the good to poor, naked creatures under an indifferent heaven? Or is the second half of the play about love, where Lear and Gloucester, essentially loners at the outset, are restored to the love of their lost children? Do we feel that the fate of Lear and his three daughters is in some way representative of humanity, that anger, rejection, madness, suffering, love, murder and arbitrary death mirror to an extreme degree our own experience of the world? Having played the part I find the play seems to say that 'life is crippled by a failure of understanding, that inequality and injustice corrode our existence, but that human nature can, even in the most extreme circumstances, rise above these. It feels to me, despite everything, a hopeful play'.[38]

4

Late plays

Janet Adelman argues that each of Shakespeare's last four sole-authored plays 'is in effect written in defensive response to the one before it; each destabilizes the resolution previously achieved, working and reworking the problematic relationship of masculine authority to the female'.[1] In this analysis all four plays are experiments, *Pericles* and *Cymbeline* being the not altogether successful try-outs for the more mature triumphs of *The Winter's Tale* and *The Tempest*. The first three plays all feature a daughter who is abandoned or banished by her father, but finally restored to him, in some sense redeeming him from a state of loss and depression brought on by his own misjudgement (*The Tempest* fits less easily into this template). All four share certain characteristics: '[s]udden tempests or disasters, separations between parents and children or between friends and lovers, wanderings and shipwrecks, wives and children lost and found, strange accidents and coincidences, encounters with the marvellous, and eventual reconciliations and reunions'.[2] Extremes of love, hate, jealousy, grief and despair are examined, though forgiveness is always paramount, and restoration seems the key-note. Above all, fathers are allowed, sometimes improbably, a second chance in their relationship with their daughters. The plays also share a challenging verse style, verbally condensed with convoluted syntax, irregular blank verse with sudden shifts of direction and a wealth of truncated metaphors, repetitions and parentheses.[3]

Pericles: Pericles, Marina and others

What attracted Shakespeare to this lurid and improbable fantasy? The bait seems to be the array of family relationships that are violated in some way, and in particular the relationships between fathers and daughters. Shakespeare may have been familiar with the Pericles story through Appolonius of Tyre, whom he had already used for *The Comedy of Errors*. Appolonius prompted the *Confessio Amantis* of John Gower (the name borrowed for the narrator), and later Lawrence Twine's *The Pattern of*

Painful Adventures (1607?), whose plot *Pericles* largely follows. The text of the *Pericles* Quarto (1609) is imperfect (the play is not included in F1), and Shakespeare's relation to the quarto is problematic in many ways. There is now a consensus that George Wilkins (c. 1575–1618) wrote the first nine scenes after his success with *The Miseries of Enforced Marriage* (pub. 1607), though claims have been made for Shakespeare as sole author, based on the improbable argument that he wrote these first scenes in a deliberately archaic style. Wilkins may have come to the King's Men with an idea, a synopsis or the completed nine or ten scenes. The vast improvement in the quality of the verse suggests Shakespeare took over in the eleventh scene, but it is impossible to tell whether he revised parts of the first nine scenes, or whether Wilkins contributed to later scenes, particularly the brothel incidents. Wilkins later produced a novelized version of the play, *The Painful Adventures of Pericles, Prince of Tyre* (1608), which perhaps incorporates recollections of performance.

Essential to the beginning of the story is the incestuous relationship of King Antiochus and his daughter, whose beauty Pericles declears 'inflam'd desire in my breast' and 'an unspotted fire of love' (1.1.21, 54). He correctly interprets the riddle set to test suitors as 'foul incest', but admits he could love her still, and though his language remains highly sexual ('touch the gate', 'fingered') he concludes, 'I care not for you'. Pericles is 'distempered' by this encounter and admits to 'dull-ey'd melancholy', but it is clear that Wilkins/Shakespeare has toned down the incest theme (1.1.21 passim; 1.2.3). Their narrator Gower merely says the King took a 'liking' to his daughter:

And her to incest did provoke.
Bad child, worse father, to entice his own
To evil should be done by none.
But custom what they did begin
Was with long use account'd no sin.

(1.Ch.26–30)

In *Painful Adventures* Wilkins heats up their union: the King's 'persuasions prevailing with his daughter, they long continued in their foul and unjust embracements'. In the play the (unnamed) daughter has only two lines, and it is not clear whether she is complicit with, or anxious to escape from, her father.

The question is whether this father–daughter incest pervades the whole play and accounts for Pericles' wayward behaviour. Ruth Nevo thinks 'the progress of the play is the haunting of Pericles by the Antiochus in himself, the incest fear which he must repress and from which he must flee'.[4] Richard McCabe finds in *Pericles* 'the most forthright contribution to the drama of father-daughter incest since the medieval *Dux Morand*'.[5] Jane Ford argues that 'the play can then be read as both an allegorical and an archetypal resolution of the father-daughter incest threat with a full range of possible solutions set out in a series of related plots'.[6] Not all commentators however are convinced that everything sexual in the play is related to Pericles' initial encounter with incest, or that every family in the play is similarly contaminated. Stanley Wells points out that the incest 'functions mainly as a plot device to set the action in motion', and that Antiochus and his daughter 'are cardboard figures lacking any depth of characterization'.[7] We observe elsewhere how Shakespeare skirts round the subject of incest (see p. 135), and from Act 3 Scene 1 onwards neither the word nor the subject is ever mentioned, until Gower in his final narration contrasts the 'joy crowned' upon Pericles, his wife and daughter with the 'just reward' (burned in their chariot) (Epilogue, 6, 2) meted out to Antiochus and his daughter. It is true nevertheless that Pericles' 'dull-ey'd melancholy' pursues him through the play, or, as Marilyn French puts it, Pericles 'gives up the masculine principle, and the power it represents, entirely'.[8] But is this done through guilt at his brief attraction for an incestuous young woman? It may be that Pericles and his family, as Janet Adelman argues, 'brought together by the sexual act, are violently put asunder, each to be desexualized and reborn purified'.[9] But Shakespeare would seem to find time and random fate a more likely author of this purification.

The next father–daughter relationship Pericles encounters is one of the most positive in the canon, though we are presumably still in Wilkins territory. King Simonides has no desire to dominate or possess his daughter Thaisa. When she writes to him that 'she'll wed the stranger knight', he declares, like a model liberal parent:

> I like that well: nay, how absolute she's in't,
> Not minding whether I dislike or no!
> Well, I do commend her choice.

(2.5.19–21)

The bond, however, has to be tested, so Simonides accuses 'the stranger knight' of treachery and witchcraft, Pericles offers to fight, Thaisa offers up her own blood, Simonides is convinced and the scene ends with a terrible (Wilkins?) couplet:

> It pleaseth me so well, that I will see you wed;
> And then, with what haste you can, get you to bed.

(91–2)

Gower's following narration, whether Shakespeare or Wilkins, records the death of Antiochus and his daughter, and may be deliberately placed there to put an end to the theme of incest. It is no wonder that Shakespeare appears to take over with the opening lines of Act 3:

The god of this great vast, rebuke these surges,
Which wash both heaven and hell; and thou that hast
Upon the winds command, bind them in brass,
Having call'd them from the deep! O, still
Thy deaf'ning, dreadful thunders; gently quench
Thy nimble sulphurous flashes!

                                                              (3.1.1–6)

Suddenly the language has energy and concentration. The contrast of sound between the consonants of 'great vast rebuke' and the vowels of 'these surges which wash' give the undulating feeling of the sea. 'Bind them in brass' (a favourite Shakespearean word) is an unexpected image, and 'nimble sulph'rous flashes' recalls, but doesn't copy, Cordelia's 'nimble stroke / Of quick cross-lightning' (*King Lear*, 4.7.34–5).

Pericles is stunned by Thaisa's apparent death and cannot seem to cope with Lychorida's request to 'take in your arms this piece / Of your dead queen', and his speech shows an ambivalence to this 'poor inch of nature' (17–18, 34). He immediately determines to make for Tarsus to visit Cleon, 'for the babe / Cannot hold out to Tyrus; there I'll leave it / At careful nursing' (78–80). It may be that Pericles unconsciously wants to free himself from Marina, and the psychological danger she might wreak on him, but his course was quite practical. Children were often sent away to wet nurses, and then raised in another household. Informal adoptions sometimes took place, as there was no law on the subject. *Pericles* paves the way for *Cymbeline* and *The Winter's Tale,* where children are abandoned or flee from their father, nurtured by others and finally restored to their birth family. In Scene 3.4 the recovered Thaisa says she'll never see Pericles again, but gives no reason for this. In *Painful Adventures* she says she thinks 'her kingly husband to be shipwrecked', but Shakespeare leaves it unexplained, perhaps in the belief that folktales don't require rational explanations. Thaisa has been brought back to life by the 'doctor' Lord Cerimon: 'I have, / Together with my practice, made familiar / To me and to my aid the blest infusions / That dwells in vegetives, in metals, stones' (3.2.33–6). This encomium of doctoring, unlike the satirical treatment of earlier plays, may owe something to Susanna Shakespeare's marriage to (Dr) John Hall, and even to the birth of their daughter in February 1608.

Pericles leaves Marina with Cleon and Dionyza after a stay of twelve months, beseeching them to give her 'princely training', and he vows not to cut his hair till she be married, which implies that he intends to be away at least a dozen years, and leaves undetermined how a husband is to be chosen. Marina is 'by Cleon trained in music's letters', and her grace is a matter of 'general wonder', but Dionyza, feeling their daughter Philoten to be overshadowed (cf. Duke Frederick and Celia), 'a present murder doth prepare / For good Marina, that her daughter / Might stand peerless by this slaughter' (4.Ch.38–40). Dionyza later defends herself to Cleon:

> And though you call my course unnatural, –
> You not your child well loving – yet I find
> It greets me as an enterprise of kindness
> Perform'd to your sole daughter.
>
> (4.3.36–9)

This suggests Cleon had a preference for Marina, underlining the theme of the love a daughter should expect from her own father. The murder seems entirely devised by Dionyza – a forerunner of Innogen's 'wicked stepmother' – without reference to Cleon, who declares he wants to undo the deed, but his wife knows 'you'll do as I advise', and Cleon weakly caves in (51). Marina will later say, 'Cruel Cleon, with his wicked wife, / Did seek to murder me' (5.1.172–3).

Why does Pericles not contact his daughter for fourteen years, when Gower claims Marina is 'all his life's delight' (4.4.13)? Does he blame her for Thaisa's death? Is he escaping family responsibilities to re-establish his masculine identity? Does he plan to return only when Marina reaches puberty and can marry? His intention in returning to Tarsus was, according to Gower, 'to fetch his daughter home' (20). Shakespeare doesn't explain the fourteen-year gap, and leaves his discovery of Marina's apparent death to Gower and the dumb show described in 4.4. Pericles leaves Tarsus swearing 'never to wash his face, nor cut his hairs' (28), though he vowed not to cut his hair fourteen years earlier. His daughter's death leaves him not merely grief-stricken, but 'he puts on sackcloth' (29) in apparent need of penance, though he had acted in good faith in leaving her upbringing to Cleon. Shakespeare gives us tantalizing glimpses of Pericles' confused and depressed state of mind, without examining who or what is to blame for his misfortunes.

The brothel scenes (4.2 and 5.1) are given considerable space, perhaps because they were much in vogue after Dekker's *The Honest Whore* (1604) and Marston's *The Dutch Courtesan* (1605). The amount of detail of brothel husbandry, far in excess of *Measure for Measure*, suggests that Wilkins supplied material, since his own inn may well have been a haunt of prostitutes.[10] Leslie Fiedler argues that the logic of the Appolonius myth demands that the heroine be confronted by the father without recognition.[11] Incest is thus avoided in one generation, but unwittingly accomplished in the next. Twine, however, supplies a governor, Athenagoras, who likens the new arrival to his own daughter, and thus her virginity is preserved. Shakespeare, presumably trying to avoid a match between father-figure and daughter, makes his governor Lysimachus as attractive and apparently youthful as possible. He enters disguised, assures Marina that 'had I brought hither a corrupted mind, / Thy speech had alter'd it', but that he came 'with no ill intent', and calls Bolt a 'damned door-keeper' (4.6.101–2, 107, 116). Wilkins' *Painful Adventures* brings some hard-nosed reality into his visit, admitting that 'I hither came with thoughts intemperate, foul and deformed', and Gary Taylor, the editor of the Oxford *Pericles* edition, incorporates some of this by referring to Lysimachus' 'foul thoughts' and that he had meant 'but to pay the price, / A piece of gold for thy virginity' (19.129, 131–2). Shakespeare, it would seem, could not stomach his heroine marrying such a man, and makes his governor on a routine investigation into iniquity in the Duke Vincentio mode. His Lysimachus refers to Marina's 'sacred physic' as if she were some kind of saint.

Marina's role in all this is clear: she appears bent on destroying Mytilene's sex industry, as the Bawd and Bolt recognize: 'She makes our profession as it were to stink afore the face of the gods' (4.6.133–4). She speaks like Isabella when she says to Lysimachus:

If you were born to honour, show it now;
If put upon you, make the judgement good
That thought you worthy of it ... That the gods
Would set me free from this unhallow'd place,
Though they did change me to the meanest bird
That flies i'th' purer air!

(89–91, 96–9)

She then persuades Bolt to set her up as a teacher of singing, weaving, sewing and dancing (180). She is remarkably resilient for a fourteen-year-old, but, though the whole sequence is a utopian fantasy giving the audience some erotic titillation before the virtuous conclusion, it does suggest that her forthright way of dealing with vice is the herald to her ability to redeem her father from his depressed inaction. Throughout the play she holds a mirror up to men's better selves. To Leonine, sent to kill her, she declares, 'You have a gentle heart' (4.1.86); to Lysimachus, about to rape her, 'If you were born to honour, show it now' (4.6.89). The Cordelia figure pervades the later plays, and Marina is the first and prime example, but like Cordelia she does not emerge as a fully rounded character. Anne Barton observes: 'Shakespeare appears to be using Marina less as a character than as a kind of medium, through which the voice of the situation can be made to speak.'[12]

The recognition scene (5.1) between father and daughter is understandably regarded as the high point of Shakespeare's writing in the play. It is, however, seen almost entirely from Pericles' point of view: Marina has no reason to recognize a father whom she has never seen since her birth. It is a long scene, some 180 lines, with great variations in mood which are difficult to play: it clearly interested, even obsessed, the writer. Pericles arrives from Tyre, having not spoken for three months, 'nor taken sustenance', his hair and beard not clipped for fourteen years, as he had promised. Marina is brought in as a form of therapist to 'make a batt'ry through his deafen'd ports' (5.1.47), sings to him, but Pericles at her first greeting grunts 'Hmh, ha!' and, as he later admits, 'pushes her back' (84, 127). Here Shakespeare has considerably toned down his sources. In Gower, 'Her with his hand he smote', and in Twine he 'fell in a rage … rose up suddenly, and stroke the maiden on the face with his foot, so that she fell to the ground, and the blood gushed plentifully out of her cheeks'. This 'rage' at a blameless young woman suggests a profound, possibly guilty, misogyny, and gives their relationship in Twine's version a dangerous intensity. Shakespeare wants to preserve the intensity, but lessen the physicality and give it more psychological nuance.

Marina does not react to his assault, but shrewdly takes the line, reminiscent of Viola, that she 'may be hath endur'd a grief / Might equal yours', and that she too has royal parentage (88–92). Pericles is intrigued and asks her to look at him, an indication that her eyes have been modestly downcast (or that Pericles has been staring elsewhere). He immediately sees the resemblance to Thaisa, 'and such a one / My daughter might have been' (108–9). Here the scene might end, but Shakespeare has a great deal more to explore. Unable to believe that his buried daughter can be alive, Pericles questions her closely. Marina seems part aware that she is acting in a romance: 'If I should tell my history, 'twould seem / Like lies, disdain'd in the reporting' (119–20). Through suffering Pericles sees them taking one another's place:

> Tell thy story;
> If thine consider'd prove the thousandth part
> Of my endurance, thou art a man, and I
> Have suffer'd like a girl.

(135–8)

He is at last acknowledging her: 'Yet thou dost look / Like Patience gazing on king's graves, and smiling / Extremity out of act' (138–40). He has been at death's door, has struck her, and she has redeemed him with her gentleness. This has given rise to a riot of post-Jungian interpretation. Roger Grainger writes, Pericles is 'searching for his own soul: for the hidden female presence which alone is responsible for spiritual wholeness in the male psyche'.[13] Coppelia Kahn sees 'a striving for balance and spiritual harmony – the healing of ruptures between masculine and feminine parts of the psyche'.[14]

When Marina reveals her name and that she is daughter to a king, Pericles still thinks she may be a spirit, a 'fairy': 'This is the rarest dream that e'er dulled sleep / Did mock sad fools withal' (162–3). Marina then tells him how the pirates rescued her from certain death, and Pericles accepts that she is indeed his living daughter. But, as in so many of the later plays, pleasure and pain are mixed. Pericles asks Helicanus to strike him:

Lest this great sea of joys rushing upon me
O'erbear the shores of my mortality,
And drown me with their sweetness!

(193–5)

This prefigures the riddling line, 'Thou that beget'st him that did thee beget' (196). The daughter has given rebirth to the grieving father; their roles are reversed. The mother is found in the daughter, as in *King Lear*. Shakespeare is writing at the very top of his abilities, in a form so condensed as to be difficult to interpret, on a subject apparently close to his approaching old age – the interdependence of parent and child.

Even at this point Pericles still wants the assurance that Marina knows his wife's name, but Marina at last asserts herself and demands to know *his* name. She then kneels, gives Thaisa's name, stands and is kissed, but is given no more to say. Shakespeare is not much concerned with the daughter's discovery of her father: the joy is explored entirely on the father's side. This is accompanied by heavenly music, which only Pericles hears, indicating that reunion of parent and child is an other-worldly experience. The late romances are to be filled with gods and goddesses revealing the machinations of a benevolent providence. Diana directs Pericles to Ephesus where he will discover Thaisa, but Shakespeare is too experienced a dramatist to give equal weight to this second reunion. Pericles recounts his tale, Thaisa immediately recognizes him, faints, Cerimon recounts his opening of the coffin, Thaisa recovers, checks that Pericles has her father's ring and they embrace and kiss. Marina is allowed one line of joy at discovering her mother, is embraced by Thaisa and Pericles blesses Diana for her vision (5.3.1–69). It is dispatched as briskly as possible: Shakespeare is decidedly more concerned with paternal love than restored marital happiness. Wilkins makes Pericles die 'in the arms of his beloved Thaisa', but Shakespeare wants to keep his protagonist father alive, as he does with Leontes and Cymbeline. The family, however, are not to remain united. Pericles decrees that he and Thaisa will retire to Pentapolis, while Lysimachus and Marina shall reign in Tyre. Shakespeare accepts that daughters must go with their husbands, as Perdita will with Florizel, Miranda with Ferdinand – and Susanna with John Hall (albeit in the same town). Unlike those daughters, however, Marina expresses no desire to marry Lysimachus; the match is entirely arranged between father and suitor. Pericles is apparently not interested in Lysimachus' motivation in visiting brothels. Anne Barton argues in favour of a pragmatic dramatist: 'He is a young man of rank in search of a sound whore, because that is what the situation demands. Afterwards, he is not – because he is going to marry Marina.'[15]

Pericles is a hard play to interpret. Shakespeare was presumably prepared to accept Wilkins' first nine scenes, and thereafter follow the outline of the fantastical folktale. At times he seems bored by the mechanics of it, at other times he explores and embellishes, intent on turning a penny-dreadful shocker into a tuppence-coloured psychological drama. Commentators, however, are determined to find a meaningful structure. As Richard McCabe writes: 'The final act is carefully designed as the thematic obverse of the first, and the gradual progress from damnation to redemption is meticulously executed.'[16] What is not in doubt, however, is that Pericles is confronted with different images of fatherhood as he tries to work out his own position, and that the many variants of fathers and daughters take centre stage.

The Winter's Tale: Leontes and Perdita

The Winter's Tale begins where many of Shakespeare's earlier comedies had ended. 'Friendship, no longer love's rival, has found a spacious if subordinate place for itself within the domain of marriage.'[17] Leontes, Polixenes and Hermione are friends; their children, Mamillius and Florizel, exist; Perdita will soon be born. All is set fair, to be shattered in an instant by an act of jealousy, possibly long suppressed, but apparently instantaneous. As in *Pericles* the father dominates the first three acts and then retreats into many years of despair, while the daughter, now grown to puberty, takes over the play in Act 4. The final reunion of father and daughter, described so extensively in *Pericles*, is summarily dealt with – as it will be in *Cymbeline*. Both *Pericles* and *The Winter's Tale* are based on Greek romances, and Shakespeare gives both casts Greek names, but *The Winter's Tale* derives more specifically from Robert Greene's most popular prose story *Pandosto, The Triumph of Time*, which had gone into six editions by 1609 – though Shakespeare is using the original 1588 edition, a presumed favourite, to which he makes some significant changes.[18]

Leontes' first relationship with his daughter is as a swelling in Hermione's body. When he is presented with the baby he declares, in his confused anger, 'This brat is none of mine; / It is the issue of Polixenes' (2.3.92–3). Carol Chillington Rutter writes: 'Pregnancy confirms potency, confers paternity, makes a man a man – or maybe not; instead a dupe, a cuckold. It produces legitimacy, an heir – or the cuckoo in the nest, a bastard. It settles a man's sense of self ... or throws him into a sexual panic, masculine crisis, self-doubt.'[19] Up till now 'her mother has many times told me she is mine' has been a defensive joke in several plays; now it is plagued with real uncertainty. Paulina insists the baby is 'the whole matter / And copy of the father', and then invokes 'good goddess Nature' in the hope that the goddess will 'order' both his eyes and mind (98–105). But Leontes refuses to accept the clear evidence that nature provides (always significant to Shakespeare), and wants the baby consumed with fire, as if she were a female traitor. It is only on the entreaties of his lords that he tells Antigonus to leave her in 'some remote and desert place' (175). When the oracle later reveals the truth, Leontes is full of remorse for his treatment of Hermione, Polixenes and particularly Camillo (he goes on at length about the wrong he's done his loyal servant), but of his now legitimate daughter he makes no mention. It takes Paulina to remind him that a devil would have wept at 'the casting forth to crows thy baby daughter' (3.2.189). But no command is sent to try to stop Antigonus leaving the country, despite the fact that, with his wife and son dead, the baby girl is his only heir and hope of progeny, although Shakespeare may have intended a time lapse between Antigonus' departure and the news from Delphi. But it is hard to escape the conclusion that baby girls were of little interest to fathers – Pericles had given his away to be nurtured for fourteen years. Antigonus, in his impassioned defence of Hermione's fidelity, throws an unexpected light on male attitudes to daughters:

> Be she honour-flaw'd,
> I have three daughters: the eldest is eleven;
> The second and third, nine and some five:
> If this prove true, they'll pay for't. By mine honour
> I'll geld 'em all; fourteen they shall not see
> To bring false generations: they are co-heirs,
> And I had rather glib myself, than they
> Should not produce fair issue.
>
> (2.1.143–50)

Antigonus is in a reckless emotional state, but so confident is he of Hermione's innocence that he can risk the threat of castration for his own daughters.

The baby girl does find a foster-father in the Old Shepherd, who takes her up 'for pity', and this before he finds the gold that would make it worth his while. The Old Shepherd is in this way set up as a deliberate contrast to both Leontes and Polixenes. He is introduced from the start as one who knows that youths 'between ten and three-and-twenty' spend their time 'getting wenches with child, wronging the ancientry, stealing, fighting' (3.3.59–63). He assumes the baby is a bastard, the issue of 'some stair-work, some trunk-work, some behind-door-work', but thinks no less of her (73–4). With the gold she brings 'we'll do good deeds on't' (132–3). When sixteen years later he observes that Florizel loves his daughter and she him, he is willing for them to make a handfasting and he 'will make her portion equal his' – he has perhaps saved her gold all this time (4.4.387–8). The Old Shepherd is another of Shakespeare's elderly widowers: he tells us he is eighty-three and that his 'old wife' is dead (whereas in *Pandosto* she has a name and personality), but he proves himself everything a surrogate father should be.

As in *Pericles* Time is a vital factor in the play, both destructive and creative. The play's imagery, so convoluted in the first half, so lyrical in the second, passes not only through the youth and age of succeeding generations, but the winter and summer of the seasons. Even Perdita is aware of the passage of time: to Florizel she regrets, 'I would I had some flowers o'th' spring, that might / Become your time of day' (4.4.113–14). Paulina, while knowing that Hermione is still alive, insists that time cannot redeem Leontes from his sense that the gods have forsaken him:

> A thousand knees,
> Ten thousand years together, naked, fasting,
> Upon a barren mountain, and still winter
> In storm perpetual, could not move the gods
> To look that way thou wert.
>
> (3.2.208–12)

Perdita gets the biggest build-up of any young woman in the canon. Time announces that she is 'now grown in grace / Equal with wond'ring' (4.1.24–5). Florizel calls her the goddess Flora, a 'piece of beauty' and 'queen of the sheep-shearing'. Fertility symbolism surrounds her, though she rejects being 'prank'd up' as a goddess, and will later say 'I'll queen it no inch farther' (4.4.451). Polixenes addresses her as 'gentle maiden', 'a fair one are you', and 'the prettiest low-born lass'. Camillo says 'she is the queen of curds and cream'. Shakespeare is at pains to emphasize her natural aristocracy, as he does with Marina in the brothel and with Cymbeline's two sons in their cave.[20] Polixenes himself says 'Nothing she does or seems / But smacks of something greater than herself, / Too noble for this place' (157–9), and Shakespeare gives her verse that seems a world away from the prose of Mopsa and Dorcas. In fact Perdita and Florizel share some of the most sensual and eloquent love poetry that Shakespeare ever wrote dramatically.[21] Perdita, like Hermione, accepts that sexual love is a good and natural practice. When Florizel objects that Perdita's wish to 'strew him o'er and o'er with garlands' is 'like a corpse' (128–9) she replies:

> No, like a bank, for love to lie and play on:
> Not like a corpse; or if – not to be buried,
> But quick, and in mine arms.
>
> (130–2)

But though their desires are clearly physical, Florizel claims his 'run not before mine honour, nor my lusts / Burn hotter than my faith' (34–5).

In *Pandosto*, by contrast, Dorastus is ashamed of his love for Fawnia, who relishes upsetting the natural order and becoming queen, and the Shepherd doubts that Dorastus' intentions are honourable. Shakespeare has transformed this more realistic model into an idealized courtship between prince and naturally aristocratic shepherdess, which he then gives an ironic twist by the nature/nurture argument between Perdita and Polixenes, where both argue against their own position and intentions. Perdita rejects the 'bastard' gillyvors in favour of naturally wild flowers, while Polixenes argues that nature itself can make improvements by grafting 'a gentler scion to the wildest stock' (93). This discussion is central to Shakespeare's treatment of his heroines in the late romances. Polixenes then rejects his defence of cross-breeding by threatening to have the Old Shepherd hanged and Perdita's 'beauty scratched with briers' (427), not being aware that she is in fact the gentlest of scions. On Polixenes' exit Perdita's reaction is defiant but defeated: on the one hand to assert that the sun shines on court and cottage alike, on the other to accept that 'I'll queen it no inch further, / But milk my ewes and weep' (451–2). However, yet another father-figure steps forward, the wise counsellor: Camillo contrives a plan to get himself back to Sicily, do Florizel 'love and honour' and, rather grudgingly, allow him to 'enjoy your mistress'. He is then won over by Perdita's intelligence – 'she seems a mistress / To most that teach' – for as Florizel reiterates, 'She is as forward of her breeding as / She is i'th' rear our birth' (582–5).

After nearly a thousand lines Shakespeare returns to the Sicilian court, where Leontes goes on at length about Hermione – 'She I killed! I did so' (5.1.17) – but makes no mention of the daughter he really did order to be killed. Nor does Paulina berate him about his daughter, whom she genuinely believes to be dead, but does find space to mention Mamillius, 'jewel of children'. Dion raises the subject of Leontes marrying again: 'Consider little, / What dangers, by his highness' fail of issue, / May drop upon his kingdom, and devour / Incertain lookers on' (26–9). Paulina has to head off such a proposal, possibly made many times in the intervening sixteen years, but it is a rare instance in the canon of a discussion about the necessity of a patriarch remarrying to produce heirs. Second and third marriages were common, and would help to explain how the elderly Lear, Capulet and others come to have such young daughters.

When Perdita arrives at the Sicilian court her build-up continues. The servant describes her to Leontes as 'the fairest I have yet beheld' and 'the most peerless piece of earth, I think, / That e'er the sun shone bright on' (87, 94–5). More remarkably, he eulogizes her cross-gender appeal:

> Women will love her, that she is a woman
> More worth than any man; men, that she is
> The rarest of all women.

> (110–12)

Leontes greets Florizel as his 'father's image' and Perdita as 'your fair princess, – goddess!' (130). Perdita symbolizes both virginity and erotic appeal, uniting Leonato's divided attitudes to women. Looking at Florizel he sees Polixenes and how his old friend's goodness merits a son, and so it triggers in him thoughts of his own dead son and, at long last, his daughter:

> I lost a couple, that 'twixt heaven and earth
> Might thus have stood, begetting wonder, as
> You, gracious couple, do.
>
> (131–3)

He goes on to lament his own folly:

> What might I have been,
> Might I a son and daughter now have look'd on,
> Such goodly things as you!
>
> (175–7)

When a lord reports that Polixenes is in the city and Perdita is no Libyan princess, Florizel begs Leontes to intercede: 'At your request, / My father will grant precious things as trifles.' Leontes replies: 'Would he do so, I'd beg your precious mistress, / Which he counts but a trifle' (220–3). At this point Shakespeare diverges from Greene's original, where Pandosto 'contrary to his aged years began to be somewhat tickled with the beauty of Fawnia', and has Dorastus imprisoned. Greene devotes several pages to Pandosto, 'boiling at the heat of unlawful lust' and telling Fawnia 'my power is such as I may compel by force'. Fawnia replies that she would 'rather choose death than dishonour', and Pandosto rages that 'he would forget all courtesy and compel her to grant by rigour'. Fawnia's honour is only saved by the intercession of Egistus/Polixenes. Shakespeare, therefore, retains the idea that Leontes is attracted by his daughter (the double of his wife?), but immediately cuts it short by making Paulina intervene:

> Your eye hath too much youth in't. Not a month
> 'Fore your queen died, she was more worth such gazes
> Than what you look on now.
>
> (224–6)

Leonted puts forward the reason/excuse, 'I thought of her, / Even in these looks I made' (226–7). Shakespeare has watered down the incest threat as thoroughly as he can. Florizel has already reminded Leontes of his youthful wooing, 'since you ow'd no more to time / Than I do now' (218–19). Leontes sees Perdita as Florizel's 'precious mistress', not as a 'trifle'. Her appearance reminds him of Hermione, a factor enhanced by an occasional tradition since the nineteenth century of the parts being doubled. His attraction is touching rather than predatory, and Paulina's admonition usually defuses the moment with audience laughter – Shakespeare knew how to place a gag.

The revelation of Perdita's birth and her reunion with her father were clearly going to be a high point in the story. In Greene's version Pandosto 'suddenly leapt from his seat, and kissed Fawnia, wetting her tender cheeks with his tears, and crying, "My daughter Fawnia, ah sweet Fawnia, I am thy father, Fawnia"'. General rejoicing and eighteen days of sports followed, and the happy couple and the Old Shepherd set sail for home. 'But Pandosto (calling to mind how first he betrayed his friend Egistus, how jealousy was the cause of Bellaria's death, that contrary to the law of nature he had lusted after his own daughter) moved with these desperate thoughts, he fell into a melancholy fit, and to close up the Comedy with a Tragical stratagem, he slew himself ...'. Shakespeare, however, had quite a different stratagem in mind, and in order not to pre-empt the reunion of Leontes and his wife has a gentleman report the meeting of Leontes and his daughter. He had learnt perhaps from his experience with *Pericles* that in dramatizing two reunions it is best to abbreviate one. So he has Paulina's steward relate how 'our king, being ready to leap [echoing Greene's verb] out of himself for joy of his found daughter, as if that joy were now become a loss, cries, "O, thy mother, thy mother!" then asks Bohemia forgiveness; then embraces his son-in-law; then again worries he his daughter with clipping her' (5.2.50–5). It is significant how quickly his thoughts turn from Perdita to Hermione, and how he worries (harasses?) his daughter by embracing her.

Hermione's magical reappearance after sixteen years, the very human Paulina standing in for the gods of *Pericles* and *Cymbeline*, is the high point of the denouement. Ovid's *Metamorphoses* has a number of instances of statues coming to life, but it is remarkable that this is the only tragicomedy that withholds the key to the story's resolution. Many have found Leontes' 'O, she's warm!' the most moving moment in the canon, and the dramatist therefore has difficulty in giving equal weight to the reunion of mother and daughter, but he makes what efforts he can. Leontes emphasizes that it is not just himself but also his daughter who are keen to see Hermione's statue. Viewing the statue, Leontes thinks himself 'more stone than it', and sees that his 'admiring' daughter stands 'like stone with thee' (5.3.38, 41–2). Father and daughter are united in their sense of still wonder. Perdita kneels to implore the statue's blessing, careful to deny that this is superstitious, and asks to kiss her hand, which Paulina has to forestall. When Hermione comes down from her plinth she embraces Leontes, and Paulina movingly tells her, 'Turn, good lady, / Our Perdita is found' (120–1) – the use of 'our' suggesting that everyone has had a stake in her survival. Paulina urges Perdita to 'kneel and pray your mother's blessing' (119–20). Hermione responds rather formally at first, in keeping with the religious aura of her survival:

> You gods, look down,
> And from your sacred vials pour your graces
> Upon my daughter's head!

(121–3)

She then demands to know Perdita's story, 'Where hast thou been preserved?, Where lived?' as 'the Oracle / Gave hope thou wast in being', but Paulina decrees 'there's time enough for that' (123–8), and Perdita has no further lines. Her reunion with her mother is thus acknowledged, but given the minimum permissible space. In fact as a pro-active character Perdita is sidelined once she arrives at the Sicilian court. She is almost smothered by her welter of new relations: her father – her lover, her mother and Paulina, another surrogate mother. Her forthright, perceptive character has been muted by her new surroundings and her dependence on Florizel, and we learn little of what the rediscovery of her parents means to her. Like Marina she is not central to the final winding-up of the story; the patriarch and his concerns always have the last word. Where *The Winter's Tale* is exceptional is that Hermione emerges as the ideal wife and mother, and she, Perdita and Paulina have the largest and most active female roles in any of Shakespeare's later plays. Though the play ends with redemption apparently achieved, there is an insistent sense of sorrow and loss. Shakespeare no longer believes in unblighted, happy endings. Mamillius and Antigonus are dead, and Perdita and Camillo cannot finally replace them. Perdita will leave for Bohemia with Florizel and Polixenes, and it may be that Leontes will, like Prospero, feel 'every third thought shall be his grave'.

Cymbeline: Cymbeline and Innogen

Cymbeline is a further experiment in tragicomedy, though it is printed in F as a tragedy. It is a fantastical fairytale to which Shakespeare tries to bring a degree of psychological realism – with mixed results: as in *Pericles* character and relationships are too often subordinate to narrative. Innogen's story is the real heart of the play, and is undoubtedly the attraction for Shakespeare. The plot seems to owe much to *The Rare Triumphs of Love and Fortune* (1589), in which a princess loves a foundling whom the king banishes. She then escapes into the wilds, meets a hermit falsely exiled and Jupiter intervenes to bring a happy ending. The 'Snow White' legend is an obvious source, where the princess has a wicked stepmother who tries to poison her, she flees into the country and becomes housekeeper to mysterious forest folk, apparently dies from a magic potion, but wakes and is restored to her rightful place and her handsome lover. Beaumont and Fletcher's *Philaster*, performed in 1610, has many similarities, but it is doubtful if it influenced the writing of *Cymbeline*, which was in the Globe repertoire in 1611.

Old fashioned romance was in vogue on all sides, and writing was more consciously literary.

The Innogen story would have been sufficient for most writers, but Shakespeare as usual grafted on further elaborations. The Iachimo wager plot is probably taken from Boccaccio's *Decameron* (and Iachimo eventually became the star male part). Holinshed provided Shakespeare with the quasi-historical Cymbeline who reigned from 33 BC for thirty-five years, was brought up in Rome, battled with the Romans and had various altercations over tribute. The complication of this wealth of material made for an unwieldy plot and one of Shakespeare's least successful last scenes, where there are some thirty denouements, all but one of which the audience knows already.[22] A prime sufferer in all this was the father–daughter relationship of Cymbeline and Innogen, one of the most cursorily examined in all late Shakespeare.

Innogen starts out as an important and highly regarded figure in her father's court, strong-willed and decisive as his only living heir. Harriet Walter, who played her at the RSC in 1987, found in her 'a quality of self-dramatization ... She casts herself in a noble role, and in playing that to the hilt, she cannot be seen to give in or let herself down.'[23] She is unusual among Shakespeare's heroines in being already married, albeit secretly, but there is some doubt whether the marriage has been consummated. Anne Barton argues that she is still a virgin, but Stanley Wells points out that this depends on the interpretation of 'oft': when Posthumus says, 'Me of my lawful pleasure she restrain'd, / And pray'd me oft forbearance' (2.4.161–2), it can be construed that Innogen is asking for moderation, not abstinence.[24] It may be that Shakespeare left it deliberately vague, hoping to leave the impression that she is still virginal, a state he preferred for his young heroines. She and Posthumus come across as adolescent lovers, who relate mainly through poeticizing and courtly games of love (1.4.25–35).

From the start of the play Shakespeare short-changes the father-daughter relationship. Cymbeline is not allowed a scene where he discovers Innogen's secret marriage and vents his fury on Posthumus: instead two gentlemen report it. Innogen is outspoken from the start. Though she fears her father's anger, she's not afraid of what he can do to her: 'A touch more rare [a deeper pain?] / Subdues all pangs, all fears', and Cymbeline cuts in, 'Past grace? obedience?' – the two virtues a daughter should have (1.2.66–7). He accuses her of disloyalty and laments, like Lear, that she 'shouldst repair my youth' (80). When he says she could have had his stepson Cloten, she replies that he's a puttock to Posthumus' eagle, and boldly goes on to blame her father for breeding Posthumus 'as my playfellow', and to declare she'd rather be a neatherd's daughter than a princess. Like Helena, men would label her 'difficult', or, as Harriet Walter writes, 'the smutty child grown to wilful adult with Amazon potential'.[25] Cymbeline thinks her mad and, in true fairytale mode, his final words are:

> Away with her,
> And pen her up ...
> Let her languish
> A drop of blood a day, and, being aged
> Die of this folly.

(83–4, 87–9)

This sets the tone of their relationship. Innogen likens her father to 'the tyrannous breathing of the north' that 'shakes all our buds from growing' (1.4.36–7), and later calls him 'a father cruel' (1.7.1). Cymbeline shows no sign of relenting. He is completely in thrall to his queen and her son Cloten, whom he assures that Innogen will forget Posthumus in time, 'and then she's yours' (2.3.45). But Shakespeare fails to breathe new life into their relationship. Innogen sees her father as cruel and tyrannous, Cymbeline thinks her lacking in all the essential daughterly virtues – loyalty, obedience and comfort. It is familiar territory, and Shakespeare is barely interested in re-examining either the *senex* model or the Lear-like dependence.

Shakespeare is, however, interested in building up Innogen. When Pisanio receives Posthumus' letter accusing Innogen of adultery he declares:

> She's punish'd for her truth; and undergoes,
> More goddess-like than wife-like, such assaults
> As would take in some virtue.

(3.2.7–9)

At times she is made to stand for Britain, and she bears the name of the wife of Brute, the legendary British king. She herself speaks of Britain's place in the world, of its being the special seat of grace and beauty, as the image of the swan's nest suggests (3.4.139). The repentant Posthumus says of 'my lady's kingdom: 'tis enough / That, Britain, I have kill'd thy mistress' (5.1.19–20). By contrast Shakespeare bathes her in floral imagery: she is 'fresh lily', 'sweetest, fairest lily'; her face is like 'the pale primrose', her veins like the 'azured harebell'. At the same time she is assertive and down to earth: when she decides to go to Milford Haven she demands 'a riding-suit; no costlier than would fit / A franklin's housewife' (3.2.76–7).

All this is overturned by her discovery that Posthumus has sent Pisanio to kill her. Shakespeare uses Posthumus to further examine male insecurity about betrayal and cuckoldry. The gullible Posthumus has blamed all the vices of the world on 'the woman's part' – lying, flattery, deceit, lust, revenge, ambition, coverings, pride, slander, mutability; 'all faults that name, nay, that hell knows' (2.4.174–9). Faced by this rampant misogyny Innogen is at first incandescent in her anger:

Poor I am stale, a garment out of fashion,
And, for I am richer to hang by th' walls
I must be ripped: – to pieces with me! – O,
Men's vows are women's traitors!

(3.4.50–3)

But this quickly descends into a masochistic self-sacrifice as she orders Pisanio to go ahead and kill her, as she is too 'craven' to take her own life. It is a turning point, where her self-determination is finally crushed, and tragedy is at hand. Pisanio's solution is, however, the stock device of comedy – male attire – and he charges her to 'forget to be a woman: change / Command into obedience'. He continues, in a telling comment on the way women were perceived: '[change] fear, and niceness / (The handmaids of all women, or, more truly, / Woman it pretty self) into a waggish courage' (154–7). The emotionally jagged verse of Innogen's plea for death turns to the textbook resolution of 'This attempt / I am soldier to, and will abide it with / A prince's courage' (182–4).

Innogen never loses courage, but 'fear and niceness' become her dominant emotions. Shakespeare sends her out into the wild countryside where, as in *As You Like It* and *King Lear*, his protagonist may find him/herself and return, sorted out and reinvigorated. But Wales turns out to be no Forest of Arden, and male attire doesn't give her the authority of a Portia. Instead she becomes a housekeeper to Belarius (a surrogate father) and his two boys, who think her an 'angel' and 'divine', but essentially womanly. She has to endure apparent death, and wake next to a headless corpse. Shakespeare is mixing melodrama, romance and realism, and is not totally in control of the experiment. As page to the Roman Lucius she becomes Fidele, the faithful one, submerges herself into his servant persona and grows more passive and ground-down as the action proceeds. It is a sad declension from the defiant princess of the court, but Shakespeare is arguing that this is the reality of a Rosalind alone in a country in turmoil and invasion. The pastoral fantasy of Arden bears no relation to war-torn Roman Wales, or to the darkening perception of the ageing writer. Shakespeare is here interested in loss, death and grief as the transformative experience, whereby his characters learn the true value of relationships.[26]

Cymbeline could, and perhaps should, have been the centre of the play, and made it seem less diffuse and episodic. But the writing for him is perfunctory and does little more than service the plot. Like Leontes, though less well written, Cymbeline is the only person at court who cannot see the truth – that Innogen and Posthumus are well suited, the Queen is evil and her son a brute. As Edward Petherbridge, who played the part for the RSC in 1997, writes, 'It was called *Cymbeline* because it was the only way Shakespeare could persuade a decent actor to play such a rotten part.'[27] Shakespeare's lack of interest in Cymbeline is shown in the way he is constantly taken offstage before any character development can take place. After Innogen's departure from court his relationship with his wife could have been thoroughly examined, but Shakespeare sees her as no more than the nameless wicked queen/stepmother of fairytale, and consequently no realistic relationship was possible: his treatment of her is one of the clearest examples of his growing prioritization of story over character in the later plays. It is, however, essential to the plot that Cymbeline eventually shows some leadership qualities, so he is made to resist Caesar, for he 'did put the yoke upon's: which to shake off / Becomes a warlike people, whom we reckon / Ourselves to be' (3.1.52–4). But confronted by news of the landing of the Roman fleet his immediate reaction is: 'Now for the counsel of my son and queen, / I am amaz'd with matter' (4.3.27–8). The writing is on a par with the character's feebleness. Criticism of Cymbeline has been harsh: J. M. Nosworthy, for example, calls him 'a feeble, henpecked, credulous, boring, half-reflection of heroic anger and madness, whose sanity only serves to mock his impotence'.[28] Faced by such an analysis it is tempting to play him comedically, were it not for his vital dramatic function in presiding over the resolution of all the disparate plot threads in the final scene, though even here the comic possibilities of his amazement at each revelation are enticing.

The queen's deathbed confession reveals her treachery, but Cymbeline is reluctant to admit his lack of perception in a classic piece of male self-justification: 'O most delicate fiend! / Who is't can read a woman?' (5.5.47–8). His defence is her beauty; her flattery was so strong that his eyes and ears 'were not in fault ... nor my heart / That thought her like her seeming. It had been vicious / To have mistrusted her' (63–6). This would have been more resonant if Cymbeline had been allowed to demonstrate his great affection for her while alive. He does go so far as to admit that his daughter might call it 'folly in me' (67). Lucius then gives Fidele a big commendation, attributing to him/her all the approved female virtues – kind, duteous, diligent, tender, true, feat, nurse-like (86–8). Cymbeline is impressed by this, admits Fidele's 'favour is familiar to me' (the Jacobean audience presumably never tired of this joke) and takes him into his grace with the fulsome 'I love thee more and more' (109). Shakespeare relishes the irony of the father being more attracted to his daughter dressed as a boy than he ever was when she was demonstrably female.

Iachimo then makes his improbable repentance with much eulogizing of Innogen, Posthumus in his agony at presuming her dead calls out for her and, when Innogen/Fidele intervenes, strikes her to the ground (in a repeat of Pericles' assault on Marina). Pisanio reveals Fidele's real person, and Cymbeline declares, 'If this be so, the gods do mean to strike me / To death with mortal joy' (in another echo of Pericles and Leontes), though nothing in the play so far has suggested that he finds any joy in his daughter (234–5). Husband and wife are then reconciled, and Posthumus is given the wonderful lines, 'Hang there like fruit, my soul, / Till the tree die'. Cymbeline calls her, more prosaically, 'my flesh, my child' (263–4), and demands her attention. Innogen dutifully kneels and asks for his blessing, as Cordelia and Marina have done, and Cymbeline sheds tears before briskly moving on to the news of the Queen's death and his reaction to it – 'O, she was naught' (271). Shakespeare is more concerned to give space to the restoration of Cymbeline's two sons. On learning of their survival his response is intriguing:

> O, what am I?
> A mother to the birth of three? Ne'er mother
> Rejoic'd deliverance more.
>
> (369–71)

This interdependence of father, mother and child, or in this case a fantasy of reproduction without union with women, echoes Pericles' recognition of Marina. This male fantasy of parthenogenesis seeks to rob women of their unique and frightening power.[29] Cymbeline's next thought is that Innogen has lost her inheritance, with the unspoken implication that Britain is better off with a male heir (a thought congenial to James I). Innogen, dutiful daughter and sister, rejoices more that she has 'got two worlds by't' (375). Cymbeline is at least curious to know Innogen's story, then claims Belarius as his brother and, witnessing Posthumus' pardoning of Iachimo, declares: 'We'll learn our freeness of a son-in-law: / Pardon's the word to all' (422–3). He then does a political about-turn, submits to Caesar and promises to pay 'our wonted tribute, from the which / We were dissuaded by our wicked queen' (463–4), so he's not admitting fault there either. The Soothsayer then concludes matters by naming Posthumus as the 'lion's whelp'; 'his miseries ended' he is the hero of the hour, 'Britain be fortunate and flourish in peace and plenty'. Cymbeline is 'the lofty cedar', and his sons his branches, and Innogen 'the piece of tender air', 'mollis aer or mulier', 'this most constant wife' (441–50). Innogen has acceded to the requisite wifely virtues – constancy, devotion, tenderness.

This last scene carries the familiar motifs of the late tragicomedies: the restoration of families after separation and supposed deaths, though years have been lost through exile and suffering; general forgiveness after treachery and misunderstanding; fathers restored to, and redeemed by, their daughters; dream sequences in which gods make crucial revelations. Cymbeline is structurally central to the last scene. Freed from the malign influence of his wife and stepson he has turned into a wise and forgiving ruler, and been afforded a second chance by the improbable recovery of all three children, but this redemption carries no emotional truth. He remains two-dimensional to the last, since Shakespeare's real interests lay elsewhere – in the characters of Innogen, Posthumus and Iachimo, and the themes of survival, succession, empire and the nature of government. As Janet Adelman says: 'His absence in the play is so prominent ... because he strikes us as absent even when present, absent to himself.'[30] This absence undermines his relations with his daughter. It is a valid criticism that the passionate, shrewd comic heroine passes through housekeeper and page to passive, constant wife, but Shakespeare would have had to radically alter the transformation demanded by the Snow White template. The success of the play lies in his reaction to every twist of Innogen's fortune, a jagged progress for which Helena in *All's Well* had paved the way. As Anne Barton writes, Innogen is 'passionate and chilly, timorous and aggressive, sometimes intensely feminine, sometimes not'.[31] At times she seems little more than a symbol, a fairytale princess, at others she springs back to life as an individual, quirky, resourceful young woman under extreme pressure. Actors have found her one of the most demanding and rewarding parts to play, but for all her complexity she never seems as inhabited a creation as Viola or Rosalind.

The Tempest: Prospero and Miranda

The Tempest is a short play, and in some respects very simple. The plot is Prospero's plot, uncomplicated in comparison with *Pericles* and *Cymbeline*. There are unforeseen developments, which Prospero is able to defeat or accommodate, but fundamentally he achieves his objectives – revenge, forgiveness, his daughter's marriage and his return as Duke of Milan – within four hours. Yet Shakespeare raises, or at times part-buries, a host of other issues. Anne Barton sees the play as 'an extraordinarily obliging work of art. It will lend itself to almost any interpretation, any set of meanings imposed upon it: it will even make them shine.'[32] The island can be seen as an image, a metaphor, the Globe Theatre, a state of mind, an experimental laboratory, a pastoral fantasy, a masque, a play within a play, a dream. Prospero 'plays' at achieving mastery, perfecting his art and perfecting Miranda. Greenblatt argues that 'the central preoccupation of almost all [Shakespeare's] plays are there in *The Tempest*', and Peter Brook, who directed a famous production with John Gielgud at Stratford in 1957 (my first experience of the play), concluded: 'Shakespeare includes all the themes from his earlier work – kingship, inheritance, treachery, conscience, identity, love, music, God – he draws them together as if to find the key to it all, but there is no such key.'[33]

After the various failings of Pericles, Leonato and Cymbeline as rulers and fathers, Shakespeare apparently set out in *The Tempest* to write a wise patriarch with a loving relationship with his daughter, but in his determination to create a three-dimensional character, as opposed to Cymbeline, he loads his Prospero with failings and inconsistencies which humanize him but also make him difficult to interpret. He can appear a self-centred loner, plagued by anxiety and anger, irritable and tyrannical, a haughty magician, an inveterate role-player and eavesdropper. Or he can seem a fundamentally good and learned man and father, struggling with himself to choose virtue over vengeance, freedom over oppression. In this way he can be seen as a summation of Shakespeare's ambivalent feelings about patriarchy. Miranda, though a less complex character, can also be played in a number of ways: an intelligent paragon, a hoyden, a feral child of nature or a rebellious adolescent, perhaps also reflecting Shakespeare's feelings about daughters.

Shakespeare dispenses with the first half of the plot, the usurpation by Antonio, Prospero and Miranda's escape and the taking over of the island: a perhaps deliberate reversal of *The Winter's* Tale, which might have started with Florizel and Perdita's arrival in Sicily. The subject of a magician prince and his daughter on an island has many antecedents in folk-lore, romance and even *commedia del'arte*. Shakespeare also knew that shipwreck in the Bermudas and the colonization of Virginia, described in 1610 pamphlets, were hot topics, though he was careful to place Prospero's island between Naples and Tunis. Prospero is a contentious figure in Jacobean terms. He has, like Vincentio, neglected his duties as a ruler and retired to his library, where his study has not been the approved course for a ruler, the enhancement of his political understanding. Worse still, in seventeenth-century eyes, he has delegated his responsibilities to his younger brother, who, like many a Renaissance prince, has taken advantage of this and deposed him. In his library Prospero has dabbled in white magic, regarded by many as the highest form of natural philosophy, which allowed him 'to energise in the gods or to control other beneficent spiritual intelligencies in the working of miraculous effects'.[34] However beneficent, all forms of magic were expressly forbidden by James 1, though Prospero might have had a particular appeal to a king who wrote 'I am the husband and the whole island is my lawful wife; I am the head, and it is my body.'[35] Shakespeare seems uncertain of the extent of Prospero's powers, but he is always a human with limitations, never a god. He's adept at putting people to sleep and can, to some extent, control nature, though he needs Ariel's help in manipulating the weather, and, at times, Ariel seems like a surrogate son. Despite Ariel's claim that he has fetched dew from the Bermudas, their joint power extends only to the island and its vicinity: Alonso's fleet was not summoned, it fortuitously happened to be passing. Shakespeare adds to the confusion by adopting in his speech 'Ye elves of hills, brooks, standing lakes and groves' (5.1.33–57) Ovid's Medea speech, recognized as the acme of witchcraft, which concentrates mainly on controlling nature but also includes waking sleepers from their graves. Prospero has given no hint of such a major power, which would certainly constitute *black* magic. If so, it would suggest either the writer's carelessness or Prospero's empty boast, though it may also reflect Shakespeare's vanity, since as playwright he had brought both Thaisa and Hermione back to life from apparent death. It is often hard to determine Prospero's inner thoughts since Shakespeare has, apparently deliberately, given him no outright soliloquies.

Many modern commentators see Prospero as a colonial exploiter. Caliban certainly thinks so: he claims the island was his until Prospero made himself 'king' and 'here you sty me / In this hard rock' (343–4). Prospero argues that he initially treated Caliban well, tutored him as a surrogate father might 'till thou didst seek to violate / The honour of my child' (1.2.348–9). In the same way Prospero released Ariel from the cloven pine Sycorax had penned him in, but only to make him his servant in magic. Prospero is, however, no textbook colonist: he came to the island by chance and against his will, and has no desire to carry away its riches. Nevertheless he now regards Caliban as a 'poisonous slave' and has turned him into a typical seventeenth-century household servant – 'He does make our fire, / Fetch in our wood, and serves in offices / That profit us' (312–14). There can be little doubt that Shakespeare was influenced by Montaigne's essay 'Of the Caniballes': Gonzalo's proposal to organize an ideal common-wealth is taken directly from it (2.1.148–65). The essay perhaps prompted Shakespeare not only to give Caliban some marvellous verse, but also to see Prospero's 'usurpation' from Caliban's point of view.[36]

Prospero's primary fixation is to be revenged on his 'perfidious' brother Antonio, and on Alonso, King of Naples, 'being an enemy / To me inveterate' (1.2.121–2). Once he has them in his power his thoughts turn to repentance and forgiveness – 'They being penitent, / The sole drift of my purpose doth extend / Not a frown further' (5.1.28–30) – but it is not clear that he does fully forgive Antonio – 'Most wicked sir, whom to call brother / Would even infect my mouth' (132–3) – or indeed that the silent Antonio does repent. In keeping with the ethic of these final plays reconciliation is the order of the day, but Shakespeare seems here to be uneasy with a conventional fairytale ending – Prospero is no Cymbeline. It may be that he was influenced by Montaigne's essay 'On Repenting': 'My doings are ruled by what I am and are in harmony with how I was made. I cannot do better: and the act of repenting does not properly touch such things as are not within our power.'[37]

Prospero's secondary fixation is with chastity and fertility, and this at times dominates his attitude to Miranda. He seems to see himself as both father and mother (he has presumably helped her through her menarche), and even describes their voyage to the island in what appears to be a birth fantasy (cf. Cymbeline and Pericles):

When I have decked the sea with drops full salt,
Under my burden groaned, which raised in me
An undergoing stomach to bear up
Against what should ensue.

(1.2.155–8)

Through observing the unities of time and place Shakespeare is forced into making Prospero recount a considerable backstory, in a stripped-down

verse of many elisions and tortured syntax. This long narration has tried
the patience of many actors and audience: Olivier famously refused to play
the part on the grounds that 'there was not a laugh in it'.[38] It does, however,
serve to set up his relationship with Miranda in some detail. She knows
of her father's magic arts, but has the courage and the 'piteous heart' to
rail at his apparent destruction of ship and crew. The pity she instinctively
shows for other characters' suffering throughout the play can be seen as
softening her father's attitude to revenge. Prospero tells her 'I have done
nothing but in care of thee, / Of thee, my dear one, thee, my daughter'
(16–17), and the emphatic repetition is significant. Prospero then asks her,
'Canst thou remember / A time before we came unto this cell?' (38–9). This
may seem a commonplace enquiry, but it is a rare instance in the canon
of a father asking what his daughter remembers of her past. Miranda can
remember women who 'tended' her, but not apparently her mother whom
she never mentions. Since she was 'not / Out three years old' (40–1) she
is now apparently fourteen, a year older than Juliet and the same age as
Marina. Prospero tells Ferdinand she is 'a third of mine own life', so this
would appear to make him mid-forties, around the same age as Shakespeare
when he wrote the play, and approaching old age in Jacobean terms. He
then reveals to her that he was formerly Duke of Milan and that she is
a princess, a fact that he held back presumably so that she should grow
up unencumbered with dreams of grandeur. Her response to the news of
their exile is to ask whether it was foul play or a blessing, a sophisticated
enquiry. Her second thought is to imagine the 'teen' (trouble) that she, a
small child, must have put her father to (60–1, 64).

Prospero develops at length his bitterness at his brother's duplicity and
three times checks that Miranda and, of course, the audience are listening,
but this would seem to be a technical device to break up his speech while
keeping Miranda in the scene, rather than indicating her lack of attention,
since these revelations are of enormous concern to her. When he finally
asks her 'if this might be a brother?' her response is again sophisticated: 'I
should sin / To think but nobly of my grandmother; / Good wombs have
borne bad sons' (118–20). This reflects the unusual amount of tutoring that
Prospero has been able to lavish on his daughter (172–4). Miranda may
be naive about the outside world, but her perception and moral integrity
indicate an exceptional education. When Prospero comes to the story of
their being forced out to sea in a 'rotten carcass of a butt', Miranda again
laments, 'Alack, what trouble / Was I then to you?', but her father's reply is
unequivocal, 'O, a cherubin / Thou wast that did preserve me. Thou didst
smile, / Infused with a fortitude from heaven' (151–4). Prospero implies
that he might have given in to despair and allowed himself to drown but
for his trusting toddler daughter, a remarkable statement of the inspiration
a child can give to a father (perhaps inspired by Shakespeare's feelings
for his three-year-old granddaughter, Elizabeth Hall?). It seems clear that
Shakespeare is setting up what, in seventeenth-century eyes, would be

an ideal relationship between father and daughter, however much some modern interpreters would see Prospero as a typical patriarch and Miranda as unduly submissive and anxious to please. David Sundelson refers to the play's 'paternal narcissism: the prevailing sense that there is no worthiness like a father's, no accomplishment or power, and that Prospero is the father *par excellence*'.[39]

When Prospero threatens Ferdinand with manacles 'neck and feet', and Miranda begs him, 'Make not too rash a trial of him', her father's reply is crushing: 'What, I say, / My foot my tutor?' (468–70). This 'foot' image has made Miranda appear an oppressed victim, however much Prospero is playing out the role of heavy father berating a new suitor. Rank paternalism is further enhanced by the importance attached to Miranda's virginity, as it is with Marina and Perdita. Caliban's attempted rape seems to hover throughout the play.[40] The following speech, assigned to Miranda in F (our only text), claims that the speaker spent hours teaching Caliban language (355–6), though his 'profit on't / Is I know how to curse. The red plague rid you / For learning me your language' (364–6). This very assertive speech is in Prospero's idiom, and Caliban is more likely to wish the red plague on his master than on Miranda. On the other hand it does lend a new dimension to Miranda's character, which actors have gratefully seized upon. It is possible that Shakespeare wrote the speech for Prospero, but then decided it was more interesting to assign it to Miranda, though it seems more probably yet another example of Shakespeare's growing lack of interest in consistent characterization in favour of, as Anne Barton writes, 'the impersonal quality of a moment of dramatic time. What the situation, as opposed to maidenly decorum and the pliability of her own nature, would seem to demand.'[41] Saved from Caliban, Miranda is ripe to be wife to Prince Ferdinand – 'sexual bait' some would now argue. As soon as they meet she sees 'a thing divine', he sees a 'goddess', and his 'prime request' is 'if you be maid or no?' Reassured on that score Ferdinand declares:

> O, if a virgin,
> And your affection not gone forth, I'll make you
> The Queen of Naples.

> (448–50)

Though they have been brought together through Prospero and Ariel's agency, Prospero is determined to test Ferdinand, 'lest too light winning / Make the prize light' (452–3), and charges him with the same crimes as Antonio, treason and usurpation. Then by making him carry logs, Caliban's normal servitude, Prospero seems bent on conquering his sense of male superiority.

When Miranda and Ferdinand next meet she is, like Perdita, unusually candid about both her chastity ('my modesty / The jewel in my dower'), and her own sexual desires. She cries for not daring to offer 'what I desire to give, and much less take / What I shall die to want' (3.1.53–4, 78–9). It is a genuine love scene between equals, and Prospero, as eavesdropper, is 'surprised' but 'glad' at his daughter's behaviour. It may also represent Miranda's bid for freedom, both from the island and her father, for, as Ferdinand posits, there is freedom to be found in willingly accepting the 'bondage' of marriage (89). Assured that Ferdinand 'do love, prize, honour' her, she declares: 'I am your wife, if you will marry me; / If not, I'll die your maid' (83–4). Miranda shows herself equally assertive in proposing marriage to a man she thinks her father dislikes, and in rejecting sex outside marriage. In this she is her father's daughter: Prospero is the most impassioned of all Shakespeare's fathers that a would-be lover should not take advantage of his daughter. He appears almost unbalanced in this obsession:

If thou dost break her virgin-knot before
All sanctimonious ceremonies may
With full and holy right be ministered,
No sweet aspersions shall the heavens let fall
To make this contract grow; but barren hate,
Sour-eyed disdain and discord shall bestrew
The union of your bed with weeds so loathly
That you shall hate it both.

(4.1.15–22)

The plot of *The Tempest* does not allow Miranda the same scope as Marina, Innogen or even Perdita enjoy: no outside force threatens her, she has no physical journey to make. She has the customary build-up of the late heroines, though this is mainly supplied by Ferdinand. She is 'admired', 'perfect', 'peerless', 'one who outstrips all praise', but Shakespeare gives her an intelligence and positive spirit that rises above the stereotype of fair and dutiful princess. She is, in common with other late-Shakespearean heroines, more forthright in language and intention than her male partner. 'Discovered' playing chess with Ferdinand, a symbol of intellectual equality, she immediately accuses him of cheating; and confronted by the six lords her wonder knows no bounds: 'How beauteous mankind is! O brave new world / That has such people in't' (5.1.184–5). It is an unwitting rebuke to her father's view of the world, and occasions Prospero sardonically to take up the half-line, ''Tis new to thee.' Father and daughter's interdependence has been shattered and, as Ruth Nevo writes (forgetting the disruptive threat of Caliban), they must be saved

from the loveliest of all fantasies. To live thus, father and daughter, alone and together, with no rival to challenge, no rebellion to threaten, no sexual turmoil to overthrow the beatific enjoyment of beauty, of obedience, of affection, of consideration ... What is this but the wishful fantasy of a Lear, who would sing like a bird in a cage in prison with Cordelia, or the fantasy of any parent.[42]

But Prospero's purpose has always been to ensure that Ferdinand and Miranda's child will eventually rule in both Naples and Milan. If revenge is his short-term objective, his long-term is undoubtedly his heirs' succession. The masques are partly aimed at Ferdinand – 'no bed-right shall be paid / Till Hymen's torch be lighted' (4.1.96–7) – but in general they invoke the cooperation of nature's plenty to bless the marriage and assure the couple's fertility. His two objectives realized, Prospero is ready to abandon his magic and release Ariel. Since 'every third thought shall be my grave' (5.1.313) he knows that magic should play no part in his final years, and certainly not as the restored Duke of Milan. His 'old brain is troubled', perhaps by the impossibility of subduing everything to his will, perhaps by the realization that 'we are such stuff as dreams are made on' (4.1.156–7), and that only by renouncing magic can he become fully human. Despite his care of Miranda, Prospero has been a solitary figure, his reliance on Ariel and other spirits further cutting him off from humanity. To step away now from magic at the height of his powers seems a kind of ethical victory.

Of course it is tempting to adopt the old chestnut and see Shakespeare himself in Prospero, and Miranda as the dream relationship he perhaps never had with his own daughters. As he feels his powers may soon fail (he was forty-seven in 1611 and had five years to live) he acknowledges the need to leave the dream world of the theatre, perhaps sell his share in the King's Men rather than invest in the rebuilding of the Globe (though he would contribute to three further plays), and return to the fraught realities of Stratford and his family, but this is wishful conjecture. The Epilogue does not directly play into this interpretation. Prospero remains in character and asks to be released from the island, yet his 'project ... which was to please' must be that of the author and actor – or all three rolled into one. In a return to his former self 'I want / Spirits to enforce, art to enchant', but he knows the harsh reality is 'my ending is despair, / Unless I be relieved by prayer', which, in an astonishing image, 'pierces so that it assaults / Mercy itself, and frees all faults'. Prospero/Shakespeare asks for the prayerful indulgence, not of God, but of the audience. Do they have the 'spell' to keep him on the island, trapped in his actor and writer's role, or free him into the world? It is not finally an entreaty or summation that yields up a precise meaning. The play raises myriad questions, and Prospero's 'despair' is not to be relieved by easy answers.

Three Fletcher collaborations

After *The Tempest* Shakespeare wrote three further plays in collaboration with John Fletcher, fifteen years his junior and his successor as the company playwright. Only *All is True* (*Henry VIII*) was included by Heminges and Condell in F1, and *The Two Noble Kinsmen* and *Cardenio* were omitted, probably on the grounds that Fletcher was the senior collaborator, possibly because they couldn't get hold of the rights. *All is True* contains a special hymn of praise of father to daughter, albeit the consensus has Fletcher as the author. The King is anxious that Archbishop Cranmer should attend to 'a fair young maid that yet wants baptism' (5.2.195) – the future Queen Elizabeth. Cranmer duly launches in to a forty-line panegyric foretelling the glory of both Elizabeth and James 1, and Henry declares:

> Thou hast made me now a man; never before
> This happy child did I get anything.
> This oracle of comfort has so pleased me,
> That when I am in heaven I shall desire
> To see what this child does, and praise my maker.

> (5.4.63–7)

This speech has an ironic ring for those in the audience aware how desperate Henry was to be succeeded by a son rather than a daughter. The structure of the play is awkward: Wolsey and Queen Katherine fare better than Henry, who is given little character development.

Cardenio is a lost play, though the story, clearly based on a tale in Cervantes' *Don Quixote*, rehearses various themes that interested Shakespeare all his life. Over a century later Lewis Theobald claimed that his play *Double Falsehood: or The Distressed Lovers* (1728) was based on three manuscripts (now lost) of versions or adaptations of Shakespeare and Fletcher's play. Two male friends are rivals in love; one woman is seduced, another forced into a wedding which is broken off; Act 4 moves to the countryside where the seduced woman is cross-dressed and the blighted wife is sprung from a convent; the seducer is finally moved to repent and the Duke ensures that all ends happily. It is familiar territory for both writers. Fletcher is the more likely instigator, since ten of his plays are based on Spanish sources, but Shakespeare could also have read the story in Thomas Shelton's 1612 translation of *Don Quixote*. Macdonald D. Jackson, having studied the stylistic evidence, thinks that some of Leonora's verse sounds either Shakespearean or a collage of Shakespearean scraps:[43] 'Patient! What else? My flames are in the flint. / Haply to lose a husband I may weep; / Never to get one. When I cry for bondage, / Let freedom quit me' (1.2.113–16). It is tempting to think Shakespeare wrote some of the father Don Bernard's prose: 'Set such price upon yourself to him as many, and much his betters, would buy you at (and reckon those virtues in you at the rate of their scarcity), to which if he come not up, you remain for a better mart' (1.2.209–13); and even some of Leonora's verse:

> How may I be obedient and wise too?
> Of my obedience, sir, I cannot strip me,
> Nor can I then be wise, Grace against grace!
> Ungracious if I do not obey a father,
> Most perjur'd if I do.

(3.2.96–100)

But though several reconstructions have been recently attempted, most notably by Gregory Doran for the RSC in 2011, it may well be that, as Jackson writes, 'scarcely a line of Shakespeare's verse survives intact'.[44]

The Two Noble Kinsmen was probably first performed in 1613, after the burning of the Globe on 29 June. The main Palamon-Arcite-Emilia plot was based on Chaucer's *The Knights' Tale*, to which Fletcher and Shakespeare added a subplot of the Jailer and his Daughter. This story was of their own devising, though the woman who frees a prisoner out of love and is later abandoned dates back, once again, to Ovid's *Metamorphoses*, where Ariadne betrays her father Minos by showing the prisoner Theseus the way in and out of the labyrinth – the disguised Julia in *The Two Gentlemen of Verona* claims to have played Ariadne, 'passioning / For Theseus' perjury, and unjust flight' (4.4.164–5) – so Shakespeare had been holding the story in reserve for over twenty years. The tale clearly appealed to both writers, since they shared its development, Shakespeare apparently writing the first six scenes and thus introducing the characters in both plots. He then seems to have written all the scenes of the main plot in the last act and, more contentiously, some of the scenes in Acts 3 and 4.

Shakespeare introduces the Jailer and his Daughter in a prose scene, where the Jailer is presented as a model father, explaining to the unnamed Wooer that he has little money as 'great ones ... seldom come' to the jail (and hence he doesn't get a cut of their lavish expenses), but on his death his daughter will get all he has. The Wooer accepts this, and 'will estate your daughter in what I have promised'. The Jailer then checks whether he has 'a full promise of her', and the Wooer says he has, though the Daughter never gives any indication of this (2.1.2–15). The Daughter is very taken with the imprisoned Palamon and Arcite 'making misery their mirth and affliction a toy to jest at' (34–5), but expresses no preference. Shakespeare then gives her a sophisticated conceit: 'Yet sometime a divided sigh, martyred, as 'twere, i'th' deliverance, will break from one of them – when the other presently gives it so sweet a rebuke that I could wish myself a sigh to be so chid, or at least a sigher to be comforted (40–5)'. She then ends the short scene, echoing Goneril's 'O, the difference of man and man!' (*King Lear*,

4.3.26) with, 'It is a holiday to look on them. Lord, the difference of men!' (55–6), which seems to imply a slight on the Wooer.

Fletcher then writes her four soliloquies in direct, rather plain verse, arguably more in keeping with her class and background than Shakespeare's maiden wishing herself 'a sigh to be so chid':

> Why should I love this gentleman?
> 'Tis odds he never will affect me:
> I am base, My father the mean keeper of his prison,
> And he a prince. To marry him is hopeless;
> To be his whore is witless.
>
> (2.4.1–5)

Cyrus Hoy apportions the third soliloquy (3.2), as her mind begins to disintegrate and she contemplates suicide, to Shakespeare, but this seems unlikely.[45] In Fletcher's 4.1 the Jailer, facing hanging for Palamon's escape, hears that the Duke has pardoned both him and his daughter at Palamon's entreaty. The Wooer reports that he observed the Daughter gathering flowers for her father's funeral, singing nothing but 'Willow, willow, willow', and that the place

> Was knee-deep where she sat; her careless tresses
> A wreath of bull-rush rounded; about her stuck
> Thousand fresh water-flowers of several colours ...
>
> (4.1.83–5)

At the sight of her suitor she 'straight sought the flood' (95), but he was on hand to save her. She then enters, singing and obsessing about Palamon's sexual prowess:

> For I must lose my maidenhead by cocklight; ...
> There is at least two hundred now with child by him –
> There must be four – yet I keep close for all this,
> Close as a cockle; and all these must be boys; ...
> I'll warrant ye, he had not so few last night
> As twenty to dispatch – he'll tickle't up
> In two hours, if his hand be in.
>
> (112, 128–30, 136–8)

This seems more of a parody than a homage to Ophelia. Fletcher evidently thought that he could risk making a lower-class character more sexually explicit, but it is plain to see why Shakespeare did not wish to revisit such an Ophelia-like scenario.

The Daughter's following scene (4.3) may well be by Shakespeare. It reverts to prose, and the sexual obsession is replaced first by her making classical references to Dido, Aeneas, Charon and Prosperpine, and then by an evocation of hell reminiscent of *King Lear* – 'such burning, frying, boiling, hissing, howling, chattering, cursing' (31–2) – which she risks by committing suicide for love. Her next speech – 'Lords and courtiers that have got maids with child, they are in this place' (40–1) – was omitted in the 1634 Quarto, presumably deemed politically contentious. This bitter and sophisticated satire sits uneasily with the character Fletcher has developed. Shakespeare's satirical vein continues with the Doctor's farcical diagnosis and cure, larded with latinate words and pompous phrases: her sense 'may return and settle again to execute their preordained faculties, but they are now in a most extravagant vagary' (70–2).

Fletcher takes over Shakespeare's Doctor's remedy – convincing her that Palamon is waiting for her – but turns it explicitly sexual, advising the Wooer: 'When your fit comes, fit her home, and presently' (5.2.11). The Jailer is alarmed by the prescription 'Lie with her if she asks you':

JAILER	Whoa there, doctor!
DOCTOR	Yes, in the way of cure.
JAILER	But first, by your leave,
	I'th' way of honesty.
DOCTOR	That's but a niceness.
	Ne'er cast your child away for honesty.
	Cure her first this way; then if she will be honest,
	She has the path before her.
JAILER	Thank ye, doctor.

(18–23)

The Jailer shows proper concern for his daughter's propriety, but is all too easily persuaded by the learned expert. His daughter accepts the Wooer as Palamon, and they go off to make love, with her haunting proviso that if it hurts her 'I'll cry' (112). It is a strangely improbable and misogynist denouement, though it pays lip service to contemporary medical theory that women deprived of sex were prone to fall ill or even mad. The Jailer's Daughter is also presented as a counterpart to Emilia, who thinks she will never fall in love with a man, while the Daughter falls in love immediately. Cold reluctance is pitted against hopeless adoration, though neither is allowed to choose her husband. Emilia, whose great love was another woman, Flavina, realizes she must submit to the winner of the kinsmen's duel – 'I had rather see a wren hawk at a fly / Than this decision' (5.3.2–3) – and at Arcite's death she is passed on to Palamon. The Daughter in turn submits to a Palamon substitute. Both are victims of the patriarchal need for women to be 'suitably' married.

Douglas Bruster sees the Daughter as 'a pivotal figure in Jacobean drama', on the grounds that folk culture in drama was dwindling by 1613, as rural characters and situations were being replaced by court and urban plots.[46] The countryside, once celebrated in entertainments like *The Blacksmith's Daughter* (1578) and *Fair Em, the Miller's Daughter of Manchester* (1590) (note how the daughter is defined by her father's occupation), in Lyly's plays, Thomas Lodge's tales, in Mopsa in Sidney's *Arcadia* (1593) and, more recently, in *The Winter's Tale*, was now regarded as an old-fashioned subject. The two plots, however, are not really integrated. The Daughter is never seen with Palamon or any figures from the main plot. Her language is distinct from both the courtiers and the other lower-class characters, though Shakespeare and Fletcher don't seem agreed on her level of sophistication. Her father is a cipher, well-meaning, even loving, but cowed by authority. She, however, is one of the strongly emotional females beloved of Jacobean dramatists, and one who, as time has passed, audiences find the most easy to identify with. It is moving to think that Shakespeare, in possibly his final play, still concerns himself with a daughter passing through great mental suffering and a near-death experience, but who survives, apparently happily, at the last.

5

Shakespeare and his daughters

Any attempt to trace the early lives of Shakespeare's daughters, Susanna and Judith, and their relationship to their father is mostly conjecture. It is not until their respective marriages and their father's will that we have a good deal of hard evidence, and even this is difficult to interpret. In November 1582 Shakespeare married the three-month pregnant Anne Hathaway: at twenty-six/seven she was the median age for brides around Stratford; at eighteen his age was the real anomaly.[1] In the period 1570–1630 in Stratford only three men are known to have married in their teens, and Shakespeare's marriage is the only 'shotgun' instance.[2] Anne would have joined her husband in the crowded house in Henley Street, and on 26 May 1583 her first-born was baptized Susanna, a fashionable name at the time. Less than a year later Anne was pregnant again, and on 2 February 1585 her twins were born, and named after their friends Judith and Hamnet Sadler. As there is no further record of baptisms it is possible that she was damaged by this twin birth. But it is also possible that her husband was increasingly absent, working perhaps as a tutor, schoolmaster, lawyer's clerk or, most probably, as an actor/writer in London.

The two girls could have been sent to a petty school, for which there is some contemporary evidence in Stratford:[3] Susanna could both read and write; Judith, judging by her wobbly squiggle on a 1611 deed, could not write, but might well have been able to read, that being considered the more important accomplishment for a girl (see p. 166–7). Their brother, Hamnet, may well have been enrolled at the King's New School, as his father presumably had been (the records have not survived). But in 1596 Hamnet fell ill and was buried on 11 August, aged eleven, his cause of death unknown (there was no recorded plague in the area that year). If Hamnet was the younger twin he may always have been weaker than Judith, who lived to the considerable age of seventy-seven. Shakespeare wrote nothing directly about his son, unlike Ben Jonson who wrote poems on the deaths of both his son and daughter,[4] but Constance's grief over her son Arthur (*King John*, 3.4.93–7) and the prominence given to the boy William Page (*The Merry Wives of Windsor*, 4.1), both probably written in 1596–7, may reflect his sense of loss. Susanna and Judith must have suffered greatly at their brother's death. Judith in particular may have felt guilty at being the twin left alive, may even have thought that her father wished it had been her, rather than his only son, that had died. What did the girls know of their father? We have no evidence that they ever visited London, may never have seen the plays (the last recorded payment to travelling players at Stratford was made in 1593).[5] Their father may have told them the stories, read the plays or poems to them or they may have read some of his plays in quarto, but it is equally possible they knew nothing of them.

In the winter of 1597/8 the family moved out of Henley St into the much larger New Place, with its ten rooms, two gardens and an orchard. The following year, when Shakespeare wrote Rosalind in *As You Like It*, Susanna would have been sixteen. He then followed up this investment in Stratford with purchases of land and tithes in 1602 and 1605. Susanna and Judith must have felt that all this demonstrated their family's growing affluence and importance in the town.[6] On 5 June 1607 Susanna, aged twenty-four, married John Hall, eight years her senior. Hall came from the Bedfordshire village of Carlton and had taken an MA at Cambridge, though he had no doctoral degree. It is likely that he moved to Stratford at some point, for Shakespeare would not have chosen a son-in-law who was going to take his elder daughter and main heir out of the area. Hall had strong puritan leanings, and it is possible that Susanna shared these, which might account for the summons she had had the previous year to appear before the Vicar's Court for failing to take the sacrament at Easter at Holy Trinity. The case was dropped, so Susanna evidently promised to conform, and there is every sign that she continued to do so, though this incident is not conclusive evidence of her religious affiliations. The marriage agreement has not survived, and this is a great loss as it might fill in certain gaps in Shakespeare's subsequent will. A 1625 document stated that Shakespeare gave the 107 acres of land that he had bought in Old Stratford in 1602 for £320 'with his daughter in marriage to Mr Hall of Stratford', and this seems very probable. Thirty-seven and a half weeks after the marriage Susanna had a daughter named Elizabeth, baptized on 21 February 1608, so conception presumably took place after the trothplight. The couple may then have lived either at New Place or a house nearby, which cannot have been Hall's Croft, since dendochronolgical evidence shows it was not built till 1613.[7] It was a period of both joy and mourning for the family, as Shakespeare's favourite younger brother Edmund had died in December 1607 and Shakespeare's mother Mary was buried on 9 September 1608.[8] With the Globe shut for sixteen months through plague, Shakespeare may have spent much of 1608 in Stratford. Whether he ever formally retired to Warwickshire is a much debated issue, but by 1613 both his remaining younger brothers, Gilbert and Richard, had died, and he may have accepted that his own powers were waning.

Susanna had no further children after Elizabeth, or at least none that survived long enough to be baptized. Shakespeare's hopes of heirs now rested on this one granddaughter, or any children that Judith might produce. But six years after Susanna's marriage a scandal threatened her position. In June 1613 John Lane 'reported' (we don't know how) that Susanna 'had the running of the reins and had been naught with Rafe Smith at John Palmer'. Accusations of adultery were a common way of attacking women at the time, and it may represent either jealousy or misunderstanding on Lane's part. Katherine Duncan-Jones suggests that Hall may have been treating Susanna for infertility, and that this was misconstrued as venereal disease, 'especially since John Hall often made use of the New World bark called "quiacum" originally imported as a treatment for syphilis'.[9] It is possible that Lane, from an old gentry family, was using it as a way of attacking the puritan Halls. In any event the Halls brought a suit in the Consistory Court at Worcester five weeks later, and Lane was declared excommunicate.

All through her twenties Judith remained unmarried, though she too, as the wealthy Shakespeare's daughter, was a good catch. Finally on 10 February 1616 she married Thomas Quiney. On the face of it this was a perfectly acceptable match. The families had been friends for decades and had many connections. The Quineys were mercers, sellers of fine cloth, but when trade declined they had turned to malting and had been caught, like Shakespeare, hoarding malt in 1598. In October of that same year Richard Quiney, Thomas's father, wrote to Shakespeare, his 'loving good friend and countryman', for a loan of £30, though the letter may never have been sent. In 1602 Richard, as Stratford bailiff, was killed while trying to stop a brawl. His youngest son, George, was then only two, and it is possible that Judith, then aged seventeen, entered the Quiney household to help out and perhaps learn the country mercer's trade,[10] though the only evidence for this is her mark on a 1611 Quiney deed. She might therefore have known Thomas, aged thirteen in 1602, from his early teens. At thirty-one she was an elderly bride, but it is possible that they had had an understanding for some years.

Nevertheless there are various factors that make the marriage seem hastily put together and, perhaps in Shakespeare's eyes, undesirable. There was no prior reading of the banns. They applied for a licence to allow them to marry in Lent not from the Bishop of Worcester, as Shakespeare had, but from the vicar of Holy Trinity. A month later, on 15 March, Walter Nixon informed against them to the Consistory Court of Worcester for marrying without the correct licence. Thomas did not attend the hearing and was excommunicated. Ten days later the probable reason for the hasty wedding became evident. On 26 March Thomas was called before the Vicar's Court in Stratford to answer for one Margaret Wheeler's pregnancy and subsequent death in childbirth. Thomas confessed, was condemned for fornication and his penance was to stand at the church door in a white sheet for three Sundays. This was later commuted to giving a crown to the poor of the parish, and even this may have been waived later. Judith's hasty marriage may, therefore, have two possible explanations. Realizing that her father was dying and had made a will, she may have wanted to marry to regularize her situation, and perhaps persuade her father to make her a larger settlement (she must have known how generous he had been to Susanna in her marriage settlement). In fact the day before the Vicar's Court hearing, Shakespeare had altered his will to ring-fence his settlement on Judith, thus making it harder for Thomas to benefit. Secondly, Judith, knowing that Thomas had had a relationship with Margaret Wheeler and got her pregnant, may have thought it best to wed him before he became a father and felt duty bound to marry the mother.

Shakespeare may have approved the Quiney match, and understood Thomas's temptation in his mid-twenties to sow some wild oats. But it seems more likely that he was not happy with his daughter's choice. Thomas was not on the face of it a good match. Even if Judith had not lived in the Quiney household, her mark on the 1611 deed shows that she knew the family well. Why then this long delay? The deed was for the sale of a house in Wood Street, and with the money Thomas took on the lease of the Atwood tavern in High Street, not a position with strong prospects. There may have been some form of understanding between them even then, which she knew her parents did not approve. It is also possible that Judith's feeling for Thomas were not reciprocated until Thomas, desperate at Margaret Wheeler's pregnancy, thought marriage to the daughter of a wealthy father was the best way out of his situation, and Judith grabbed the opportunity. Either way it suggests that there was some long drawn-out tension or rift between Judith, her parents and Thomas over her future.

In January 1616 Shakespeare got his friend and attorney, the elderly Francis Collins, to make a draft of his will, though it was not then signed and executed. It seems to indicate his attitude to his two daughters. Susanna and John Hall were the sole executors, Anne and Judith were ignored. Susanna was left New Place, the two tenements in Henley Street and all his 'barns stables orchards garden lands tenements and hereditaments' in Stratford, Old Stratford, Bishopton and Welcombe, plus the Blackfriars London house bought in 1613. After Susanna's decease these were to go to her heirs male, and Shakespeare allowed for seven of them, so he evidently had not abandoned the thought of grandsons. To John Hall and Susanna he left 'all the rest of my goods chattels leases plate jewels and household stuff'. Susanna's daughter, Elizabeth (then aged seven) was left all his plate. There is no mention in this January draft of Anne Shakespeare. If she was entitled to one third of the estate under 'dower right' – and there is dispute about whether this operated in the Midlands – there is no mention of it. The fact that Shakespeare's £140 purchase of the Blackfriars tenement in 1613 was put in the hands of trustees suggests that it was not to be included in her dower rights. The Halls may have joined Anne in New Place, though Greer suggests she may have gone into a Chapel Lane cottage which Judith had been made to surrender in return for £50.[11]

The first legatee mentioned is in fact Judith, perhaps because her portion was hedged about with far more provisos than her sister's. This first page was also rewritten, so it presumably already contained a number of changes. Even so there are further alterations. One hundred and fifty pounds is left to 'my son in L', which is crossed out and 'daughter Judith' substituted, suggesting that Shakespeare knew of the impending marriage, approved the choice and then changed his mind, presumably when the Margaret Wheeler scandal broke. If his executors decide, Judith can be paid £10 per annum, and here is later inserted 'in discharge of her marriage portion', which implies that Susanna can ensure her sister, or her husband, doesn't spend it all in one go. Judith is also to get a further £150 if she, or her children, are living three years after Shakespeare's death, and this was also to be in trust at £15 per annum. If Judith died without issue then £100 went, not to her husband, but to Elizabeth Hall, and the remaining £50 to Shakespeare's sister Joan, who otherwise had to make do with £20, Shakespeare's 'wearing apparel' and £5 for each of her children – not a generous legacy to his only surviving sibling.

It is clear that Shakespeare was making every effort to preserve the family money for the Halls, Judith and their children. Thomas Quiney, however, could not be entirely left out, perhaps at the insistence of the Quiney family. At the end of three years if any husband Judith has can 'assure unto her and the issue of her body lands answerable to the [£150] portion', then the £150 can be paid to the husband. This was presumably to ensure that if the Quineys couldn't come up with such a sum, Thomas wouldn't be able to get his hands on any of Judith's money. There are a number of other not over-generous additions, mainly to buy rings for friends, including Heminges, Condell and Burbage, and also, most famously, the second-best bed to his wife. If Anne was to move into the Chapel Lane cottage, perhaps this was to ensure she took their favourite bed with her. The will draft has certain tantalizing omissions: the absence of any mention of Shakespeare's books and papers (though a 'study of books' was eventually left to Thomas Nash),[12] of his shares in the theatre company (unless they had been sold in 1611) and of any specific bequests to Anne apart from the bed.

Susanna is his main heir and, by Stratford standards, a very wealthy woman, or to be more exact the Halls are a wealthy couple. Shakespeare hopes very much she will have further sons. It may be, as Stephen Greenblatt conjectures, that 'the woman who most intensely appealed to Shakespeare in his life was twenty years younger than he: his daughter Susanna'.[13] Younger daughters usually come off badly, and it is difficult to assess the significance of Judith's £25 per annum. On the one hand it is a very handsome dowry by local standards, on the other it is strikingly less than her sister's. The will, however, does take great care to ensure her interests are safeguarded: it does not suggest that Shakespeare disliked or distrusted Judith, merely that he had reservations about her marriage. Of course it would be dramatically tidy to characterize the first-born Susanna as his favourite daughter, reliable, conscientious and determined, ready to marry a pillar of the community of her father's choosing, and Judith as the problem second-born, difficult and rebellious, marrying against her parents' wishes a man with little vocation, but the evidence is hardly conclusive. Fathoming Shakespeare's relationship with Anne has similar problems. Some form of settlement must have been devised for her, but the evidence has not survived. The absence in the will, however, of any conventional loving appellation, such as 'my beloved wife', is chilling, and suggests the relationship had been distant, even troubled, for some time.

Shakespeare's apparent concern about Judith's marriage proved justified. In July 1616, with Judith's inheritance secure, the Quineys moved from the Atwood tavern to a larger tavern/wine shop at the corner with Bridge Street Thomas began to climb the civic ladder, becoming burgess, constable and then town chamberlain, but his accounts were rejected as defective in 1623 and he progressed no further. In 1631 he was fined for swearing and 'suffering townsmen to tipple in his house' at forbidden times. Two years later his lease was taken over by John Hall and Elizabeth's husband, Thomas Nash. Judith presumably still had her £25 per annum, but they may have been given an allowance by Thomas's wealthy brother Richard or, more improbably, by the Halls. Judith's first son, Shakespeare, born in November 1616, died in infancy on 8 May 1617. The choice of name would suggest that Judith wished to proclaim her connection to her famous father, or even, less charitably, to advertise to Susanna her ability to bear a son. Two more boys followed, but both were to die in 1639 without issue, aged only twenty-one and nineteen. Judith lived on through the Civil Wars to die in February 1662.

Elizabeth remained Susanna's only child, and married young in 1626 at the age of eighteen to the considerably older Thomas Nash. After his death in 1647 she married again, and died in 1670 as Lady Barnard, still childless and having abandoned New Place. The direct line of descent from Shakespeare died out after two generations. John Hall died in 1635 at the age of sixty, having sold off the Stratford tithes and the Blackfriars tenement to no great profit. The inscription on his tomb in the chancel of Holy Trinity records that he married Susanna, 'the daughter of Will Shakespeare, gent'. There is an addition in smaller print after 'daughter' of '& co-heir', which, if Judith was the instigator, may imply that she felt she was being written out of the family history. If so, it suggests a fraught relationship between the sisters. Susanna, who is described as 'faithful wife', lived on another fourteen years, dying in July 1649 at the age of sixty-six. She lies by her husband in the chancel. There was no room left for Judith, whose tomb out in the churchyard is now lost. Susanna's tombstone records (perhaps written by herself, perhaps by her sister?) that she was 'witty above her sex' – an epitaph sufficiently unusual to be taken seriously – and that 'some of Shakespeare was in that', an interesting testament to the continuing status and popularity of her father's writings.

6

Fathers and daughters in contemporary society

There is no other shift but women must needs stoop and understand the ruin and confusion of mankind came in on their side ... There is no other way but for them to stoop and to bear patiently the subjection God laid upon them

CALVIN

The Bible, and in particular the story of Adam and Eve, was often quoted to uphold the subjection of women. Eve was the weak, insubordinate, untrustworthy daughter, who disobeyed her Heavenly Father and caused all future generations to be deprived of an earthly paradise. Morality and Saints plays had for centuries divided women into whore and virgin, either weak, irrational and shrewish, or patient, silent and chaste. John Knox railed against the 'monstrous regiment' of women in 1558: 'Nature, I say, doth paint them forth to be weak, frail, impatient, feeble and foolish: and experience hath declared them to be unconstant, variable, cruel and lacking the spirit of counsel and regiment.'[1]

James I learnt from his master, writing in his *Satire against Women*:

Even so all women are of nature vain
And cannot keep no secret unrevealed
And where at once they do conceive disdain
They are unable to be reconciled
Fulfilled with talk and clatters but respect
And often times of small or none effect.

But the late sixteenth-century saw a strong reaction to this assault. On the biblical front it was pointed out that even Paul wrote, 'There is neither male and female; for ye are all one in Christ Jesus' (Gal. 3.28), and that both Adam and Eve sinned against God, both their eyes were opened and both were expelled from Eden. Christopher Newstead wrote of Eve in 1620: 'What if she were an instrumental cause of our fall, was she not as much the cause of our rising? But we all sooner forget benefits than injuries; we are eagle-eyed in espying their faults, but dark-sighted owls in perceiving their virtues.'[2]

Puritan writers argued for the spiritual equality of man and wife and for domestic comradeship, but stopped short of social, political and economic equality. Robert Cleaver insisted that the family was a political unit; 'A household is as it were a little commonwealth, by the good government whereof God's glory may be advanced.'[3] The household was, however, largely under male domination. William Whateley, a popular puritan divine, wrote in his *Bride Book* (1617), 'the wife is indeed an inferior, but very near and very familiar'. Few would have been as liberal as Montaigne when he wrote:

> I saw that male and female are cast in the same mould: save for education and custom the difference between them is not great. In *The Republic* Plato summons both men and women indifferently to a community of all studies, administration, offices and vocations both in peace and war ...[4]

Women had to be cast in the inferior mould in order of course that men could remain superior. Edmund Tilney, Master of Revels, wrote in *The Flower of Friendship* (1568): 'For indeed both divine and human laws in our religion giveth the man absolute authority over the woman in all places'. Religious and secular texts emphasized the same dichotomy: men rule, women obey; men speak, women are silent; men provide through outside work, women keep the house. St Paul was adamant: 'Wives, submit yourselves unto your own husbands, as unto the Lord. For the husband is the head of the wife, even as Christ is the head of the church' (Eph. 5.22–3). Daughters, therefore, knew what their marital obligations would be – as Katherine and Portia clearly express. Unmarried, the law gave them virtually no rights. On the contrary both law and custom gave their fathers wide powers of coercion and authority. The legal rights of all women were defined only in terms of their marital status, when at least the law governing dowries gave them some financial control. The paterfamilias in theory reigned supreme. James I wrote: 'The state of monarchy is the supremest thing upon earth ... Kings are compared to fathers in families: for a king is truly *parens patriae*, the politic father of his people.' King and father, however, do have obligations. 'The father, of his fatherly duty, is bound to care for the nourishing, education and virtuous government of his children: even so is the king bound to care for all his subjects.'[5] Not that James was a good example of paternal care: he had little time for his wife or for his intelligent, accomplished daughter Elizabeth.

By the mid-sixteenth century the father's role as unquestioned patriarch was under pressure. Children were increasingly questioning their father's absolute power. Local court records showed considerable preoccupation with women who were a threat to the patriarchal system.[6] The many shrill denunciations of young women and men's independence of mind and action suggest that youthful autonomy was on the march. Keith Thomas argues that 'the sixteenth and seventeenth centuries are conspicuous for a sustained desire to subordinate persons in their teens and twenties and to delay their equal participation in the adult world'.[7] The great increase in the population also meant that parents were often outnumbered by their children and were uncertain about controlling them – that is if the parent were still alive. Life expectancy in London has been calculated at as little as 22.3 years, so that by the age of twenty 47 per cent of London women had suffered the death of their parents, and in particular their mothers, since so many died in child-birth. One in four households with a new-born child had a single male parent, but when mothers survived they often outlived their husbands, as Anne did Shakespeare. Consequently there are many instances of mothers arranging their daughters' marriages, a situation Shakespeare's plays mostly avoid.[8] Wealthy fathers, uncertain about living long enough to see their daughters married, often made bequests conditional upon strict obedience, sometimes even nominating a husband. The second Earl of Southampton ordered both portion and maintenance to be cut off if his daughter disobeyed her executors.

Although fathers might still see themselves as demi-gods, even James I allowed that they had responsibilities. In 1598 Robert Cleaver wrote that parents had four duties: to instruct their children in the fear of the Lord; to rear them to love virtue and to hate vice; to be examples of godliness to them; and to keep them from idleness. The influential writer Giovani Michele Bruto argued that fathers and mothers were not the best people to bring up their children because 'their wisdom and virtue is often overcome ... by the great affection they bear unto them'.[9] Bruto goes on to assert that daughters should be kept away from all men, prattling serving maids and children of their own age (though others thought it permissible for children to play with their own sex). Parents must never kiss or embrace their children, and must not condone or laugh at unseemly behaviour. The girl's bed should be clean and hard, her diet simple, of common, unspiced food, her only drink water and her clothing simple. Above all, she should never be idle. Whether she should ever be beaten was a subject of much debate. Whether many families adhered to this strict regimen is doubtful, but it gives some idea of the disciplined upbringing a daughter of a reasonably affluent family might endure.

Montaigne had a far more gentle view in 'On the Affection of Fathers for Their Children', which may be more typical of the liberal intelligentsia:

> I condemn all violence in the education of tender minds which are being trained for honour and freedom ... Leonor, an only daughter ... has reached the age of six or more (her mother's gentleness readily predis-posing her that way) without our having used in her upbringing and in the punishment of her childish faults anything but words – gentle ones at that. Do we want to be loved by our children? Do we want to remove any occasion for their wishing us dead ... then let us within reason enrich

their lives with whatever we have at our disposal ... I would try to have
gentle relations with my children and so encourage in them an active love
and unfeigned affection for me, something easily achieved in children of
a well-born nature.[10]

In any age the daughter occupies a unique position in the family; she is the
exchangeable figure, the 'temporary sojourner'. She will only acquire status by
leaving the family through marriage. Father and daughter are the two figures
'most symmetrically proportioned in terms of gender, age, authority and
cultural privilege'.[11] As Lévi-Strauss was later to write: 'The total relationship
of exchange which constitutes marriage is not established between a man and
a woman ... but between two groups of men, and the woman figures only as
one of the objects in the exchange, not as one of the partners.'[12]

If the father controls the transaction, even chooses his daughter's
husband, then he retains in some measure his primary claim. He has not
been defeated by a rival male, his daughter has not been allowed to choose
another male over him, he has made a magnanimous gift. This notion of
the daughter as an object of exchange is explored by Shakespeare in a
succession of plays, from *The Two Gentlemen of Verona* to *The Tempest*.

One of the prime threats to paternal authority was a daughter's sexuality.
Female chastity was a prerequisite of the patriarchal order, since it was
recognized that sexual desire could not finally be controlled. Montaigne
thought, as Shakespeare also clearly did, that sex was at the centre of
things: 'All the world's motions bend and yield to this conjunction, it is a
matter everywhere infused; and a centre whereto all lines come, all things
look.'[13] One means patriarchy had to control women was to brand them as
sexually voracious. A common condition of women was, therefore, invented
called 'womb hysteria', 'an immoderate and unbridled desire to copulate, so
strong and unquenchable that the woman appears mad and delirious as a
result of this excessive and insatiable appetite' (Mercatus).[14] Church courts
record that one in seven of the population were denounced for various
kinds of sexual deviance – as happened to both Susanna Shakespeare and
Thomas Quiney (see p. 157).[15] Men and women were, however, treated
differently: women were more commonly called whoremongers than men
were named as fornicators; JPs and constables could whip or imprison
strumpets and bawds, men often got off with public penance or a small fine.

Virginity was, therefore, essential to a daughter's position in the world,
as Laertes points out to Ophelia. Bruto held that chastity, or 'virtue',
was 'the flower of manners, the honour of the body, the ornament and
splendour of the feminine sex, the integrity of the blood, the faith of their
kind, and the proclaimer of the sincerity and candour of a fair soul'.[16] More
prosaically, in matters of inheritance it was considered vital to be certain
of the legitimacy of the first-born. Thomas Becon in his *Catechism* (1564)
called the Bible to witness: 'Let them remember what chanced to Dinah,
Jacob's daughter, through going abroad to see vain sights (Gen. 34.1–2).

Was she not deflowered and lost her virginity? Virginity once lost, what remaineth safe and praiseworthy in a maid? The highest, best and greatest dowry that a maid can bring to her husband is honesty ...'[17] England was commonly known abroad for sexual laxity and adultery. Illegitimate births doubled in Shakespeare's lifetime, though they remained under 5 per cent of the total number of births.[18] Small wonder that so many plays portray a father locking his daughter within the house.

Chastity might be next to godliness, but a daughter had to have further attributes. Robert Cleaver wrote in 1598 that, after chastity, the six vital feminine characteristics were report, look (outward appearance), talk, apparel, company (her associates) and education.[19] Silence, modesty and humility were the signs that a woman was chaste. Girls should let elders speak first and never interrupt them, rise when they enter a room, stand while they sit and curtsey in token of subjection. A silent and inconspicuous woman, however, presented a problem: what lay behind her inscrutability? As Milton later wrote: 'Who knows not that the bashful muteness of a virgin may oftimes hide all the unliveliness and natural sloth which is really unfit for conversation?'[20] Juan Luis Vives had written a century earlier that in her behaviour a girl could hardly win:

> If thou talk little in company folks think thou canst but little good: if thou speak much, they reckon thee light; if thou speak uncunningly, thou shalt be called a shrew; if thou answer not quickly, thou shalt be called proud or ill brought up ... if thou sit with demure countenance, thou art called a dissembler ...[21]

In Dekker and Middleton's *The Roaring Girl* (c. 1607–10) Moll Firth's declaration that 'I please myself and care not who loves me' (5.1.349) was the ultimate challenge to accepted female behaviour. Moll's dressing as a man reflected a growing trend. Philip Stubbes had complained in 1583 that some women 'have doublets and jerkins as men have ... yet they blush not to wear it: and if they could as well change their sex ... I think they would as verily become men in deed as now they degenerate from godly sober women ...'.[22] Deuteronomy 22.5 expressly called cross-dressing an abomination unto the Lord, and in the 1620s James I was forced to condemn it (Shakespeare is careful never to suggest that his cross-dressed women would prefer to be men). Demureness was probably the safest option. Acquiring any form of reputation was dangerous – 'the most honest woman is least spoken of' (Barnaby Rich). The demure Hero and the outspoken Beatrice are thus contrasted in *Much Ado About Nothing*. Beauty was attractive to suitors, but gained a woman a reputation for arrogance and profligacy. A favourite proverb ran, 'A fair woman is a paradise to the eye, a purgatory to the purse, and a hell to the soul.'

Daughters had to be kept busy. If they were idle at home they might be gossiping with servants, or reading erotic or subversive literature. If she left the house, 'as oft as a maid goeth forth among people, so often she cometh in judgement and extreme peril of her beauty, honesty, demureness, wit, shamefastness and virtue ...'.[23] It was also of paramount importance that she was prepared for what would probably be her life's work – running a household. Even an enlightened educationalist like Richard Mulcaster wrote: 'I think it, and know it, to be a principal commendation in a woman: to be able to govern and direct her household, to look to her house and family, to provide and keep necessaries ... to know the force of her kitchen.'[24] So there were a multitude of skills for a middle-class daughter to learn: sewing, spinning, weaving and turning flax and wool into clothes; milking, butter and cheese making; cooking and baking; washing and mending clothes. Unless a woman knew how to do these things herself, it was argued, how could she order and regulate her servants?

How much education was good for daughters was a fraught subject. Mulcaster thought the idea of schooling girls was important so long as it did not interfere with schooling boys. He gave four reasons: it was customary in England; it was the duty of parents to educate all their children; girls' natural abilities made them apt; and historically there had been many good results. Education had been fashionable under Katherine of Aragon, who had supervised her daughter Mary's classical education. Queen Elizabeth had turned out a paragon, knowing Latin, Greek, Hebrew, French, Dutch, Spanish and Italian; and studying maths, astronomy, politics, history, geography, architecture, rhetoric, philosophy and divinity. Thomas More had established a home school for his sons and daughters and other dependent children. His system 'gave his female students spiritual and ethical autonomy', 'a capacity for moral judgement' and 'the power of wise speech', all meant to free them from 'the bondage to male authority' characterizing 'conventional marriage'.[25] And yet for all this humanist fervour for gender equality, there were few who did not think that women were in some respects inferior. Even More subscribed to the idea that women could only achieve 'near-equality' with men. Mulcaster wrote that:

> though the girls seem commonly to have a quicker ripening in wit than boys have, for all that seeming yet it is not so. Their natural weakness, which cannot long hold, delivers very soon ... Besides, their brains be not so much charged, neither with weight nor with multitude of matters, as boys' heads be, and therefore like empty cask they make the greater noise ...

Mulcaster's four essentials for girls were 'reading well, writing fair, singing sweet, playing fine', and many an enlightened father would have agreed this was sufficient.[26] A middle-class girl might attend a petty or dame's school and learn to read, a girl of higher birth might be tutored at home. But there were many parents who thought education dangerous, as it made girls arrogant and unruly: Ovid, Catullus and Virgil were too full of illicit love and adultery. 'Books of Robin Hood, Bevis of Hampton, Troilus and such like fables do but kindle in liars like lies and wanton love.'[27] Learning had two purposes: recreation (and girls should be too busy acquiring housewifely skills); and profit (which is men's work). Schools trained boys for the law, commerce and the priesthood, and as all these were closed to girls what was the point of their even learning to write? As a result it has been calculated that little more than 10 per cent of women were literate in 1600.[28]

Marriage was, however, considered more important for a woman than celibacy: the Bible pronounced 'Whoso findeth a wife findeth a good thing, and obtaineth favour of the Lord' (Prov. 18.22). Marriage, reproduction and inheritance were the basic building blocks of society. For a girl 'marriage signified a passage into adulthood, a mark of social maturity ... It assigned new privileges, advantages and obligations. It redefined social and sexual roles, rearranged patriarchal obligations, and conferred new duties of status, authority and dependency.'[29] A woman could now raise children, hire servants, keep accounts and run a household, without rivals to her authority: small wonder then that it was the objective of most young women. Though her income and possessions would pass into the control of her husband, he had responsibilities to look after her, even to the extent of paying her debts. It has been calculated that in the sixteenth century 90 per cent of adults would marry, some several times, and yet so high was the death-rate that at any one time 50 per cent of women might be single.[30] Widows, rich and poor, populate plays of the period.

A law of 1456 laid down that 'at her 7th year the father may marry [his daughter] ... A woman married at 12 cannot disagree afterwards, but if she be married younger, she may dissent till she be 14.' Teenage marriages, however, were found only among the nobility, and by the late 1500s only 5 to 6 per cent of peers wed at fifteen or younger, so that Shakespeare's youthful brides are not representative of their class. In any case early consummation was not encouraged, as it was thought to impair a man's physical and intellectual development, enfeeble the mother and produce stunted children. Sometimes after a young marriage the girl stayed with her parents, while the boy was sent off abroad, where he was safe from being trapped in an 'unsuitable' marriage. The Canons of 1604 raised the age of consent from twelve for girls and fourteen for boys to twenty-one, thus giving parents even more control. For the bulk of the population, however, marriage came much later. It was important that the couple, in most cases the male, had the economic means to set up a household, and since apprenticeships could last seven years the mid-twenties were the more usual marriage age. In the Stratford area, of 106 known marriages between 1570 and 1630 the greatest number of men and women married at between twenty-four and twenty-six.[31]

Daughters were not to be bullied into marriage, or so the enlightened wisdom went. Luther had written: 'To force together two persons who have neither liking nor love for each other [would produce an] eternal hell and lifetime of tragedy.'[32] For Puritans marriage was a blessing, and the church at large held it should be 'free and uncompelled', and that a marriage could in extreme cases be invalidated if there was evidence of compulsion. Yet in the 1660s John Evelyn was still writing that 'so many forced matches make fained love and cause real unhappiness', so the woman's right of veto was not clearly established (and it is of course the stuff of Restoration comedy).[33] It remained, however, a father's principal duty to find a suitable match for a daughter. The Garden of Eden was often cited, where Eve had been the choice not of Adam but of God the father. Daughters might rebel, parents might disagree, siblings and relatives would sometimes interfere, causing further family splits. It was the perennial stuff of drama, though in many instances parents saw their children not as property, but as their 'comfort and delight', and were ready to accede to their wishes. The tyrannical father, beloved of playwrights, was not always in evidence, since it has been calculated 50 per cent of young people were fatherless by the time it came to marriage. Mothers, if they survived childbirth, tended to live longer than men, but many twenty-year-olds were orphans. The young woman with the greatest freedom of choice was the orphan left her portion without strings – as the Countess Olivia recklessly enjoys hers. Courtship was the young man's responsibility. He made visits, proffered gifts and made his intentions clear. The woman had to remain largely passive, but there were manifold ways of signalling or withholding her interest. Alberti counsels that the woman can prevail with a reluctant male with 'a sweet carriage of countenance, as also a comely, discreet and modest presence: one piercing look heats and enkindles the dullest desire, one modest amorous glance awakens sleepy thoughts, fetcheth fire from the flint, and maketh the heart as yielding, as your own can crave enjoying'.[34] It was difficult, however, for a young woman to know how forward to be. In Beaumont and Fletcher's *The Wild-Goose Chase* (1621) Lillia Bianca complains:

> You see, sir, though sometimes we are grave and silent,
> And put on sadder dispositions.
> Yet we are compounded of free parts, and sometimes too
> Our lighter, airy, and out fiery mettles
> Break out, and show themselves ...
> We followed your directions, we did rarely,
> We were stately, coy, demure, careless, light, giddy
> And played at all points: this, you swore, would carry.

(2.2)

If a couple were agreed a contract might be entered into, known as a handfasting, trothplighting or spousal. A contract *in verba de future* was a promise to marry in the future, expressed by the words 'I will', but usually conditional, as for example 'when I inherit my land': nevertheless this could be binding. A contract *in verba de praesenti* made an indissoluble commitment expressed by the words 'I do', or 'I do take thee to wife.' If this was before witnesses, with or without the parents present, they were legally married. Such contracts, however, were sometimes disputed through being poorly worded, inadequately witnessed or the discovery of undisclosed impediments. Angelo pulls out of his contracted marriage to Mariana when she loses her fortune, 'pretending in her discoveries of dishonour' (*Measure for Measure*, 3.1.228–9). Although these contracts were legally sanctioned in the ecclesiastical courts, the Church considered the practice inadequate. They wanted an Order of Holy Matrimony in five steps: a legal contract, a formal betrothal, banns in church, a church wedding and finally consummation. Couples who evaded this could be fined, or even excommunicated, though it didn't invalidate the marriage. This was all codified in the 1604 ecclesiastical canons. In fact most couples by 1600 did eventually go to church – and this always seems to be envisaged in Shakespeare's plays. But many contracted couples considered themselves 'married in the eyes of God', despite the fact that legally pre-marital sex was fornication and could be punished. Parish registers show that at least a fifth of all brides were pregnant when they came to church.[35]

Many married couples were no doubt loving and supportive, but the law still allowed that 'the husband hath dominion over his wife, and may keep her by force within the bounds of duty, and may beat her', though not in a 'violent and cruel manner'.[36] It was said a man might legally beat 'an outlaw, a traitor, a pagan, his villain, and his wife'. William Whateley wrote in *A Bride Bush* (1617), 'The whole duty of the wife ... is to acknowledge her inferiority, the next to carry herself as inferior.' She must obey even a drunken, brawling husband, for 'it is not for a prisoner to break prison at his pleasure, because he has met with a rough jailer'. Daughters might regard marriage as an ultimate goal, as they do in Shakespeare's plays, both comic and tragic, but they had to be aware that even the wealthy Portia, 'Lord / Of this fair mansion, master of my servants, / Queen o'er myself' (167–9), would feel obliged to tell the penniless Bassanio:

> Happiest of all, is that her gentle spirit
> Commits itself to yours to be directed,
> As from her lord, her governor, her king.
> Myself, and what is mine, to you and yours
> Is now converted.

(The Merchant of Venice, 3.2.163–7)

7

Fathers and daughters in drama 1585–1620

The Plautine model of the tyrannical *senex* and the daughter out to marry a man of her choice was the template that most dramatists of the period adopted, and though in the following decades there were sophisticated variations on this father-daughter theme no one was to break free of this model more successfully than Shakespeare. In 1590 the dramatist most concerned with the Plautine template was John Lyly, who wrote exclusively for the boys companies, and Shakespeare evidently studied his plays intensely. Lyly's comedies, written in prose noted for its wit and eloquence, are generally set in mythical worlds where heroism and enduring love predominate – not a pattern Shakespeare was to follow.[1] More to his taste was Lyly's siding with the daughter in his treatment of the father-daughter relationship. In *Love's Metamorphosis* (1586/8) a poor farmer, Erischthon, sells his daughter Protea to a rich merchant, 'who knows no other god than gold'. Protea appeals to Neptune, who obliges by turning her into a fisherman. Her father then rejoices at her escape and urges her to 'find and enjoy' her true love, Petulus. In similar vein Livia in *Mother Bombie* (1590) rebels against her father's choice with forthright eloquence:

> Our parents take great care to make us ask blessing and say grace when we are little ones, and growing to years of judgment they deprive us of the greatest blessing ... the liberty of our minds; they give us pap with a spoon before we can speak, and when we speak for that we love, pap with a hatchet ... Nature hath made me his child, not his slave.
>
> (1.3.99–100, 101–2, 111)

In *Midas* (1590) Sophronia, the embodiment of chaste affection, is openly critical of her avaricious father: 'Ambition hath but two steps: the lowest, blood, the highest envy. Both these hath my unhappy father climbed, digging mines of gold with the lives of men' (2.1.103–6). In *The Woman in the Moon* (1594?) the chief deity is female, and her most important act of creation is the first female human – not a concept to appeal to the Christian Church.

In *Galatea* (1591/2?) Lyly takes his rebellious daughters to a further extreme, beyond anything Shakespeare later attempted. Two fathers separately contrive to disguise their daughters as boys to prevent their being chosen as a peace-offering to Neptune. The two 'boys' fall in love, though each suspects the other is female. Venus decides they should marry, and to facilitate this she will turn one of them into a male (a same-sex wedding was beyond even Lyly's daring), though the audience are tantalized by Venus not revealing which one she will choose. Lyly also adds an admission of incestuous desire on the part of one father, who defends himself on the grounds that 'Old fancies crave young nurses, and frosty years must be thawed by youthful fires' (4.1.58–9). Lyly's fathers are largely stereotypes of no great interest, but his daughters are a major influence on later dramatists. They speak directly and naturally, are frank about their sexual desires and superior in wit and intellect to their male lovers.

None of Lyly's contemporaries wrote about women with the same degree of passion and insight, with the exception of Robert Greene. Thomas Kyd in *The Spanish Tragedy* (c. 1587) has Bellimperia, forced by her father to marry Balthazar, the killer of two of her former lovers, stab both Balthazar and herself. Her relationship with the grieving Hieronimo and her murdering brother Lorenzo is examined in detail, but her uncaring father is little more than a plot device. George Peele digs deep into misogyny in *The Old Wives Tale* (c. 1593) with a father whose wife's tongue 'wearied me alive', and now has two daughters, the one 'curst as a wasp', and the other 'foul and ill-faced'. Christopher Marlowe influenced all the writers of the period, and *Titus Andronicus* and the *Henry VI*s owe much to him, but daughters only feature in *The Jew of Malta* (c. 1590), where he presents Barabas and Abigail as black and white. Abigail is beautiful, scarce fourteen, obedient and devoted to her father, ready to steal back his lost money. Barabas contrives to kill off her Christian lovers, and when she converts poisons her and the entire nunnery with the comment 'I grieve because she lived so long' (4.1.9). Father and daughter are centre-stage, but their relationship becomes farcical melodrama. Shakespeare's treatment of the same plot is more nuanced and realistic, but in many ways he eschews the wild, experimental daring of both Kyd and Marlowe.

Robert Greene, however, was considerably more interested in women, and Shakespeare's comedies follow Greene in having semi-serious main plots, comic sub-plots, alternation of verse and prose, with romantic love as the focal point. In *Orlando Furioso* (c. 1591) the Emperor of Africa allows his daughter Angelica to choose freely from among six suitors, 'for trust me, daughter, like of whom thou please, / Thou satisfied, my thoughts shall be at ease' (1.1.138–9). Her choice of Orlando, the suitor of lowest status, causes her to be slandered by his rivals, and her father disowns her as a 'damned adulteress', but all ends in happy reconciliation. *Friar*

Bacon and Friar Bungay (c. 1590) has probably the closest relationship to Shakespeare's writing. Greene takes the old fable of Margaret, a keeper's daughter, beloved by both the king's son Edward and Lacy Earl of Lincoln. She is the model of upward mobility dreamt of by audiences of the 'middling sort', but she is very shrewd about class difference when Lacy proposes:

> Handmaid unto the earl, so please himself;
> A wife in name, but servant in obedience.

> (2.3.738–9)

Margaret plans to become a nun rather than an obedient servant, her loving father is distraught at losing her, but Lacy finally prevails in his suit, though only after offering her up to the prince (in an echo of Valentine surrendering Silvia to Proteus in *The Two Gentlemen of Verona*). Margaret emerges as a complex and ambiguous female character, rare for 1590. Is she a manipulative schemer, a victim of her own beauty, a male fantasy of submissiveness or a combination of all three?[2] Greene (or possibly Henry Chettlel) in attacking Shakespeare in his *Groats-worth* as an 'upstart crow' and a 'Johannes factotum' evidently recognized that Shakespeare was writing in a similar vein.

By 1594 Marlowe, Kyd and Greene were dead, and Lyly and Peele had retired, leaving Shakespeare more space to experiment and develop. Ben Jonson was later to write in his commendatory verse to F1 that he should 'tell how far thou didst our Lyly outshine, / Or sporting Kyd, or Marlowe's mighty line'. The next wave of dramatists younger than Shakespeare – Jonson, John Marston, George Chapman, Thomas Heywood and Thomas Dekker – did not make their mark till the late 1590s, by which time Shakespeare had explored father-daughter relationships in his great comedies. Marston was the dramatist most sympathetic to young women, possibly because, like Lyly, he wrote for the boys companies adept at playing them. Shakespeare's influence is evident in *Antonio and Mellida* (1599), a satire on the affectations of young lovers. Piero Sforza, Duke of Venice, intends his daughter Mellida to marry the Prince of Milan, and calls for the head of 'that carpet-boy' Antonio, her beloved. When Mellida is later revealed in page's attire, Piero exclaims in Capulet mode:

> Light and induteous! Kneel not, peevish elf,
> Speak not, entreat not. Shame unto my house,
> Curse to my honour! Where's Antonio,
> Thou traitress to my hate? What, is he shipped
> For England now? Well, whimpering harlot, hence!

> (4.1.247–51)

At the denouement Antonio, presumed dead, rises from his coffin (a favourite gimmick of the period, to which Shakespeare never descended) and Mellida is transported: 'Conceit, breath, passion, words be dumb!' (5.2.233). Piero, suddenly the model Renaissance father, is delighted: 'Possess me freely, I am wholly thine' (241). In *Jack Drum's Entertainment* (1600) Marston makes one of the boldest paternal statements of the period. Sir Edward Fortune tells his daughters:

> I do love my girls should wish me live,
> Which few do wish that have a greedy sire. ...
> Nay be free my daughters in election,
> Oh how my soul abhors informed yokes,
> Chiefly in love, where the affections bent
> Should wholly sway the father's kind consent. ...
> Choose one either of valour, wit, honesty, or wealth,
> So he be gentle, and you have my heart,
> I'faith you have: What, I have land for you both,
> You have love for yourselves.
>
> (1.100–1, 177–80, 192–5)

Fathers in drama who allow their daughters such freedom of choice are few and far between.

Jonson had little interest in the relationship. In *The Case is Altered* (1597) Jacques de Prie has a beautiful daughter Rachel (though actually abducted as a child), and locks her up in case her suitors should discover his hidden riches. Jonson's other plot concerns Count Ferneze, also in love with Rachel, and his two daughters, Aurelia and Phoenixella, but they are sidelined in favour of the Count's search for his lost son. Jonson's real interest lies in suitors vying and double-crossing one another, leaving Rachel, their prize, as little more than a gracious silence (she has only thirty-seven lines). In a much later play, *A Tale of a Tub* (1633), Jonson enjoyed poking fun at romantic comedy and clearly had Shakespeare in mind. His heroine Awdrey Turfe regards husbands as no more than a necessity, for 'I care not who it be, so I have one' (3.6.44). Polmarten, her suitor, woos her with the promise of 'a silken gown and a rich petticoat', for 'I see the wench wants but a little wit' (82, 94). He then tricks her father out of a £100, and the father cries in Shylock-parody: 'My money is my daughter; and my daughter / She is my money' (5.3.32–3).

Chapman adopts one well-worn model in *All Fools* (c.1599), where Gostanzo puts his daughter Bellanora under house arrest, but her part is very underwritten, and Chapman is much more concerned about writing for the young men. Dekker shows greater interest in putting daughters centre-stage. In *The Shoemaker's Holiday* (1599) the Lord Mayor will not let Rose be courted by Rowland Lacy, the Earl of Lincoln's cousin: 'Too mean is my poor girl for his high birth: / Poor citizens must not with courtiers wed' (1.1.11–12). Rose remains adamant, the King eventually sorts it out, telling

Lincoln, honourably if improbably: 'Dost thou not know that love respects no blood, / Cares not for difference of birth or state?' (5.5.105–6). In *The Honest Whore Part 1* (1604) Dekker creates a murderous father in Gasparo Trebazzi, Duke of Milan, who swears he'll starve his daughter Infelice on the Appenine before Hippolito shall marry her, and then gets his doctor to poison her lover: 'A noble youth he was, but lesser branches / Hindering the greater's growth, must be lopt off, / And feed the fire' (4.4).

The most examined study of fathers and daughters in the early Jacobean period is, however, a collaboration between Chapman, Jonson and Marston, *Eastward Ho* (1605). Touchstone, a goldsmith, reluctantly agrees to his daughter Gertrude's marrying Sir Petronel Flash, though the father knows she is 'of a proud ambition and a nice wantonness', as she brags 'though my father be a low-capped tradesman, yet I must be a lady; and I praise God my mother must call me Madam' (1.2.3–5). Touchstone, who is written with great vigour, tells Flash 'my hopes are faint. And sir, respect my daughter: she has refused you wealthy and honest matches, known good men, well-moneyed, better traded, best reputed' (114–16). Mildred, the younger daughter, is a dutiful paragon: 'Sir, I am all yours; your body gave me life; your care and love, happiness of life; let your virtue still direct it, for to your wisdom I wholly dispose myself' (159–61). She is, therefore, happy to marry the apprentice Golding, of 'most hopeful industry', and can see 'when titles presume to thrust before fit means to second them, wealth and respect often grow sullen, and will not follow' (31–3). Flash, of course, has no castle in the country, and immediately spends her £100 dowry, but Gertrude keeps up a front: 'Though my knight be run away, and has sold my land, I am a lady still.' Her father observes, ironically: 'Your ladyship says true, madam; and it is fitter and a great decorum, that I should curtsey to you that are a knight's wife, and a lady, than you be brought a your knees to me, who am a poor cullion and your father' (4.2.114–19). Jonson's cynicism seems at work here, particularly with regard to class, a marriage issue that Shakespeare confronted in few of his plays.

By 1611 Shakespeare was on the point of retirement, having created powerful young women like Isabella, Helena, Marina and Innogen, strong older women like Cleopatra, Volumnia and Paulina and malign influences like Lady Macbeth, Goneril and Cymbeline's Queen. A new wave of dramatists, Thomas Middleton, John Webster, Francis Beaumont and John Fletcher, were inspired to put a wide variety of women at the centre of their plays. Lisa Hopkins argues that following the enormous success of Beaumont and Fletcher's *The Maid's Tragedy* (1610/11) there is a rush of female protagonists who are not passive or victims, but active agents in their own fate – Webster's Duchess and Vittoria Corombona, Middleton's Bianca and Beatrice-Joanna, Ford's Annabella and Calantha. 'Ironic though it may seem, the staging of a constant stream of bad or fallible women worked not to reinforce misogyny, but to prise it open' and 'effect a collective transformation of understanding of the female condition.'[3] In *The Maid's Tragedy* the king thwarts Aspatia's love for Amintor by forcing him to marry the royal mistress Evadne. Aspatia's father, Calianax, a Polonius-like figure – 'old men are good for nothing' – is written entirely comedically, but stands up for his wronged daughter, though they barely have a scene together:

> My child is wronged, disgraced ... Tis high time
> Now to be valiant: I confess my youth
> Was never prone that way. What, made an ass!
> A court-stale! Well, I will be valiant,
> And beat some dozen of these whelps; I will!
>
> (2.2.91, 103–7)

Evadne eventually ties the King's arms to the bed, which he thinks a 'pretty new device', and then stabs him. When Amintor rejects her as a 'master of cruelty' she kills herself. Aspatia then dresses as a man and, pretending to be her brother, fights with Amintor, is mortally wounded, and Amintor kills himself. Calianax concludes, in a gentler version of Pandarus: 'I know not what the matter is, but I am grown very kind, and am friends with you all now. You have given me that among you will kill me quickly; but I'll go home, and live as long as I can' (5.3.303–6). It is evident neither prose nor verse compare well with Shakespeare, but though the play is a melodramatic shocker it has proved very powerful in performance.

Middleton too created fathers and daughters prepared to go to lengths not envisaged by Shakespeare. In *A Chaste Maid in Cheapside* (1611–13) Yellowhammer swears to lock up Moll, his 'disobedient strumpet' daughter, when he discovers her secretly marrying Touchwood junior. He intends her for the licentious Sir Walter Whorehound, and when he learns that Sir Walter is an 'arrant whoremaster' he confides when alone:

> I have kept a whore myself, and had a bastard ...
> The knight is rich, he shall be my son-in-law,
> No matter so the whore he keeps be wholesome,
> My daughter takes no hurt then, so let them wed,
> I'll have him sweat well e'er they go to bed.
>
> (4.1.272, 277–80)

Moll eventually feigns death, only to rise from her coffin (that gimmick again) for her marriage. In *Women Beware Women* (c. 1621) Middleton again uses an extreme variation of the *senex* plot. Fabritio is determined his daughter Isabella shall marry Guardiano's rich but foolish ward: 'Like him or like him not, wench, you shall have him, / And you shall love him' (1.2.131–2). Middleton's twist is that Isabella is not in love with a lowly youth but with her uncle Hippolito, and everything ends in general carnage.

Fathers, tyrannical, scheming or miserly, and daughters, wily, rebellious or submissive, are the stuff of drama from Plautus to *Hobson's Choice*. The outcome is usually comedic, with the daughter triumphant and the father defeated but resigned. Even in tragedy, as in *The Changeling* and *The Maid's Tragedy*, the daughter dies a heroine of sorts, while the father is humbled. What is lacking in nearly all the plays of this period is any real examination of the *relationship* between father and daughter. This is particularly true of Peele, Marlowe, Jonson, Dekker and Chapman. Sometimes this is because the dramatist is far more interested in the father's relations with his sons, as in Jonson's *The Case is Altered* or Chapman's *All Fools*. Sometimes the daughter's part, though integral to the plot, is very small, as in Dekker's *The Honest Whore*. Marston, Beaumont, Fletcher and Middleton, early seventeenth-century writers much influenced by Shakespeare's dramaturgy, give far more space to women, sometimes placing them by 1610 at the tragic centre. Yet often when the daughter's part is considerable – as in *The Maid's Tragedy*, *The Changeling* and *The Wild-Goose Chase* – the father is sidelined. No one rivals the treatment given to Polonius and Ophelia, Lear and his three daughters or Prospero and Miranda.

Conclusion

Shakespeare inherited the Plautine model of father–daughter relationships, and though he never entirely abandoned this template, he increasingly sought to subvert it. *The Two Gentleman of Verona* shows the clearest adherence to the classical model. Both the Duke and Silvia are stock figures, spasmodically convincing, and only enlivened by the Duke's intemperate anger at his daughter's rebelliousness. Baptista, however, is not a typical *senex*, but Shakespeare's first attempt at a well-meaning father, out of his depth in dealing with two strongly contrasted daughters, the elder passing from rebelliousness into apparently submissive wifehood, the younger developing from virtuous humility into domineering self-interest. Titus is by contrast a tyrannical patriarch in the Senecan mode who sets out to avenge his daughter's despoliation at whatever cost to himself and, this achieved, sacrifices her before seeking his own death.

These three early plays show the breadth and ambition of Shakespeare's search for his distinctive voice, and the importance he attached from the outset to father–daughter relationships. The culmination of this search is expressed in his treatment of the *Romeo and Juliet* story. Despite his over-reliance on the Brooke poem, he manages to make the father, and in particular the daughter, more credible and three-dimensional figures. The writing for Juliet is so free, individual and emotional that it proved a completely original way of portraying an early adolescent in love. Capulet, though still bound to the *senex* model, is introduced as the model Renaissance parent, anxious to safeguard his daughter's interests, before exterior crises push him into a volte-face, expressed in wonderfully colloquial verse. The mutability of adolescent love is then contrasted in the staggering virtuosity of *A Midsummer Night's Dream*, where the conventional anger of the despotic Egeus is sharpened by his open preference for his prospective son-in-law, and by Hermia's choice of death rather than yield to her father's choice. In both his early tragedy and comedy Shakespeare set out to explore the extremes of passion.

In the comedies that follow Shakespeare carries his experimentation into further areas, with the exception of *The Merry Wives of Windsor*, which has all the appearance of a commissioned potboiler and in which he reverts to the wily daughter outwitting her parents' schemes to marry her to wealthy dolts. Just how far Shakespeare was prepared to go in overturning preconceived notions is shown by his treatment of father and daughter in *The Merchant of Venice*. Marlowe's amoral, blood-thirsty

Jew and virtuous daughter are replaced by a stern but caring Shylock at odds with a persecuting Christian society, and a rebellious Jessica whose motives and morality are open to question. In *Much Ado About Nothing* Leonato is introduced as a typically commonplace father in the vein of Baptista and Page, anxious like Capulet to marry his daughter to any aristocrat who will propose. Though gullible in initially accepting the plot against her, he throws himself into redeeming his daughter's reputation with a manic intensity that prefigures Othello and Leontes. Hero is developed in a novel and perceptive way that shows her demurely quiet in the company of men, but spirited and assertive when alone with women. Perhaps in reaction to Leonato's domination of Hero, Shakespeare next puts a daughter at the centre of a play. Rosalind and Celia's relationship with their fathers is perfunctorily sketched in, and Rosalind is left to dominate, albeit largely in male attire. If Shakespeare had been more prepared to flout convention he would have named the play after her, as *Cymbeline* should be named *Innogen* (and indeed is so in the Globe 2016 production).

From 1599 Shakespeare breaks new ground in both tragedy and comedy, and his restless experimentation leads him to examine daughters as either defiantly independent, dominated victims, destroyers or redeemers, and fathers and surrogate fathers as either perplexed, manipulative, cruelly dismissive, heedful or unheedful. In the three 'problem' plays of 1602–5 he explores the relation between the young woman at the centre and a surrogate father figure. Orsino and Malvolio are the first tentative experiments in the genre, to be followed by Pandarus, Duke Vincentio and the King of France. Pandarus is really in love with Troilus and exploits his niece to bring him closer to the young man. Cressida, knowing that a prince is out of her sphere, is uncertain of his faithfulness, as Troilus becomes of hers, and their love is destroyed by the politics of war. Isabella is unusual in having no love interest of her own, and this allows the Duke – disguised as a friar and therefore a 'father' to his 'daughter' – to befriend her, and eventually propose marriage after various devious tests of her character. Isabella's response to her 'ghostly father's' manipulation is left in the air. Helena, by contrast, is very open about her sexual desires and is in love with her aristocratic playmate Bertram, who considers her beneath him. It is only through the intervention of the King, himself attracted to Helena, that Bertram is forced to marry her, and this enables Helena to assert herself through the bed-trick and her subsequent pregnancy to bring Bertram to submission.

The Polonius–Ophelia relationship, probably Shakespeare's invention, marks a new phase in his development of a father and daughter beset by tragedy. Polonius is a recognizable *senex*, but his caring yet exploitative treatment of Ophelia is not only unusually complex but is enlivened by the comedy of his meddling pomposity, which eventually leads to his death and, in turn, to his daughter's distracted grief. Ophelia is the first of Shakespeare's examinations of an intelligent loving daughter caught up in, and finally destroyed by, political intrigue. Desdemona is similarly destroyed, though in this case through the machinations of a psychopath. Shakespeare's innovation is to give her a father, unrelenting in his opposition to her marriage, who finally dies in grief and desperation. Shakespeare's ultimate statement on the dysfunctional family is contained in *King Lear*. Lear, fatally lacking in self-knowledge, has no understanding of his three daughters, who all rebel in their different ways. The elder two, unwisely handed power, set out to cut him down to size and finally destroy him. Cordelia, banished for her unconsidered honesty, seeks to restore her father and Lear enjoys a brief fantasy of resting in her 'kind nursery', but Shakespeare, upending his sources, destroys them both. Whether the bleakness of this vision of father and daughters is in any way redeemed by Cordelia's love is a matter of debate. By the end of *King Lear* Shakespeare's exploration of daughters as exploited innocents or tragic victims has run its course.

The three romances that follow show Shakespeare's preoccupation with an unusually consistent theme: fathers are separated from their daughters through cruel or uncaring treatment, and are finally reunited through fortuitous if improbable accidents. *Pericles* examines widely contrasting father-daughter relationships, and finally sees Pericles lifted from his depressed immobility by the re-appearance of his resourceful daughter and his divinely restored wife, though the feelings of Marina are barely examined in contrast to the attention Shakespeare gives to the father. The same formula is applied in outline to *The Winter's Tale*. Leontes sends his baby daughter to her death, though this crime is thereafter hardly discussed at court when compared to his son's death and his treatment of his wife. Perdita dominates Act 4, as Marina does, but her reunion with her father is told in reported speech and pales alongside the magical reappearance of Hermione. In *Cymbeline* the daughter lies at the centre of the play, but the relationship with her father is similarly short-changed. Cymbeline never emerges as a three-dimensional character, changing from a tyrannical *senex* under his new wife's influence to an improbably wise and liberal ruler after her death. Innogen shows great courage in her escape from her father's domination, but cannot sustain her assertiveness in war-torn countryside, and her final reconciliation with her father is upstaged by his delight at the restoration of his lost sons. *The Tempest* fits less easily into this template of loss and redemption. Father and daughter have a close, unparalleled bond, strengthened by twelve years of lonely union, which both are resolved to break by Miranda's marriage to Ferdinand. In his final sole-authored play it is the nearest Shakespeare comes to describing a complex relationship between a patriarchal father and an adolescent daughter charged by her new sexuality.

This brief chronological outline, demonstrating the ambition of Shakespeare's developing analysis of the family, throws up a number of questions. To what extent are the interactions between fathers and daughters plot devices? How far do they examine their actual relationship, as opposed to fathers and daughters operating in their separate spheres? How does Shakespeare develop his attitude to paternal responsibilities, and how far does he endorse or subvert patriarchy? How does he treat the position of young women in society, and how far does he give them a measure of equality?

All drama is, of course, dependent on plot devices. Rosalind and Innogen are driven out into the wilds in male disguise by the unjustified cruelty of uncle and husband; Ophelia is set up as a decoy to test Hamlet's sanity through Polonius' interpretation of the prince's wordless visit to her chamber; Hero is unjustly slandered in church through the machinations of Don John. All these plot developments, however, have a complicated backstory, an unexpected outcome and a resonance that belie their dismissal as a mere plot devices. At the same time Shakespeare sometimes sets his plays in motion through a plot situation that is unexplained or improbable: Lear abdicates and divides up his kingdom; Viola decides to become a eunuch at Orsino's court; Leontes becomes savagely uncertain of his wife's faithfulness. All these Shakespeare asks us to accept as a starting point for the story. Only as the plays develop is he generally careful not to make the twists and turns of fortune appear arbitrary plot necessities.

The extent of the relationship between father and daughter is a complex issue. In the Elizabethan family the father had little interrelation with his young daughter, who naturally looked to her mother as a role model and in many cases it was the mother who determined her future, but in Shakespeare's plays the mother is often absent, and it is the father who shapes the daughter's maturing and marriage. Titus has an important relationship with Lavinia, but only when she is maimed and silent. Capulet may try to broker Juliet's marriage, but his relationship with her mostly consists of exasperated commands, until she finds, as Romeo also does, that she can express her innermost thoughts and feelings to Friar Laurence, an unthreatening, asexual surrogate father – a theme that Shakespeare was to develop in the tragicomedies of 1602–5. Leonato devotes himself to rehabilitating Hero, but their previous relationship has been very formal. The real turning point comes with Polonius and Ophelia, where considerable space is given to their interrelation, however cruelly it develops, and leaves Ophelia the first daughter to express her love for her father, albeit in a form of distracted madness. *King Lear* is Shakespeare's ultimate study of the interaction between a tyrant father and three rebellious daughters, where Cordelia's love for her father finally outweighs the machinations of her elder sisters. The romances are dominated by the separation of father and daughter, however significant their reunion, until Shakespeare in *The Tempest* finally puts a father in charge of his daughter's development from infancy to maturity – a bond developed for once over many years, and not dependent on recurrent crises that have hitherto largely driven father and daughter together.

Shakespeare's attitude to the role of the patriarch is chequered. In the early plays the fathers, the Duke of Milan, Baptista, Capulet, Egeus, are shown to be wrongheaded, incompetent or even tyrannical: the *senex* template is much in evidence. The writing for Leonato shows a rejection of the model. The length of the part, the near tragic nature of his obsession and the quality of the verse indicate that Shakespeare was prepared to lavish great attention on a father championing his daughter against slander and cruelty, as Titus had with Lavinia. Page and Duke Frederick are sketched in more traditional mode, but Polonius signals Shakespeare's decision to rethink the role of the father in tragedy, as he becomes, like Brabantio, over-possessive and anxious to contain his daughter's sexuality. Shakespeare then examines the role of the surrogate father, to whom the isolated young woman, bent on striking out on her own, turns in her need for advice, protection and championing. Pandarus proves too self-interested for the task, the King of France abuses his position by forcing his ward to marry the reluctant Helena, and Duke Vincentio cruelly misleads Isabella into thinking her brother dead. Shakespeare's studies of how an older man, given paternal status, will exploit the trust of a needy young woman are unsparing.

If Polonius is the comic version of the myopic blunderer, Lear is his tragic counterpart. His favouring of his youngest daughter is unabashed, and his belief that all his daughters are there to nurture and defer to him in old age is total. He mishandles these family ties at every turn, but Shakespeare now has too much insight to suggest that he learns very much from his ill judgements. Three of the romances concentrate on the cruelties, carelessness and anxieties of fatherhood and the possibility of resulting tragic endings, Pericles from self-neglect, Leontes by suicide (as in *Pandosto*) and Cymbeline through defeat by the Romans. Only Prospero emerges as a father anxious to free himself from dependence on revenge and the supernatural, and ensure his daughter's happiness. But despite Shakespeare's many exposés and criticisms of paternal behaviour, fathers never lose their patriarchal status, and Shakespeare seems to endorse this at every turn. The plays operate within a heavy male ethos, and in the second half of his career Shakespeare seems increasingly preoccupied with the tormented uncertainties of his male protagonists: throughout his writing fathers remain the head of the household, and daughters continue to regard both fathers and husbands as their 'lords'. Marina will accept the brothel-visiting Lysimachus without comment because her father decrees it, and Isabella will presumably accept the counterfeit friar Vincentio because he has such status. Kahn argues that however much the plays 'reflect and voice a masculine anxiety about the uses of patriarchal power over women', his female characters always validate the male identity through their obedience as wives and daughters.[1] In nearly all the plays daughters are sidelined at the denouement, and it would seem that Shakespeare's overriding interest lay in the way fathers come to terms with the reconfiguration of their family. With the exception of Rosalind's epilogue, fathers have literally the last word.

Juliet Stevenson doubts that the female is ever raised to a position of equality:

> If you are playing one of Shakespeare's women you are by definition in a supporting role. You appear in a relationship to the men – as wife, daughter, mother, lover. The man is the motor, the initiator of action; he sets the pace of the play and the woman is usually in a reactive, not an active, position. There are exceptions, like Rosalind ...[2]

Fiona Shaw makes an additional point: 'There are moments when Kate's story simply isn't tenable, because she doesn't have the lines. For example, when Petruchio [586 lines] says, "Will you, nill you, I will marry you", Kate [219 lines] says nothing. How does the actress occupy that silence? Is Kate shocked? Delighted? Angry? Stunned?'[3] Juliet Dusinberre disagrees: 'Shakespeare saw men and women as equal in a world which declared them unequal ... To talk about Shakespeare's women is to talk about his men, because he refused to separate their worlds physically, intellectually, or spiritually.'[4]

In the main Shakespeare wrote for young daughters and elderly fathers. He deliberately reduced Juliet's age to thirteen, and in the comedies that follow we feel that the heroines, Jessica, Anne Page and Hero in particular, are in their mid-teens, in contrast to the more mature-seeming Lavinia and Kate. Keeping his heroines young was one way of making them more vulnerable to the perils that beset them (Silvia by rape, Hermia by death, Juliet by untested poison and her lover's suicide, Hero by humiliation and feigned death, Rosalind by Duke Frederick's anger), but it also meant they forfeited their adolescence, 'no sanctioned period of experiment with adult identities or activities'.[5] These fourteen/fifteen-year-old girls were presumably being played by fourteen/fifteen-year-old boys, and this may have been one of the attractions to a male writer, who, however talented, was bound to view women from a male perspective (a female dramatist might well have found boy players more problematic). Lisa Jardine argues that female subordination 'is polemical rather than performance-orientated, focusing on male concerns and male versions of how women should or should not behave such that *any performer of whatever age or gender* [my italics] is likely to be required to present women within its parameters'.[6] It is often argued that Shakespeare fitted his female characters to a boy player's capabilities, but, if so, with Juliet, Portia, Beatrice and Rosalind he clearly tested them to the extreme. Various theories of a filtering process attach themselves to the influence of boy players: that the heroines could say and do indecorous things which would have been less acceptable if played by women, and that, as Kabuki theatre demonstrates, male actors will instinctively play those aspects of femininity that especially appeal to men. There can also be little doubt that boy players aroused erotic interest, both homosexual and heterosexual, in the spectators.

The comedies, which centre on and culminate in marriage alliances, are not fundamentally about fathers but about their daughters' attempts to find husbands of their choice. Hero may be directed into accepting Claudio, but the young women are in the main out to choose a mate to *their* liking. It is necessary for Lodge's original plot that Rosalind and Celia should have fathers, and it seems at first that the two dukes will take an equal share in determining the story, but Shakespeare is quick to see that for his two heroines to flourish in the fantasy stage of Arden their fathers have to be sidelined. In *Twelfth Night*, Shakespeare's last attempt at a comedy unencumbered with the threat of death, fathers are removed altogether. Viola and Olivia, however helter-skelter their journeys, are left free to embrace their destinies. The writing for Rosalind, Celia, Viola and Olivia represents Shakespeare's final exploration of a young woman's search for her identity in a purely comedic setting. Rosalind and Celia may have banished themselves, albeit with plenty of money, Viola may feel imprisoned in male guise and not up to a duel with Sir Andrew, and Olivia may discover she's been making overtures to another woman, but these are not serious hazards when compared with those that will face Isabella, Helena and the daughters of the tragedies and romances. Shakespeare decided, however, that he could only explore the freedom Rosalind and Viola enjoy by making them spend the bulk of the play as young men. This not only justified Rosalind living alone with her 'sister' in the forest and Viola attending the Duke Orsino, but it enabled them to talk to their lovers in some depth without the encumbrance of directly expressed sexual attraction. Shakespeare, so interested in the feminine aspects of masculine identity, is able to explore how women respond to the male mask. Rosalind revels in it, not only by 'teaching' Orlando but by ruminating on the pros and cons of love, courtship and marriage. Viola finds disguise a 'wickedness', apparently limiting her ability to attract Orsino, though succeeding against her expectations in achieving exactly that. Whether breeches actualized a young woman's male potential or made her a more developed female is much debated.[7] But, as ever, the women's talk is dominated by love, men and marriage (to the frustration of modern actresses). By 1600 Shakespeare had come to the end of a particular journey. He perhaps felt, to adapt Bernard Shaw, that 'there are plots more pressing than which attractive young person will mate with which other attractive young person'.

The five daughters that follow are given extraordinarily varied treatment. *Hamlet* is a new departure in so many ways, not least in the space given to Ophelia. She is not the first of his 'victim' daughters, but, while the damage done to Lavinia is physical, Ophelia's suffering is psychological, a state which increasingly concerned Shakespeare. She suffers from a lover's betrayal and her father's ineptitude, and is finally destroyed by the political intrigues of the state. Cressida suffers a similar fate, again betrayed by lover and surrogate father. She is in love, but uncertain who she is and why she acts in the way she does. Isabella is fiercely principled, though Shakespeare seems as critical of her rigid ideals of conduct as he is of Cressida's wayward indecisiveness. She too succumbs to the very questionable plans of an older man. Only Helena states unequivocally that her destiny lies in her own hands, that sexual desires are paramount, and through these she proves a triumphant assertion of a young, and not altogether sympathetic, heroine's ability to dominate the narrative. Desdemona starts out as an assertive and rebellious young woman, but she has been brought up to prove an obedient and conventional wife, however abusive her husband, and Shakespeare suggests that this is a part of her undoing.

By accepting to deliver a new adaptation of *King Lear* Shakespeare knew that he was bound in by the parameters of the story, however radically he changed the ending. In the first two acts, he graphically sets out Lear's limitations as a parent, and makes as good a case as he can for Cordelia's reckless honesty and for Goneril and Regan's justifiable need to limit their father's authority. In the second half of the play, however, his reinterpretation of the daughters' case falters, as Goneril and Regan become stereotypical harridans and Cordelia, though clearly asserting her love for her father, becomes strangely muted. In the romances the anxieties and preoccupations of fatherhood dominate, as daughters are initially rejected, brutally in the case of Cymbeline and Leontes and by apparent neglect in the case of Pericles. Innogen is the only daughter at the centre of the action, and her influence and direction of the narrative dwindles as the overcompli-cated plot unfolds. Miranda is in thrall to her father for much of the play, while Marina and Perdita, though they dominate Act 4, are sidelined at the end. All three women function as doubles of their mothers, uniting chastity with fertility, but though they 'deliver' their fathers to new identities, they remain, as Kahn argues 'accessories to their fathers development as characters, rather than characters developed for their own sakes, and their spheres of action are severely restricted'.[8]

Thirty-five years ago Irene Dash claimed that Shakespeare's women 'challenge accepted patterns for women's behaviour. Compliance, self-sacrifice for a male, dependence, nurturance, and emotionalism are the accepted norms. Yet independence, self-control and, frequently, defiance characterize these women.'[9] Lisa Jardine was quick to refute this: the plays 'neither mirror the social scene, nor articulate explicitly any of the varied contemporary views on "the woman question"... I maintain that the strong interest in women ... is related to the patriarchy's unexpressed worry about the great social changes which characterize the period.'[10] Shakespeare was certainly not on a mission to create a New Elizabethan Woman, and his plays reveal a complicated picture. He varies the characterization of his women according to where the narrative and focus of the play lies, though in most cases he has a tendency to idealize them. He was, however, constricted both by societal and dramatic norms. Having chosen his story, often with a folktale or mythic origin, he was not free to radically alter the role played by the daughter. Lavinia, Hero and Ophelia couldn't be made to assert their independence and defiance throughout the play (much as modern actresses have tried) – that was the point of the story. Desdemona becomes a submissive wife, Perdita accepts she may have to milk her ewes and weep and Innogen is submerged into the role of Fidele. Long-suffering young females, from Lavinia and Julia through to Marina and Innogen, have to shift into patient resignation as they await a patriarchal resolution of the injustices done to them.

These caveats made, however, there is no denying that Shakespeare's treatment of young women was by sixteenth-century standards enlightened and progressive. Before him young heroines tended to be passive and interchangeable (Lyly's plays excluded), while his are active, enabling and sharply differentiated – Juliet and Hero, Rosalind and Viola, Isabella and Helena could hardly be less alike. How much this reflected social change, a desire for such change or a fantasy about the possibility of change is hard to determine.[11] His comedy heroines show a writer's support for a more liberated view of women's independence, where romantic love, sexual desire, free choice of partner and escape from the confines of mansion or court all challenge the restraining social order. In tragicomedy Isabella and Helena demonstrate how orphaned young women, confronted by the full authority of the state, can through their determination realize their destiny. In his tragedies Shakespeare is at pains to dispel the notion that women are merely passive victims. Ophelia is given introductory scenes to establish her sibling equality and her once loving relationship with Hamlet; Desdemona is shown to defy her father and explain her sense of divided duty to the senate; Cordelia leads an army, defeated by her sister Goneril. In the romances Marina, Innogen and Perdita endure great changes of fortune, and show immense resolve in struggling to be reunited with their families. Throughout his career Shakespeare was careful never to show daughters in thrall to, or idolizing, their fathers: 'Why talk we of fathers when there is such a lover as …' is more his motto. Perhaps the feminist critic Marianne Ney best states the bottom line: 'For all the limitations on his feminism, Shakespeare is one of the few widely honoured culture heroes who can be claimed as a supporter of women at all.'[12]

This concentration on the father-daughter relationship might make it appear Shakespeare's primary dramatic concern, when it is in fact only one of a number of themes he obsessively returned to: male rivalry, the autonomy of the individual, the limitations of power, the acceptance of mortality and so on. He was not alone in seeing the dialectic of father and daughter a useful vehicle for studying power relations within the family; the inherent friction between the aspirations of the patriarch and the marriageable daughter; the liberation of the individual from social norms; and the ongoing conflict between reason and emotion. This was not achieved through discussion between characters. Shakespeare is always more interested in what people do, than what they profess – action always outdoes theory. He is the embodiment of the modern dramatic mantra, 'Show, don't tell.' We shall never know why fathers and daughters interested him so much in his writing; and husbands and wives, mothers and children, so little. Even his examination of fathers and sons drops away as he grows older. Between June 1607 and September 1608 his daughter Susanna married and bore a daughter, and his favourite brother Edmund and his mother both died. With the Globe shut for sixteen months through plague, it seems likely that Shakespeare spent much of 1608 in Stratford, grieving at 'things dying', rejoicing at 'things new born'. His plays thereafter seem obsessed by the restoration of long-lost wives and daughters, and above all, by errant fathers being granted second chances in life. Is it possible Shakespeare longed for some second chance? How much was he filled with self-doubt about his qualities and failures as a husband and father? How much did he brood on his relationship with Anne, Susanna and Judith, and how much store did he set by the second chance of Susanna's marriage, her daughter Elizabeth and her hoped-for sons? It is possible his personal life had little bearing on his creative development, but is it merely coincidence that in his last sole-authored play he tried to create an ideal, if fantastical, relationship between a magician father and a daughter fashioned in his image? Families remained central to Shakespeare's view of society throughout his career, and the twenty-one plays that prominently feature fathers, surrogate fathers and daughters show his continually evolving fascination with the complexity of this relationship.

NOTES

Introduction

1   Jonathan Miller, *Subsequent Performances,* Faber & Faber (1986), 160–1.

2   Coppelia Kahn, *Man's Estate: Masculine Identity in Shakespeare*, University of California Press (1981), 193.

3   Stephen Greenblatt, *Will in the World: How Shakespeare Became Shakespeare*, Pimlico (2005), 127.

4   Carol Chillington Rutter, 'Shakespeare and School', *Shakespeare Beyond Doubt*, Paul Edmondson and Stanley Wells (eds), Cambridge University Press (2013), 138.

5   David Riggs, *The World of Christopher Marlowe,* Faber & Faber (2004), 86.

6   I am indebted to Professor Carol Rutter for this observation.

7   Eileen Fairweather, *Daughters and Fathers*, Lynda E. Boose and Betty S. Flowers (eds), John Hopkins University Press (1989), 2.

8   D. Eckstein and J. A. Kaufman, 'The Role of Birth Order in Personality: An Enduring Intellectual Legacy of Alfred Adler', *The Journal of Individual Psychology* 68 (2012): 75–106.

9   David Wilbern, 'Fathers and Daughters in Freudian Theory', *Daughters and Fathers*, 88.

10 Jonathan Croall, *Performing Lear: Gielgud to Russell Beale*, Arden Shakespeare (2015), 102, 195.

11 Diane Elizabeth Dreher, *Domination and Defiance: Fathers and Daughters in Shakespeare*, University Press of Kentucky (1986), 44–63.

12 Lagretta Tallent Lenker, *Fathers and Daughters in Shakespeare and Shaw*, Greenwood Press (2001), 51–161.

13 Barbara Goulter and Joan Minninger, *The Father-Daughter Dance*, HarperCollins (1993), 160–1. Mark Taylor, *Shakespeare's Darker Purpose: A Question of Incest*, AMS Press (1982), 86.

14 Oliver Ford Davies, *Performing Shakespeare*, Nick Hern Books (2007), 229.

15 All references are taken from *The Arden Shakespeare Complete Works*, Richard Proudfoot, Ann Thompson and David Scott Kastan (eds), Arden Shakespeare (2011).

16 Simon Callow, *Being an Actor*, Methuen (1984), 165.

17 Geoffrey Bullough, *Narrative and Dramatic Sources of Shakespeare*, vol. 8, Routledge and Kegan Paul (1966), 46.

Chapter 1

1 Bullough, *Sources*, 1, 225.

2 Ibid., 224.

3 Michael D. Friedman, 'To be Slow in Words is a Woman's Only Virtue: Silence and Satire in *Two Gentlemen of Verona*' (1994), *Two Gentlemen of Verona: Critical Essays*, June Schveter (ed.), Garland (1996), 217.

4 Jonathan Bate (ed.), *Titus Andronicus*, Arden Shakespeare (1995), 79–85.

5 G. Blakemore Evans (ed.), *The Riverside Shakespeare*, Houghton Miffen Co. (1974), 1021.

6 Jonathan Bate (ed.), *Titus Andronicus*, 117–21.

7 Barbara Hodgdon (ed.), *The Taming of the Shrew*, Arden Shakespeare (2010), 44.

8 This was a line taken by Jonathan Miller in his 1987 RSC production with Brian Cox and Fiona Shaw. See also Valerie Wayne, 'Refashioning the Shrew', *Shakespeare Studies* 17 (1985): 173.

9 Elizabeth Schafer (ed.), *The Taming of the Shrew*, Cambridge University Press (2002), 34.

10 *Riverside Shakespeare*, 107. Coppelia Kahn sees the speech as a satire on the male urge to control women; *Man's Estate*, 104–18.

11 Carol Rutter, 'Kate, Bianca, Ruth and Sarah: Playing the Woman's Part in *The Taming of the Shrew*', *Shakespeare's Sweet Thunder: Essays on the Early Comedies*, Michael J. Collins (ed.), University of Delaware Press (1997), 197.

12 When at Marlowe's school in Canterbury in 1957 I made my sole contribution to Shakespearean research. Dr William Urry, the cathedral archivist and author with A. Butcher of *Christopher Marlowe and Canterbury*, Faber & Faber (1988), pointed out to me that the Jack Cade Rebellion in *2 Henry VI* refers to 'Best's son, the tanner of Wingham' and 'the clerk of Chatham' (4.2.24–5, 86). Best is a well-known local name (there is still a Best Lane in Canterbury), and F has the 'clearke of Chartam' – Chartham is a small village two miles outside Canterbury – which was presumably amended in later editions to the more recognizable 'Chatham'. I therefore cycled over to Wingham, some five miles away, where in the parish archives I found an Elizabethan Best, though his trade was not given. It is therefore possible that Shakespeare asked Marlowe for some Kentish names that would get an audience reaction, and Marlowe obligingly offered the (lecherous?) clerk of Chartham and the (trickster?) tanner Best (Marlowe's father was a rival tanner). The *New Oxford Shakespeare* has now decided to give Marlowe collaborative status in all three *Henry VI* plays.

13 Bullough, *Sources,* 1, 330 *passim*.

14 Irene G. Dash, *Wooing, Wedding and Power: Women in Shakespeare's Plays*, Columbia University Press (1981), 74.

15 Michael Billington, *Guardian*, 2 April 1976.

16 Thomas Morsan, 'Gender and Patriarchy', *In Another Country: Feminist*

Perspectives on Renaissance Drama, Dorothea Kehler and Susan Baker (eds), Scarecrow Press (1991), 115.

17 Anna Freud, 'On Adolescence', *The Psychoanalytic Study of the Child,* 13 (1958), 260. Simone de Beauvoir, *The Second Sex*, H. M. Parshley (ed. and trans.), Penguin (1983), 360.

18 Morsan, 'Gender and Patriarchy', 131.

Chapter 2

1 Alan C. Dessen, 'The Elizabethan Stage Jew and Christian Example', *Shylock*, Harold Bloom (ed.), Chelsea House (1991), 254.

2 Quoted in *The RSC Much Ado about Nothing*, Jonathan Bate and Eric Rasmussen (eds), Macmillan (2009), 122–3.

3 Bullough, *Sources,* 2, 137.

4 Ibid., 120.

5 David Mann, *Shakespeare's Women: Performance and Conception*, Cambridge University Press (2008), 32.

6 Claire McEachern (ed.), *Much Ado about Nothing*, Arden Shakespeare (2006), 42.

7 Mihoko Suzuki, 'Gender, Class, and the Ideology of Comic Form: *Much Ado about Nothing* and *Twelfth Night*', *A Feminist Companion to Shakespeare*, Dympna Callaghan (ed.), Oxford University Press (2000), 129–36.

8 Carol Thomas Neely, *Broken Nuptials in Shakespeare's Plays*, University of Illinois Press (1993), 45.

9 Lesley Anne Soule, 'Subverting Rosalind: Cocky Ros in the Forest of Arden', *New Theatre Quarterly* 726 (1991): 128.

10 Bullough, *Sources* 2: 158–256, for Thomas Lodge's *Rosalynde*.

11 It has since become perhaps the most popular comedy: between 1970 and 2013 the RSC mounted twelve new productions.

Chapter 3

1 Paul Edmondson, 'Comical and tragical' *Shakespeare: An Oxford Guide*, Stanley Wells and Lena Cowen Orlin (eds), Oxford University Press (2003), 268.

2 Michael Ratcliffe in *Observer*, 19 March 1989.

3 Tony Church, 'Polonius in Hamlet', *Players of Shakespeare 1*, Philip Brockbank (ed.), Cambridge University Press (1985), 103–14.

4 Bullough, *Sources*, 7, 64.

5 Bullough, *Sources*, 7, 44–5.

6   Frank Kermode, *Shakespeare's Language*, Allen Lane, The Penguin Press (2000), 109–10.

7   Louis B. Wright (ed.), *Advice to a Son: Precepts of Lord Burghley, Sir Walter Raleigh, and Francis Osborne*, Literary Licensing, LLC (2011).

8   John Masefield, quoted in Dreher, *Domination and Defiance*, 77.

9   Deborah Barker and Ivo Kamps (eds), *Shakespeare and Gender: A History*, Verso (1995), 121.

10 Kaara L. Peterson and Deanne Williams (eds), *The Afterlife of Ophelia*, Palgrave Macmillan (2012), 1.

11 R. D. Laing, *The Divided Self*, Penguin (1965), 195 n.

12 David Leverenz, 'The Woman in Hamlet: An Interpersonal View', 117–18, quoted in Bert O. States, *Hamlet and the Concept of Character*, Johns Hopkins University Press (1992), 140.

13 Jan Kott, *Shakespeare our Contemporary*, Methuen (1964), 65.

14 Marilyn Williamson, *The Patriarchy of Shakespeare's Comedies*, Wayne State University Press (1986), 105.

15 Stanley Wells and Gary Taylor with John Jowett and William Montgomery, *William Shakespeare: A Textual Companion*, Oxford Unversity Press (1987), 126–7.

16 Kay Stanton, 'All's Well in Love and War', *Ideological Approaches to Shakespeare: The Practice of Theory*, Robert P. Merrix and Nicholas Ranson (eds), Edwin Mellen (1992), 86.

17 Sheldon P. Zitner (ed.), *All's Well That Ends Well*, Harvester Wheatsheaf (1989), 102. Robert S. Miola, 'New Comedy in *All's Well That Ends Well*', *Renaissance Quarterly* 46 (1993), 37.

18 Sean Benson, *Shakespeare, Othello and Domestic Tragedy*, Continuum (2012), 6–7. A. D. Nuttall, *Shakespeare the Thinker*, Yale University Press (2007), 253.

19 Bullough, *Sources*, 7, 242–5.

20 Stephen Greenblatt, *Renaissance Self-fashioning: From More to Shakespeare*, University of Chicago Press (1980), 237–52.

21 Dash, *Wooing, Wedding and Power*, 104.

22 R. A. Foakes (ed.) *King Lear*, Arden Shakespeare (1997), 29–30.

23 Jonathan Croall, *Performing King Lear: Gielgud to Russell Beale*, Arden Shakespeare (2015), 39.

24 Ibid, 32.

25 Ibid, 37.

26 Quoted in Simon Callow, *Charles Laughton: A Difficult Actor*, Methuen (1987), 266.

27 Croall, *Performing King Lear*, 212.

28 Richard Burton, *The Anatomy of Melancholy* (1676 edn), 63, 67.

29 For quotations from *King Leir* see Bullough, *Sources* 6: 336–44.

30 Foakes, *King Lear*, 38.

31 Coppelia Kahn, 'The Absent Mother in *King Lear*', *New Casebook*, Kiernan Ryan (ed.), Macmillan (1993), 99.

32 Croall, *Performing King Lear*, 65.

33 Ibid, 190.

34 Oliver Ford Davies, *Playing Lear*, Nick Hern Books (2003), 54.

35 Nuttall, *Shakespeare the Thinker,* 309.

36 Freud, 'The Theme of the Three Caskets' (1913), *Complete Works*, vol XII, The Hogarth Press (1958), 301.

37 Howard Felperin, *Shakespearean Representation: Mimesis and Modernity in Elizabethan Tragedy*, Princeton University Press (1977), 105.

38 Ford Davies, *Playing Lear*, 184.

Chapter 4

1 Janet Adelman, *Suffocating Mothers: Fantasies of Material Origin in Shakespeare's Plays,* Hamlet *to* The Tempest, Routledge (1992), 194.

2 R. A. Foakes, 'Romances', *Shakespeare: An Oxford Guide*, Oxford University Press (2003), 249.

3 Russ McDonald, *Shakespeare's Late Style*, Cambridge University Press (2006), 33.

4 Ruth Nevo, *Shakespeare's Other Language*, Methuen (1987), 42.

5 Richard A. McCabe, *Incest, Drama and Nature's Law 1550–1700*, Cambridge University Press (1993), 176.

6 Jane M. Ford, *Patriarchy and Incest from Shakespeare to Joyce*, University of Florida Press (1998), 47.

7 Stanley Wells, *Shakespeare, Sex & Love*, Oxford University Press (2010), 224.

8 Marilyn French, *Shakespeare's Division of Experience*, Abacus (1983), 295.

9 Adelman, *Suffocating Mothers*, 186.

10 Charles Nicholl, *The Lodger: Shakespeare on Silver Street*, Allen Lane (2007), 204.

11 Leslie A. Fiedler, *The Stranger in Shakespeare*, Croom Helm (1973), 219.

12 Anne Barton, 'Leontes and the Spider', *Essays, Mainly Shakespearean*, Cambridge University Press (1994), 168.

13 Roger Grainger, *Theatre and Relationships in Shakespeare's Later Plays*, Peter Lang (2008), 102.

14 Coppelia Kahn, *Pericles: Critical Essays*, David Skeele (ed.), Garland Publishing (2000), 11.

15 Barton, 'Leontes and the Spider', 170.

16 McCabe, *Incest, Drama and Nature's Law*, 180.

17 Barton, 'Leontes and the Spider', 162.

18 Bullough, *Sources*, 8, 156–99.

19 Carol Chillington Rutter, *Shakespeare and Child's Play: Performing Lost Boys on Stage and Screen*, Routledge (2007), 120–1.

20 Kermode, *Shakespeare's Language*, 283.

21 Wells, *Sex and Love*, 231.

22 Ros King, *Cymbeline: Constructions of Britain*, Ashgate (2005), 1.

23 Harriet Walter, *Players of Shakespeare 3*, Russell Jackson and Robert Smallwood (eds), Cambridge University Press (1993), 204.

24 Barton, '"Wrying but a Little": Marriage, Law and Sexuality in the Plays of William Shakespeare', *Essays*, 24.Wells, *Sex and Love*, 231.

25 Jonathan Bate and Eric Rasmussen (eds), *Cymbeline*, RSC Shakespeare (2011), 181.

26 Ibid., 190.

27 Edward Petherbridge, *Slim Chances and Unscheduled Appearances*, Indepenpress (2011), 396.

28 J. M. Nosworthy (ed.), *Cymbeline*, Arden Shakespeare (1955), xlv.

29 Kiernan Ryan (ed.), *Shakespeare: The Last Plays*, Longman (1999), 107. Adelman, *Suffocating Mothers*, 200.

30 Adelman, *Suffocating Mothers*, 109–10.

31 Barton, '*As You Like It* and *Twelfth Night*: Shakespeare's "Sense of an Ending"', *Essays*, 112.

32 Anne Barton (ed.), *The Tempest*, Penguin (1968), 22.

33 Greenblatt, *Will in the World*, 378. J. C. Trewin, *Peter Brook: A Biography*, MacDonald (1971), 135.

34 Walter Clyde Curry, *Shakespeare's Philosophical Patterns*, Louisiana State University Press (1937), 167.

35 The 1603 address to Parliament.

36 Michel de Montaigne, *The Essays: A Selection*, M. A. Screech (ed.), Penguin (1993), 79–92.

37 Ibid., 241.

38 BBC television interview with Patrick Garland, July 1985. John Goodwin (ed.), *Peter Hall Diaries*, Hamilton (1983), 12.

39 David Sundelson, 'So Rare a Wonder'd Father', *Representing Shakespeare: New Psychoanalytic Essays*, Murray M. Schwartz and Coppelia Kahn (eds), Johns Hopkins University Press (1980), 53.

40 A view undoubtedly enhanced by my experience as a fourteen-year-old in a rehearsal of an outdoor school production, attended by the veteran Shakespearean actor Robert Atkins. He remained largely silent, until he suddenly roared, 'You've left out the best line in the play', and seizing an overhanging branch hauled his portly body swinging into the air, the bough threatening to break at any moment, and thundered: 'Would't had been done; thou didst prevent me, I had peopled else this isle with Calibans.'

41   Barton, 'Leontes and the Spider', 167.

42   Nevo, *Shakespeare's Other Language*, 133–4.

43   MacDonald P. Jackson, 'Looking for Shakespeare in Double Falsehood: Stylistic Evidence', *The Quest for Cardenio: Shakespeare, Fletcher, Cervantes and the Lost Play*, David Carnegie and Gary Taylor (eds), Oxford University Press (2012),161.

44   Jackson, 'Looking for Shakespeare', 161.

45   Lois Potter (ed.), *The Two Noble Kinsmen*, Arden Shakespeare (1997), 25.

46   Douglas Bruster, 'The Jailer's Daughter and the Politics of Madwoman's Language', *Shakespeare Quarterly* 46 (1995): 277.

Chapter 5

1   Park Honan, *Shakespeare: A Life*, Oxford University Press (1998), 354.

2   Jeanne Jones, *Family Life in Shakespeare's England: Stratford-upon-Avon 1570–1630*, Sutton Publishing: The Shakespeare Birthplace Trust (1996), 90.

3   Paul Edmondson and Stanley Wells (eds), *The Shakespeare Circle: An Alternative Biography*, Cambridge University Press (2015), 75.

4   Ben Jonson, *Poems*, Ian Donaldson (ed.), Oxford University Press (1975), 26.

5   Jones, *Family Life*, 111.

6   Germaine Greer, *Shakespeare's Wife*, Bloomsbury (2007), Ch. 10.

7   *The Shakespeare Circle*, 88, quoting *Dendrochronological Results for Hall's Croft*, Shakespeare Birthplace Trust (1990).

8   Edmund was only three years older than Susanna, so may have become a surrogate brother. He came to London as an actor, presumably under his brother's patronage. A document of 1597/8 lists an apprentice 'Ned', and this could be Edmund, who was seventeen at the time (Jonathan Bate, *Soul of the Age: The Life, Mind, and World of Shakespeare*, Penguin Viking (2008), 48). When he died in December 1607, probably of the plague, and was buried at Southwark, it must have been Shakespeare who paid the large sum of 20s. for him to be buried 'in the church' and for 'a forenoone knell of the great bell' of St Saviour's to mark his passing.

9   Katherine Duncan-Jones, *Ungentle Shakespeare: Scenes from his Life*, Arden Shakespeare (2001), 260. Peter Whelan's play *The Herbal Bed* (RSC 1996) suggests a possible scenario for Rafe Smith's involvement with Susanna.

10 *The Shakespeare Circle*, 112.

11 Greer, *Shakespeare's Wife*, 327.

12 *The Shakespeare Circle*, 129.

13 Greenblatt, *Will in the World*, 389.

Chapter 6

1   Kate Aughterson (ed.), *Renaissance Women: A Sourcebook Constructions of Femininity in England*, Routledge (1995), 138. John Knox, *The First Blast of the Trumpet against the Monstrous Regiment of Women* (1558).

2   Christopher Newstead, *An Apology for Women* (1620).

3   Robert Cleaver, *A Godly Form of Household Government* (1598), 1.

4   Montaigne, *The Essays,* 329.

5   Lawrence Stone, *The Family, Sex and Marriage 1500–1800*, Weidenfeld & Nicolson (1997), 152.

6   *The Cambridge Companion to Shakespeare*, Margreta de Grazia and Stanley Wells (eds), Cambridge University Press (2001), 106–7.

7   Keith Thomas, 'Age and Authority in Early Modern England', *Proceedings of the British Academy*, 62 (1976): 214.

8   Barbara Gottlieb, *The Family in the Western World from the Black Death to the Industrial Age*, Oxford University Press (1993), 133.

9   Carol Camden, *The Elizabethan Woman*, Paul P. Appel (1975), 39–40.

10 Montaigne, *Essays*, 153–4, 157.

11 Boose, *Daughters and Fathers*, 20.

12 Claude Lévi-Strauss, *The Elementary Structures of Kinship*, Beacon Press (1969), 115.

13 Montaigne, *Essays*, Florio translation, 772, quoted in Bate, *Soul of the Age*, 413.

14 Ludovic Mercatus, *On the Common Conditions of Women*, Venice (1587).

15 *The Cambridge Companion to English Renaissance Drama*, A. R. Branmuller and Michael Hattaway (eds), Cambridge University Press (1990), 109.

16 Camden, *Elizabethan Woman*, 41.

17 Aughterson, *Renaissance Women*, 27.

18 David Cressy, *Birth, Marriage and Death: Ritual, Religion, and the Life-Circle in Tudor and Stuart England*, Oxford University Press (1997), 277.

19 Camden, *Elizabethan Woman*, 72.

20 John Milton, *The Doctrine and Discipline of Divorce* (1643).

21 Juan Luis Vives, *The Instruction of a Christian Woman* (1540), quoted in Aughterson, *Renaissance Women*, 71–2.

22 Philip Stubbes, *The Anatomy of Abuses* (1583), quoted in Aughterson, *Renaissance Women*, 76.

23 Vives, *Instruction,* quoted in Aughterson, *Renaissance Women*, 71.

24 Richard Mulcaster, *Positions concerning the Training up of Children* (1581), 178.

25 Kent Cartwright, *Theatre and Humanism: English Drama in the Sixteenth Century*, Cambridge University Press (1999), 136–7.

26 Cressy, *Birth, Marriage and Death*, 110.

27 Henry Bullinger, *The Christian State of Matrimony* (1541).

28 Cressy, *Birth, Marriage and Death*, 106. Aughterson, *Renaissance Women*, 167.

29 Cressy, *Birth, Marriage and Death*, 287–8.

30 Ann Jennalie Cook, *Making a Match: Courtship in Shakespeare and his Society*, Princeton University Press (1991), 17–18.

31 Jones, *Family Life*, 90.

32 Martin Luther, *Letters of Spiritual Counsel*, Westminster Press (1955), 264.

33 John Evelyn, *Evelyn Mss.* 143, 48, Christ Church, Oxford.

34 Camden, *Elizabethan Woman*, 73.

35 Martin Ingram, 'Love, Sex and Marriage', *Shakespeare: An Oxford Guide*, 122.

36 Ibid, 254.

Chapter 7

1 Cartwright, *Theatre and Humanism*, 168.

2 Ibid., 236.

3 Lisa Hopkins, *The Female Hero in English Renaissance Tragedy*, Palgrave Macmillan (2002), 2–3.

Conclusion

1 Kahn, *Man's Estate*, 9.

2 Carol Rutter, *Clamorous Voices: Shakespeare's Women Today*, The Women's Press (1988), xxiv.

3 Ibid., xxv.

4 Juliet Dusinberre, *Shakespeare and the Nature of Women*, 3rd edn, Palgrave Macmillan (2003), 30.

5 Kahn, *Man's Estate*, 93.

6 Quoted in David Mann, *Shakespeare's Women: Performance and Conception*, Cambridge University Press (2008), 51.

7 Mann, *Shakespeare's Women*, 223, 231. Dusinberre, *Nature of Women*, 233.

8 Kahn, *Man's Estate*, 195.

9 Dash, *Wooing, Wedding and Power*, 1.

10 Lisa Jardine, *Still Harping on Daughters: Women and Drama in the Age of Shakespeare*, Harvester Press (1983), 6

11 Ibid, 182.

12 Kathleen McCluskie, 'The Act, the Role, and the Actor: Boy Actresses on the Elizabethan Stage', *New Theatre Quarterly* III[10] (May 1987), 130.

SELECT BIBLIOGRAPHY

Adelman, Janet, *Suffocating Mothers: Fantasies of Material Origin in Shakespeare's Plays,* Hamlet *to* The Tempest, Routledge (1992).

Aughterson, Kate (ed.), *Renaissance Women: A Sourcebook, Constructions of Femininity in England,* Routledge (1995).

Barker, Deborah and Ivo Kamps (eds), *Shakespeare and Gender: A History,* Verso (1995).

Barnes, Dana Ramel (ed.), 'Fathers and Daughters in Shakespeare', *Shakespearean Criticism* 36 (1997).

Barton, Anne, *Essays, Mainly Shakespearean,* Cambridge University Press (1994).

Bate, Jonathan, *Soul of the Age: The Life, Mind, and World of Shakespeare,* Penguin Viking (2008).

Benson, Sean, *Shakespeare, Othello and Domestic Tragedy,* Continuum (2012).

Boose, Lynda E. and Betty S. Flowers (eds), *Daughters and Fathers,* Johns Hopkins University Press (1989).

Branmuller, A. R. and Michael Hattaway (eds), *The Cambridge Companion to English Renaissance Drama,* Cambridge University Press (1990).

Brockbank, Philip (ed.), *Players of Shakespeare 1,* Cambridge University Press (1985).

Bruster, Douglas, 'The Jailer's Daughter and the Politics of Madwoman's Language', *Shakespeare Quarterly* 46 (1995).

Bullough, Geoffrey, *Narrative and Dramatic Sources of Shakespeare,* vols 1–8, Routledge and Kegan Paul (1966).

Callaghan, Dympna (ed.), *A Feminist Companion to Shakespeare,* Oxford University Press (2000).

Callow, Simon, *Being an Actor,* Methuen (1984).

Camden, Carol, *The Elizabethan Woman,* Paul P. Appel (1975).

Carnegie, David and Gary Taylor (eds), *The Quest for Cardenio: Shakespeare, Fletcher, Cervantes and the Lost Play,* Oxford University Press (2012).

Cartwright, Kent, *Theatre and Humanism: English Drama in the Sixteenth Century,* Cambridge University Press (1999).

Chaucer, Geoffrey, *The Complete Works of Geoffrey Chaucer,* Walter W. Skeat (ed.), Oxford University Press (1951).

Cook, Ann Jennalie, *Making a Match: Courtship in Shakespeare and his Society,* Princeton University Press (1991).

Corum, Richard, *Understanding Hamlet,* Greenwood Press (1998).

Cressy, David, *Birth, Marriage and Death: Ritual, Religion, and the Life-Cycle in Tudor and Stuart England,* Oxford University Press (1997).

Croall, Jonathan, *Performing King Lear: Gielgud to Russell Beale,* Arden Shakespeare (2015).

Curry, Walter Clyde, *Shakespeare's Philosophical Patterns*, Louisiana State University Press (1937).

Dash, Irene G., *Women's Worlds in Shakespeare's Plays*, University of Delaware Press (1997).

Dash, Irene G., *Wooing, Wedding and Power: Women in Shakespeare's Plays*, Columbia University Press (1981).

Davies, Stevie, *The Feminine Reclaimed: The Idea of Women in Spenser, Shakespeare and Milton*, University Press of Kentucky (1986).

Dreher, Diane Elizabeth, *Domination and Defiance; Fathers and Daughters in Shakespeare*, University Press of Kentucky (1986).

Duncan-Jones, Katherine, *Ungentle Shakespeare: Scenes from his Life*, Arden Shakespeare (2001).

Dusinberre, Juliet, *Shakespeare and the Nature of Women*, 3rd edn, Palgrave Macmillan (2003).

Eckstein, D. and J. A. Kaufman, 'The Role of Birth Order in Personality: An Enduring Intellectual Legacy of Alfred Adler', *The Journal of Individual Psychology* 68 (2012).

Edmondson, Paul and Stanley Wells (eds),*The Shakespeare Circle: An Alternative Biography*, Cambridge University Press (2015).

Erickson, Peter, *Patriarchal Structures in Shakespeare's Drama*, University of California Press (1985).

Felperin, Howard, *Shakespearean Representation: Mimesis and Modernity in Elizabethan Tragedy*, Princeton University Press (1977).

Fiedler, Leslie A., *The Stranger in Shakespeare*, Croom Helm (1973).

Ford, Jane M., *Patriarchy and Incest from Shakespeare to Joyce*, University of Florida Press (1998).

Ford Davies, Oliver, *Playing Lear*, Nick Hern Books (2003).

Ford Davies, Oliver, *Performing Shakespeare*, Nick Hern Books (2007).

French, Marilyn, *Shakespeare's Division of Experience*, Abacus (1983).

Gottlieb, Barbara, *The Family in the Western World from the Black Death to the Industrial Age*, Oxford University Press (1993).

Grainger, Roger, *Theatre and Relationships in Shakespeare's Later Plays*, Peter Lang (2008).

Grazia, Margreta de and Stanley Wells (eds), *The Cambridge Companion to Shakespeare*, Cambridge University Press (2001),

Greenblatt, Stephen, *Renaissance Self-Fashioning: From More to Shakespeare*, University of Chicago Press (1980).

Greenblatt, Stephen, *Will in the World: How Shakespeare Became Shakespeare*, Pimlico (2005).

Greer, Germaine, *Shakespeare's Wife*, Bloomsbury (2007).

Gross, John, *Shylock: Four Hundred Years in the Life of a Legend*, Chatto and Windus (1992).

Honan, Park, *Shakespeare: A Life*, Oxford University Press (1998).

Hopkins, Lisa, *The Female Hero in English Renaissance Drama*, Palgrave Macmillan (2002).

Hoy, Cyrus, 'Father and Daughter in Shakespeare's Romances', *Shakespeare's Romances Reconsidered*, Carol McGinnis Kay and Henry E. Jacobs (eds), University of Nebraska Press (1978).

Ingram, Martin, 'Love, Sex and Marriage', *Shakespeare: An Oxford Guide*, Stanley Wells and Stephen Orlin (eds), Oxford University Press (2003).

Jackson, MacDonald P., *Defining Shakespeare: Pericles as Test Case*, Oxford University Press (2003).

Jackson, MacDonald P., 'Looking for Shakespeare in Double Falsehood: Stylistic Evidence', *The Quest for Cardenio: Shakespeare, Fletcher, Cervantes and the Lost Play*, David Carnegie and Gary Taylor (eds), Oxford University Press (2012),

Jardine, Lisa, *Still Harping on Daughters: Women and Drama in the Age of Shakespeare*, Harvester Press (1983).

Jones, Jeanne, *Family Life in Shakespeare's England: Stratford-upon-Avon 1570–1630*, Sutton Publishing: The Shakespeare Birthplace Trust (1996).

Kahn, Coppelia, *Man's Estate: Masculine Identity in Shakespeare*, University of California Press (1981).

Kahn, Coppelia, 'The Absent Mother in *King Lear*', *New Casebook*, Kiernan Ryan (ed.), Macmillan (1993).

Kehler, Dorothea and Susan Baker (eds), *In Another Country: Feminist Perspectives on Renaissance Drama*, Scarecrow Press (1991).

Kermode, Frank, *Shakespeare's Language*, Allen Lane, The Penguin Press (2000).

King, Ros, *Cymbeline: Constructions of Britain*, Ashgate (2005).

Kott, Jan, *Shakespeare Our Contemporary*, Methuen (1964).

Laing, R. D., *The Divided Self*, Penguin (1965).

Lévi-Strauss, Claude, *The Elementary Structures of Kinship*, Beacon Press (1969).

Luther, Martin, *Letters of Spiritual Counsel*, Westminster Press (1955).

Mann, David, *Shakespeare's Women: Performance and Conception*, Cambridge University Press (2008).

McCabe, Richard A., *Incest, Drama and Nature's Law 1550–1700*, Cambridge University Press (1993).

McDonald, Russ, *Shakespeare's Late Style*, Cambridge University Press (2006).

McLuskie, Kathleen, 'The Act, the Role, and the Actor: Boy Actresses on the Elizabethan Stage', *New Theatre Quarterly* III[10] (May 1987).

McLuskie, Kathleen, 'The Patriarchal Bard: Feminist Criticism and Shakespeare: King Lear and Measure for Measure', *Political Shakespeare: Essays in Cultural Materialism*, Jonathan Dollimore and Alan Sinfield (eds), 2nd edn, Manchester University Press (1994).

Miller, Jonathan, *Subsequent Performances*, Faber & Faber (1986).

Montaigne, Michel de, *The Essays: A Selection*, M. A. Screech (ed.), Penguin (1993).

Morsan, Thomas, 'Gender and Patriarchy', *In Another Country: Feminist Perspectives on Renaissance Drama*, Dorothea Kehler and Susan Baker (eds), Scarecrow Press (1991), 115.

Mulcaster, Richard, *Positions concerning the Training up of Children* (1581).

Neely, Carol Thomas, *Broken Nuptials in Shakespeare's Plays*, University of Illinois Press (1993).

Nevo, Ruth, *Shakespeare's Other Language*, Methuen (1987).

Newman, Karen, *Fashioning Femininity and English Renaissance Drama*, University of Chicago Press (1991).

Nicholl, Charles, *The Lodger: Shakespeare on Silver Stret*, Allen Lane (2007).

Novy, Marianne, 'Patriarchy, Mutuality and Forgiveness in King Lear',
     Shakespeare's King Lear, Harold Bloom (ed.), Chelsea House (1987).
Novy, Marianne, 'Multiple Parenting in Pericles', *Pericles: Critical Essays*, David
     Skeele (ed.), Garland Publishing (2000).
Nuttall, A. D., *Shakespeare the Thinker*, Yale University Press (2007).
Ogden, James and Arthur Scouten (eds), *Lear from Study to Stage*, Associated
     Universities Presses (1997).
Ovid, *Metamorphoses*, A. D. Melville (trans.), Oxford University Press (1987).
Petersen, Kaara L. and Deanne Williams (eds), *The Afterlife of Ophelia*, Palgrave
     Macmillan (2012).
Potter, Nicholas, *Shakespeare's Late Plays*, Palgrave Macmillan (2009).
Rose, Mary Beth, 'Where are the Mothers in Shakespeare?: Options for Gender
     Representation in the English Renaissance', *Shakespeare Quarterly* 42[3] (1991).
Rutter, Carol, *Clamorous Voices: Shakespeare's Women Today*, The Women's
     Press (1988).
Rutter, Carol, 'Kate, Bianca, Ruth and Sarah: Playing the Woman's Part in *The
     Taming of the Shrew*', *Shakespeare's Sweet Thunder: Essays on the Early
     Comedies*, Michael J. Collins (ed.), University of Delaware Press (1997).
Rutter, Carol Chillington, *Enter the Body: Women and Representation on
     Shakespeare's Stage*, Routledge (2001).
Rutter, Carol Chillington, *Shakespeare and Child's Play: Performing Lost Boys on
     Stage and Screen*, Routledge (2007).
Rutter, Carol Chillington, 'Shakespeare and School', *Shakespeare Beyond Doubt*,
     Paul Edmondson and Stanley Wells (eds), Cambridge University Press (2013).
Ryan, Kiernan (ed.), *Shakespeare: The Last Plays*, Longman (1999).
Sinfield, Alan, *Shakespeare, Authority, Sexuality: Unfinished Business in Cultural
     Materialism*, Routledge (2006).
Soule, Lesley Anne, 'Subverting Rosalind: Cocky Ros in the Forest of Arden', *New
     Theatre Quarterly* 7[26] (1991).
States, Bert O., *Hamlet and the Concept of Character*, Johns Hopkins University
     Press (1992).
Stone, Lawrence, *The Family, Sex and Marriage 1500–1800*, Weidenfeld &
     Nicolson (1977).
Sundelson, David, 'So rare a wonder'd father', *Representing Shakespeare: New
     Psychoanalytic Essays*, Johns Hopkins University Press (1980)
Sundelson, David, *Shakespeare's Restoration of the Father*, Rutgers University
     Press (1983).
Taylor, Mark, *Shakespeare's Darker Purpose: A Question of Incest*, AMS Press
     (1982).
Thomas, Keith, 'Age and Authority in Early Modern England', *Proceedings of the
     British Academy* 62 (1976).
Traub, Valerie, 'Gender and Sexuality in Shakespeare', *The Cambridge
     Companion to Shakespeare*, Margreta de Grazia and Stanley Wells (eds),
     Cambridge University Press (2001).
Trewin, J. C., *Peter Brook: A Biography*, MacDonald (1971).
Van Es, Bart, *Shakespeare in Company*, Oxford University Press (2013).
Warren, Roger, *Staging Shakespeare's Last Plays*, Oxford University Press (1990).
Wayne, Valerie, 'Refashioning the Shrew', *Shakespeare Studies* 17 (1985).
Wells, Stanley, *Shakespeare, Sex & Love*, Oxford University Press (2010).

Wells, Stanley and Gary Taylor with John Jowett and William Montgomery,
    William Shakespeare: A Textual Companion, Oxford (1987).
Williamson, Marilyn, *The Patriarchy of Shakespeare's Comedies*, Wayne State
    University Press (1986).
Wright, Louis B. (ed.), *Advice to a Son: Precepts of Lord Burghley, Sir Walter
    Raleigh, and Francis Osborne*, Literary Licensing, LLC (2011).

I have also benefited from many of the introductions in the relevant Arden,
New Cambridge, Norton, Oxford, Penguin, Riverside and RSC editions of
Shakespeare's plays.

INDEX

Page references in bold denote the section devoted to that play.

Adelman, Janet 125, 127, 144–5
adultery 133, 159
An Age of Kings (BBC TV) 31
All Fools (Chapman) 179
All's Well That Ends Well 2, 75,
    97–102
  Bertram 97–102, 182
  Countess of Rossillion 2, 97–8, 102
  Helena 2, 6, 68, 96, 97–102, 140,
    145, 182, 188
  King of France 97–102, 182
Almeida Theatre 5, 79, 107–8
'an actor's perspective' 8, 31–44,
    52–64, 73–87, 107–24
Anatomy of Melancholy, The (Burton)
    109
androgyny *see* cross-dressing
anima 5, 117
anti-semitism 45, 47–9
Antonio and Mellida (Marston)
    175–6
Appolonius of Tyre 125, 129
Arden, forest of 64, 67, 142
Ashcroft, Peggy 52–3
As You Like It 2, **64–9**, 142, 182
  Celia 66–8
  Duke Frederick 8, 65–6
  Duke Senior 65–8
  Orlando 65–9
  Rosalind 64–9, 70, 98, 142, 145,
    158, 182
audibility 32, 120
audience
  Elizabethan 8, 46, 48, 68
  Jacobean 96, 151
Austen, Jane 3

Barton, Anne 23, 130, 132, 140, 145,
    149
Barton, John 53, 74, 115, 120
bastardy 54, 133–4, 167
bawdy 22, 24
Beaumont, Francis 177
Becon, Thomas 166–7
bed-trick 94, 99, 182
Belleforest, Francois: *Histoires*
    Tragiques 53, 54, 58, 61, 69,
    74–5
Bhattacharjee, Paul 53
Bible 163–6, 169–70
Birmingham Rep 31–2, 65
Birth Order 5, 24, 118, 161–2
Blakemore, Michael 108
Boas, F. R. 73
Boccaccio, Giovanni 11, 15, 87, 140
boy players 4, 38, 55, 67, 186–7
boys companies 173, 175
Branagh, Kenneth 55, 82
Bride Book, A (Whateley) 164, 171
Brighouse, Harold 4
Britain 141, 144
Brook, Peter 19, 96, 107–8, 111,
    145
Brooke, Arthur 32–40, 42, 44
brothels 78, 84, 129–30
Bryant, Michael 74, 78
Bruto, Giovani Michele 165, 166
Bullough, Geoffrey 7–8
Burbage, William 93, 120, 122, 161
Burden, Suzanne 113, 115, 123
Burleigh, William Cecil, first Baron 75,
    76, 80
Burton, Richard 73

Calder-Marshall, Anna 32, 39–40
Callow, Simon 7
Calvin, John 29, 163
Cardenio **152–3**
Carroll, Nancy 112, 114, 122–3
Case is Altered, The (Jonson) 176, 179
Cervantes, Miguel de 152
Changeling, The (Middleton and
    Rowley) 179
Chapman, George 175, 176
Charleson, Ian 73
Chaste Maid in Cheapside, A
    (Middleton) 178
chastity/virginity 30, 57, 62, 82, 94,
    97, 98, 140, 147, 149–50
Chaucer, Geoffrey 29, 154
    Troilus and Criseyde 87–8, 90
Chekhov, Anton 3–4
Chettle, Henry 85, 175
Christianity 95, 122, 171
Church, Tony 74
Cinthio, Giraldi 94, 103, 106
Cleaver, Robert 164, 165, 167
colonialism 147
Comedy of Errors, The 23
Connery, Sean 31
Coriolanus 18, 39
Cox, Brian 32, 108
countryside 67, 136, 142, 152, 156
courtly love 14
courtship 22, 27–8, 68, 100, 170
Cymbeline 11, **139–45**
    Cymbeline 140–5, 183
    Cymbeline's Queen 141–4
    Innogen 68, 139–45, 183
    Posthumus 140–4

Daneman, Paul 13
Dash, Irene 188
daughters, upbringing of 165–7
Day-Lewis, Daniel 73
De Beauvoir, Simone 40
Dekker, Thomas 94, 175
Dench, Judi 31, 53, 109
Devine, George 108
Dews, Peter 31–2
doctors 128, 155, 158
Doran, Gregory 73–4, 153
Downie, Penny 73

dowries 22, 26, 54, 110, 113, 158,
    160, 164
Dreher, Diane Elizabeth 5–6
Duncan-Jones, Katherine 159
Dusinberre, Juliet 186
Dutch Courtesan, The (Marston) 129

Eastward Ho (Chapman, Jonson and
    Marston) 177
Edinburgh University 8
Edmondson, Paul 73
education 2, 3, 68, 105, 157
    for girls 168–9
Elizabeth I, Queen 28, 152, 168
elopement 24, 105, 107
epilogues 28, 67, 151, 186
Evelyn, John 170

Fairweather, Eileen 4
Fawn, The (Marston) 94
Felperin, Howard 124
Ffrangcon-Davies, Gwen 40
Fielding, Susannah 62–4
Fletcher, John 152–6, 177
Foakes, W. A. 107, 125
Ford, Jane M. 126–7
Ford, Petronella 52
Ford Davies, Oliver
    as Capulet 32–9
    as King Lear 5, 107–24
    as Leonato 53–61
    as Polonius 73–87
Fratricide Punished 75
Freud, Sigmund 4–5, 123
Friar Bacon and Friar Bungay
    (Greene) 175

Galatea (Lyly) 174
Gale, Mariah 73, 79–80, 82, 84–5
Gambon, Michael 32
Gielgud, John 52–3, 108, 145
Gilliatt, Penelope 53
Globe Theatre 8, 68, 139–40, 145,
    151, 153, 190
Goulter, Barbara 6
Grainger, Roger 131
Graves, Robert 53
Greek drama 3
Greenblatt, Stephen 1, 145, 161

Greene, Robert 27, 174–5
Greer, Germaine 160

Hall, Elizabeth 128, 148, 158, 160,
       162, 190
Hall, John 128, 132, 158, 160–2
Hall, Peter 74
Hall, Susanna *see under* Shakespeare
Hamlet 1, 3, 7, **73–87**
    Claudius 7, 75–6, 79–81, 83–5
    Gertrude 7, 75, 80–1, 83–4
    Hamlet 3, 75–86, 92
    Ophelia 6, 74–87, 92, 154, 182–3,
       187–8
    Polonius 6, 73–87, 182
Hardy, Robert 31
Hardy, Thomas 39
Hare, David 107
Heminges, John 38, 152, 161
Higgins, Anthony 32
Holinshed, Raphael 109–10, 140
Holm, Ian 108
homoeroticism 31
Honest Whore, The, Part 1 (Dekker)
       129, 177, 179
Hopkins, Anthony 107–8
Hopkins, Lisa 177
Hordern, Michael 117
housekeeping 168
Howard, Alan 107
Hoy, Cyrus 154
humanism 164, 165, 168
Hytner, Nicholas 53, 61 63

illegitimacy *see* bastardy

Jack Drum's Entertainment (Marston)
       176
Jackson, Glenda 86
Jackson, Macdonald D. 152–3
Jacobi, Derek 120
James I, King of England 102, 111,
       144, 146, 163–4, 167
    Basilikon Doron 94, 114
Jardine, Lisa 186, 188
Jefford, Barbara 96
Jennings, Alex 74
Jew of Malta, The (Marlowe) 45–6,
       174

Jonson, Ben 3, 4, 157, 175, 176, 177
Jung, Carl Gustav 5, 131

Kahn, Coppelia 1, 131, 185, 188
Kemp, Will 38
Kendal, Felicity 43
Kent, Jonathan 108–9, 116, 120
Kermode, Frank 18, 135
King Henry IV, Part 1 28
    Falstaff 1, 31, 37, 82
King Henry V 27–8
King Henry VI, Part 1 26–7
King Henry VIII 152
King John 157
King Lear 1, 2, 8, **107–24**, 142, 155,
       183, 188
    Cordelia 5, 6, 8, 109–23, 128, 130,
       183, 188
    Fool 112, 115–16
    Goneril 8, 109–21, 123, 153, 183,
       188
    Kent 110, 113, 117
    King Lear 4, 7, 20, 107–24, 183,
       185, 188
       and madness 7, 108, 110, 120
    Regan 109–21, 123, 183, 188
King Leir 109–10
King Richard II 1, 79
King's Men 126
King's School Canterbury 3, 31
Knox, John 163
Kott, Jan 89
Kyd, Thomas 17, 75, 175
Kyle, Barry 39

labelling characters 6, 24, 26
Laing, R. D. 86
Laughton, Charles 107–8, 120
Leigh, Vivien 19
Lenker, Lagretta Tallent 6
Leverenz, David 86
Lévi-Strauss, Claude 166
life expectancy 165
Lodge, Thomas 65 *see also Rosalynde*
London 157, 158
Love's Labours Lost **28–9**
Love's Metamorphosis (Lyly) 173
Luscombe, Christopher 52
Luther, Martin 170

Lyly, John 12, 173–4

Macbeth 2, 114
McInnerny, Lizzy 118
Maid's Tragedy, The (Beaumont and
    Fletcher) 85, 177–8, 179
Marlowe, Christopher 13, 17, 27, 45,
    174, 175
marriage arrangements 169–71
    settlements 25, 27, 35, 166
Marston, John 94, 175
masques 151
Measure for Measure **92–7**
    Angelo 93–7
    Claudio 93–7
    Duke Vincentio 29, 93–7, 130, 182
    Isabella 28, 68, 93–7, 130, 182,
        188
Merchant of Venice, The **45–50**, 182
    Jessica 5, 7, 8, 45–50, 182
    Portia 6, 48–50, 70, 98, 142, 171
    Shylock 5, 7, 45–9, 175, 182
Merry Wives of Windsor, The 2, **50–2**,
    157, 181
    Anne Page 2, 50–2, 181
    Fenton 50–2
    Page 50–2
    Mrs Page 2, 50–2
Midas (Lyly) 173
Middleton, John 7, 94, 177–8
Midsummer's Night Dream, A **29–31**,
    181
    Egeus 29–31, 181
    Helena 16, 30, 98
    Hermia 29–30, 181
    Theseus 29, 30
Miller, Jonathan 1, 117, 120
Montaigne, Michel Eyquem de 147,
    165–6
More, Thomas 168
Morsan, Thomas 40
Mother Bombie (Lyly) 173
Much Ado About Nothing 2, **52–64**,
    167, 182
    Beatrice 6, 52, 56–64, 69
    Benedick 52, 56–64
    Claudio 54–64
    Don John 7, 8, 52, 54, 57–62
    Don Pedro 54–62

Hero 53–64, 182
Leonato 6, 8, 52–64, 104, 182, 184
Mulcaster, Richard 168
music 14, 28, 132

National Theatre 53, 107
Nashe, Thomas 27
Nevo, Ruth 126, 150
Newstead, Christopher 163
Ney, Marianne 189
Noble, Adrian 93
Nosworthy, J. M. 143
Nunn, Trevor 39, 65
Nuttall, A. D. 121–2

Old Wives Tale, The (Peele) 174
Olivier, Laurence 5, 107, 117, 148
O'Neill, Eugene 4
Orlando Furioso (Greene) 53, 174
Osborne, John 4
Othello **102–7**
    Brabantio 30, 103–5, 183
    Desdemona 6, 102–7, 183, 188
    Emilia 106–7
    Iago 103, 105–7
    Othello 59, 102–7
Ovid 15, 146
    Metamorphoses 3, 4, 17, 20, 21,
        138, 153

Palace of Pleasure, The (Painter) 39,
    98, 99–100
Pandosto (Greene) 5, 133–4, 135–8
Pattern of Painful Adventures, The
    (Twine) 125–6, 128–9, 131
Pearce, Joanne 86
Peele, George 17
Pennington, Michael 74, 108
Pericles 5, **125–33**, 183
    Lysimachus 29, 129–30, 132
    Marina 4, 6, 29, 128–32, 183
    Pericles 6, 126–33, 183
    Thaisa 127, 132
period setting 52, 76, 108–9
Petherbridge, Edward 142
petty school 157, 168
Philaster (Beaumont and Fletcher) 139
Philomel 16, 17, 21, 40
Phoenix Theatre, Leicester 52

plague 157, 158, 190
Plautus 2
    Plautine plot 2, 12, 173
Playing Lear (Oliver Ford Davies)
        108–9, 124
prostitutes 92, 99
Pryce, Jonathan 5
puritanism 158, 159, 170

Quiney, Judith *see under* Shakespeare
Quiney, Richard 159
Quiney, Thomas 159–62, 166

racism 45, 103
Raleigh, Sir Walter 76
rape 15, 18, 21, 149
Rape of Lucrece, The 18
Renaissance
    man 33, 84, 146, 181
    thought 120
    woman 24, 62, 68
Restoration comedy 16, 170
Ritter, Sonia 20
Roaring Girl, The (Dekker and
        Middleton) 167
Romeo and Juliet **31–44**, 181
    Capulet 4, 6, 28, 31–44, 59, 104,
        181
    Friar Laurence 38, 40–1, 43–4
    Juliet 3, 6, 30, 32–44, 68, 98, 107,
        181
    Lady Capulet 2, 32–9, 41–3
    Romeo 7, 33–4, 38–9, 40, 42, 98
Rosalynde (Lodge) 65–6
Royal Shakespeare Company (RSC)
        6, 12, 20, 65, 73, 108, 140,
        142, 153
Royle, Carol 86
Russell-Beale, Simon 53, 74, 108
Rutter, Carol 133

St Paul 163–4
Saxo Grammaticus 74
Scofield, Paul 73, 108, 116
Seneca 2, 17, 18, 20, 119
Shakespeare, Anne (née Hathaway)
        157, 160–2, 165, 190
Shakespeare, Edmund 158, 190
Shakespeare, Hamnet 70, 118, 157–8

Shakespeare, Judith 70, 118, 157–8, 190
    inheritance 161–2
    marriage 159–60
Shakespeare, Susanna 63, 118, 132,
        157–8, 166, 190
    inheritance 160–2
    marriage 158–9
Shakespeare, William (WS)
    dramatic writings
        absent wives and mothers 2, 4,
            55, 110, 184
        adolescence 40–1, 44, 98–9,
            105, 134, 140, 146, 186
        age of daughters 33, 39, 53,
            104, 130, 134–5, 148, 186
        age of fathers 4, 33, 122, 148
        ambiguity in 6, 26, 45, 111, 115
        backstory 103, 114, 147
        class differences 35, 50, 55–6,
            68, 90, 98–100, 102
        classical knowledge 4–5, 13, 40,
            155
        collaborators 17, 27, 152–6
        cross-dressing 6, 11, 46, 49,
            67–70, 142–3, 187
        daughters
            defiant 14, 30, 40, 46, 50,
                115, 118
            divided duty 68, 104–5, 112
            dominated 62, 82, 84, 107
        fairytale in 99, 139–40, 143,
            147
        family, dramatist of 1, 35, 39,
            42, 74, 76, 79, 109, 119, 190
        folktale in 21–2, 47, 109–10,
            120, 128, 133, 146, 189
        half-hearted husbands 54, 62,
            141
        imagery 17, 19, 51, 59–60, 99,
            113, 135, 151
        incest 6, 112, 115, 126–7, 129,
            137–8
        irony 23, 65, 115
        magic 30, 103, 138, 145–6, 151
        marriage settlements 35, 56,
            153, 158, 160
        mirroring 1, 14, 48, 81
        misogyny 91, 106–7, 141, 144,
            155, 174

multiple plots 11, 110, 140
nature 67, 133–4, 136
opacity 6, 95, 97
parthenogenesis 132, 144, 147
pastoral 65, 67, 15–6, 142
paternalism 26, 71
    attitude to daughters 29,
        37, 51, 56, 64, 77, 114,
        149
    head of family 23, 41, 67,
        164
patriarchy 15, 46, 65, 74, 149
    examined 107, 113, 145–6,
        166, 183
    upheld by WS 48, 185–6
playwriting characters 6, 95,
    145
plot devices 13, 184
psychological complexity 21, 26,
    86, 96, 119, 131
rebirth in 61, 138, 146
religion 93, 96
rhetoric 17, 59, 76, 93, 114
rhythmic prose 37, 69
role-playing 6, 26, 64, 78
same-sex bonds 11, 16, 29, 31
second chances 125, 144, 190
soliloquy 41, 83, 84, 89, 93,
    114, 146, 154
spying 78, 80–2
surrogate fathers
    in comedy 1. 28, 71, 94, 97,
        134, 185
    in tragedy 43, 88
surrogate mothers 30, 39, 139
tragic hero 86, 107, 109
verse development 8, 13, 34,
    36–7, 42, 59–60, 100–1, 128,
    135
usurpation 65, 147, 149
life
    grandaughter 148, 158–60, 190
    land purchases 158, 160
    relations with Anne 160, 162
    relations with daughters 158–62
    retirement 158, 190
    will 157, 160–2
Shaw, Fiona 23, 186
Shaw, George Bernard 4, 187

Shoemaker's Holiday, The (Dekker)
    176–7
Sidney, Sir Philip 93
Sinden, Donald 53
Smith, Maggie 53
Sonnets 40, 102
Southampton, Henry Wriothesley,
    second Earl 165
Southampton, Henry Wriothesley,
    third Earl 75
Spanish Tragedy, The (Kyd) 174
Stephens, Robert 53, 108
Stevenson, Juliet 186
Stratford-upon-Avon 158–62, 169
    Holy Trinity Church 157, 158,
        159
    King's New School 3, 148–9, 157
    New Place 158, 160, 162
Stride, John 31
Stewart, Patrick 73, 81
Stubbes, Philip 167
Syal, Meera 53
syphilis 88

Tale of a Tub, A (Jonson) 176
Taming of a Shrew, The (Anon.) 21–4
Taming of the Shrew, The 3, 8, 21–6,
    186
    Baptista 6, 21–6, 181
    Bianca 3, 24–6
    Kate 8, 21–6, 186
    Petruccio 8, 21–6
Taylor, Don 13
Taylor, Gary 130
Taylor, Mark 6
Tempest, The 145–51
    Caliban 147, 149
    Ferdinand 148–51
    Miranda 4, 6, 145–51, 183
    Prospero 4, 6, 145–51, 183, 185
Tennant, David 73
Theobald, Lewis 152
Thomas, Keith 164–5
Titus Andronicus 3, 16–21
    Lavinia 16–21
    Saturninus 17–18
    Tamora 18, 20
    Titus Andronicus 16–21, 181
tragicomedy 72, 93

Troilus and Cressida 84, **87–92**
  Cressida 87–92, 182, 188
  Diomedes 87–8, 91–2
  Pandarus 88–92, 182
  Troilus 87–92
trothplight/handfasting 21, 56, 134,
    170–1
Twelfth Night 10, **69–71**
  Malvolio 71
  Olivia 69–71, 170
  Orsino 8, 70–1
  Viola 8, 69–71, 98, 131, 145
Two Gentlemen of Verona, The 3,
    11–16, 175, 181
  Duke of Milan 11–16, 181
  Julia 3, 14–16, 98, 153
  Proteus 11–16, 98
  Silvia 11–16, 181
  Valentine 11–16
Two Noble Kinsmen, The 29, 85,
    153–6
  Jailer 153–5
  Jailer's Daughter 153–6

university wits 13
Ur-Hamlet 75, 85

Vicar's Court 158, 159–60
Victor, Benjamin 15
Virgil 3
Vives, Juan Luis 167

Wales 142
Walter, Harriet 6, 140
Wanamaker, Zoë 53
wardship 102
Warner, David 73
Warner, Deborah 20
Webster, John 177
Wells, Stanley 127, 140
Westminster School 3
Whateley, William 164, 171
Wilbern, David 5
Wild-Goose Chase, The (Beaumont
    and Fletcher) 170, 179
Wilkins, George 126, 127, 129, 130
Williams, Clifford 31
Winter's Tale, The 2, 5, **133–9**, 146
  Hermione 133–4, 136–9, 146, 183
  Leontes 5, 133–9, 142, 183
  Paulina 136–9
  Perdita 4, 5, 133–9, 183
witchcraft 30
Wolfit, Donald 108
Woman in the Moon, The (Lyly)
    173–4
Women Beware Women (Middleton)
    178
Wood, John 5, 108
Woodall, Andrew 54

Zefferelli, Franco 31, 53
Zitner, Sheldon P. 102